COMMUNICATION PROBES

Brent D. Peterson, Brigham Young University

Gerald M. Goldhaber, University of New Mexico

R. Wayne Pace, University of New Mexico

SRA

SCIENCE RESEARCH ASSOCIATES, INC.
Chicago, Palo Alto, Toronto, Henley-on-Thames, Sydney, Paris

A Subsidiary of IBM

© 1974, Science Research Associates, Inc. All rights reserved.
Printed in the United States of America

Library of Congress Catalog Card Number: 73–93238
ISBN 0-574-19135-6

Contents

Component 2: The Message   37

Appropriate verbal and nonverbal symbols are essential to effective communication.

The words you use should adequately symbolize what you want to say.

Nonverbal cues can help you read messages.

You can communicate with plants and animals.

Component 3: The Environment   63

Social trends and technological advancements influence your life.

The conflict between what you want and the environment in which you live produces stress in your life.

Relationship 1: Dyadic   89

Relationship 2: Serial   121

Relationship 4: Speaker-Audience 173

The Ending 207

Photo Essays

Preface

A song popular a few decades ago asserted that fish gotta swim and birds gotta fly. If we were to define people by something they characteristically do, we might say that people gotta talk. To communicate or not to communicate is a decision that defies human capabilities. All of us communicate—even when we choose not to speak.

We consider *Communication Probes* to be an introductory book, since it avoids the deep, involved analysis of technical aspects of physiology, language, speech, and behavior. Rather than expound at length and in detail on academic principles, we have chosen materials from books, magazines, and newspapers as well as cartoons, advertisements, songs, and poems. These selections (probes) examine, with some precision, basic concepts and issues concerning communication.

Although this book is less a continuous essay than a collection of many different types of messages, the important ideas are developed much as they would be in a regular textbook. A key topic (probe) is stated and then explained and illustrated. The writings of scholars as well as of clever social commentators are combined in unique sequences suitable for an initial exposure to the field. You may disagree with some of the probes, but more often you will probably find them disturbingly accurate.

To discourage you from taking any principles too seriously, we have attempted to incorporate some humor into our presentation. Enjoy yourself as you read. As editors, we want this book not only to introduce the fundamentals of communication theory and practice, but also to be fun to read.

Unusual as is the content of this book, so also is its design in order to present properly the relationships among the selections. As you read them, you will note that, in general, articles that come from scholarly sources or that discuss the concepts presented in this book are set in a serif typeface; they are positioned in the inner one or two columns, when other types of material are present. Selections that come from more popular sources and serve largely to illustrate certain concepts are in a sans serif typeface. These are positioned in the outer one or two columns. Footnotes for the scholarly type of article are usually collected at the end of it.

For the most part, the people whose materials we have been privileged to use should be credited with providing the substance of this book. We are indebted to them for their comments and observations. As editors, we share responsibility for the weaknesses that overshadow the brilliant work of the contributors. In no way should our ineptness diminish their genius.

To our many friends and colleagues we give our thanks for their inspiration and guidance in steering us to probe this fascinating, satisfying, and troublesome field of study. We wish to acknowledge the self-sacrifice and support of our wives, Arlene, Marylynn, and Gae. We also wish to thank May Polivka for pounding her typewriter through confounding confusion to the end of this manuscript. With deep appreciation, we recognize the keen efforts of Frank Geddes in facilitating the creation of this book. With few bruised feelings, we wish to recognize the editorial prowess exhibited by Gretchen Hargis in shaping up this manuscript for publication.

Like knights in search of the fabled city of El Dorado, many of us seek places of wealth, abundance, and opportunity. Sadly we learn through small triumphs and great disappointments that El Dorado is not a spot of ground; it is our relationships with people. The treasures we seek can be found in how and what we do with others.

To understand how people communicate and why they fail may be man's most important objective.

The ability to communicate effectively paves the road to El Dorado—personal satisfaction as well as recognition, money, and material goods. Out of effective communication may come success in influencing others. Of course, not all communication involves power. Sometimes you may want pleasant relationships. You may seek to be understood and to understand others and to help them achieve what they want. At other times you may seek neither power nor love but only to give accurate information.

Through practicing the principles of speech communication you can exert influence, express and evoke love, and help others get good information. No other body of concepts and abilities offers so much for both good and evil. Through communication, people find, establish, and foster close relationships; world powers negotiate treaties and make decisions that affect millions of people; industrialists coordinate the efforts of thousands to produce goods and services; protests are expressed; social clubs are formed and sustained; civilization is created; wars are waged and civilization destroyed; people are hurt and love is crushed.

Communication is intimately tied in with language and other types of symbols such as pictures and drawings. We define *symbol* as something that stands for something else. The word *friend* represents, points to, and stands in the place of an actual friend. When we call someone a friend, we are saying that he or she behaves, looks, and talks in a manner consistent with our image, or concept, that accompanies the word *friend*.

Concept refers to a mental picture that each of us creates of things, people, happenings, creations, and reactions—real or imagined. A concept begins with a perception, a sensory impression, of some activity, object, or person. This mental image is a person's neurological record of what he or she heard, saw, felt, smelled, or tasted. We call these preliminary impressions *percepts*. As a group of percepts merge into an identifiable object, we form a concept and assign symbols (often called labels or names) to the whole concept and each of its parts.

Consider the question "How did Sir Fleming know that he had discovered penicillin?" This question is humorous because it assumes that the word came before the concept. Sir Fleming did not know that he had discovered penicillin; he simply called his discovery by that name. From sensory experiences with the object evolved percepts that developed into a concept that was given a name.

You may have some rather vague percepts for which you have no names, but it is very unlikely that you will have even one concept for which you have no name or symbol. Take a moment now to try to think of such a concept. You may have a concept that is incomplete or subject to change, but you probably have a name even for it.

Concepts consist of both mental images and feelings about them. If, for example, an acquaintance whom you identify as a friend borrows fifty dollars and fails to repay the loan, you may be angry. This anger, a negative feeling, becomes associated with your concept of friend and is likely to affect your responses to other would-be friends. Even if an event has the possibility of producing some desirable consequence for us, we may not like it because of a negative feeling associated with it. It is true that sometimes we react to feelings more vigorously than to events separate from us. Generally, however, feelings are associated with concepts, which we react to whether or not they are labeled and spoken.

Words usually evoke the concepts they stand for. Sometimes we react to words as if the real event (not just the concept) were happening to us. If you habitually call a person handsome or brilliant, he or she may begin to react to the words without asking what they refer to. Even more important, he or she may forget that such words may not accurately describe his or her actual behavior.

Actions such as gestures and facial expressions usually indicate how we feel about concepts. If a friend comes to visit unexpectedly and I blush as I say, "It's a pleasure to see you," his arrival may be not only unexpected but also inconvenient. The blush reveals more about how I feel than about the concept of a friend visiting. To refer to both the same concepts and the same feelings as those with whom you communicate, you must interpret nonverbal as well as verbal behavior.

The Beginning

To communicate, a person must be able to evolve a concept of something, give it a name, and develop a feeling about it. Effective communication with another person implies that the concept, name, and feeling are similar to what that person has in mind. In other words, effective communication means you and I refer to the same things when we talk. If we are communicating effectively and I say, "Meet me at 7 o'clock near the gym," you visualize the same gym as I do, you fix the same time of day as I do, and you identify the same relationship associated with meeting people as I do.

In effective communication, you develop and share accurate meanings with others.

What kinds of clues help us know what people mean when they talk to us? What kinds of clues can we give others so that they can know what we mean? I can ask you directly "What do you mean?" or "What are you referring to?" If you can physically point out your referent, I have a good chance of finding out what you mean. Many things that we talk about, however, are difficult to point to physically: feelings, hopes, plans, experiences. How do we determine what a message means when we cannot look at what is being referred to? In such a case we need to describe to each other the concepts we have created inside ourselves.

It must be remembered, however, that communication is a process in which events are not controlled to any great extent. As I say something to you, I interpret your behavior; you react nonver-

bally to some parts of what I say and verbally to others. While you are reacting, you are also formulating what you will say when I finish. You might even interrupt me. At the same time, I might react to a concept inside of me that sprang to prominence by some movement you made and that is somewhat unrelated to our immediate conversation. The moments when we respond directly to what each of us means are few and precious. Effective communication depends in part upon our abilities to sense and respond to these fleeting revelations at just the right moment.

There are three basic components of the communication process—people, messages, and environment. The personal component concerns the personalities of both the initiator (sender) of a message and the responder (receiver) to it. The initiator is the human source of verbal and nonverbal symbols, and the responder interprets them. Of course, objects and events may also serve as sources of information to which people react; but unless the responder interacts with the initiator, the latter may as well be talking to himself. Personality includes beliefs and values, self-perceptions, attitudes, abilities, and self-esteem.

The message component deals with the use of verbal and nonverbal symbols. We are able to create messages because of our ability to symbolize—to make words, behaviors, and things stand for something else. Messages are collections of symbols that reveal information. Language is the most common type of symbol in human communication, but all types of nonverbal symbols are part of our daily lives. Advertising campaigns, political parties, corporations, and service clubs use them.

The type (form) of a message refers to the specific way in which an idea is presented—e.g., in a memo or a speech, by telephone or letter, over a public address system or on a bulletin board. Many times we study the form of a message when we should be trying to make better decisions about which form to use. The principles explained and illustrated in this book relate to many different types of messages. The primary focus is on face-to-face forms, however, rather than on written ones.

The environmental component of human communication concerns the conditions that evoke a climate or atmosphere in which communication occurs. Most of us live in an environment molded by institutions and mass media. It is an environment of unrest and stress. As people change, the environment in which they live changes and thus also the climate in which communication takes place. Part of the environment is the social context, or cultural milieu, which consists of the physical surroundings, setting, and location. For three people in a room their immediate environment might be the room (its shape, size, and furnishings), the air (its circulation, temperature, and humidity), the sounds (their tone, frequency, and quality). This environment is, of course, within a cultural context determined by community, state, national, and international affairs. Each person interacts with

---

To understand human communication, you need to know its components and the relationships between communicators.

---

others within the context of both immediate and broader cultural environments.

Relationships consist of the connections between individual communicators. They influence how, to whom, when, and why people communicate. In each set of relationships, individuals are connected by expectations, norms, rules, and other circumstances. Four significant relationships deserve close examination.

1. Intimate relationships are usually created between two human beings. When you interact with another person, the encounter is dyadic. Relating to another person on a deeply personal basis requires great awareness and ability. Those who work in management, supervision, selling, and in many service occupations depend upon the quality of their dyadic relationships to accomplish their objectives. These relationships are fundamental in daily affairs.

2. When a second person reproduces a first person's message for a third person and that person in turn reproduces the message for a fourth person and so on, communication becomes serial. The messages that determine policy and day-to-day operations in formal organizations are disseminated through serial relationships.

3. A small group relationship occurs when a relatively small number of individuals interact face-to-face for the purpose of making a decision. Everyday we are involved in small groups. Many people use small groups in order to carry out productive goals and to learn about themselves.

4. When a large number of people gather to listen to a speaker, a speaker-audience relationship occurs. Speaking to an audience allows a person to structure messages carefully and to control nonverbal behavior so as to produce a specific response in several people at once—perhaps to assert his own power.

These components and relationships of communication are the major concerns of the book. A chapter is devoted to each of them. Information about them will, we hope, help you understand about communication and how to communicate effectively with others. Within these pages you will find out how to prepare messages and interact with people in order to establish personal, intimate relationships; how to participate in and work with small groups; how to reduce the loss of information that occurs when a chain of communicators reproduce messages; and how to prepare and give a public speech.

Communication Probes seeks to do more, however, than introduce the basic theory of human communication and demonstrate its application. This book also raises questions and encourages you to answer them. Each selection may be considered a probe, an investigative tool. The highlighted statements may also be considered probes in that they initiate further comment. At the end of each component and relationship (and this chapter, too) are prods—questions, problems, and exercises that relate back to the probes and urge you to apply them to your own life.

Since in this book we are attempting to provoke you, the reader, to probe how you communicate, we speak to you directly. Although we realize that what we say here applies to us as well, we have avoided the editorial *we* in favor of directly addressing you, so that you will focus on your own behavior. We want you to take responsibility in communicating with other people and to analyze your own behavior to find out how you can improve your communication.

Prods

1. Why is it important to understand how communication takes place? (If your answer is "to make money," reread the beginning. If your answer is "to reduce loneliness," continue to component one. If your answer is "to be able to make changes in your own communicative behavior," give yourself a prize and take a break. Of course, you might have chosen some other answer, too.)

2. What aspects of communication are part of the environmental component?

3. Which kind of relationship is most important in your life? Dyadic? Serial? Small group? Speaker-audience? Why?

4. How does one create a communication gap? Experiment with your answer by creating such a gap and closing it. Try this exercise: talk to yourself but don't answer. What happened?

Your values and attitudes are part of your personality and serve as guidelines for how you behave and what you perceive.

Your self-concept develops through contact with others.

Self-disclosure and feedback can help you form close relationships with others.

Your perceptions may be a prime obstacle to effective communication.

Component

1

The Person

The Responsibility of Communicators

The Role of Human Values in Communication

Virgil L. Baker

Professor of Speech, University of Arkansas, Fayetteville, Arkansas

Your values and attitudes are part of your personality and serve as guidelines for how you behave and what you perceive.

A value, we learn, is a concept of the desirable. The Greeks had no word for value, but they did have a close synonym, *axios*, meaning worth. A value thus is anything of worth. Values, as we define them, are the goods of life, life resources. Values are all those things both objective and subjective without which we cannot be human beings.

What are the chief human values and how may we structuralize them for use in our communications? While we might well trace all human values to their first origins in our primitive ancestors, we now look to the Western World for our modern, more highly developed value system. From the Greek civilization of the fifth century B.C. came that classic value triad: the good, the true, and the beautiful. From the Hebrew-Christian cultures come the values incorporated in the Ten Commandments, the seven virtues (faith, hope, charity, prudence, justice, fortitude, and temperance), and the seven mortal sins (pride, wrath, envy, lust, gluttony, avarice, and sloth). Finally, modern scientific technology has added a host of values ranging all the way from the scientific method itself to better health, longer life expectancy, and to technology that fills our homes with labor-saving devices and comforts, including electronic communications that make incidents from any spot on earth "no sooner done than said."

Perhaps no more realistic way of structuralizing a human value system can be found than that of indicating the values our institutions gather, nurture and disseminate. Says Harold Lasswell, "Values are shaped and shared in patterns that we call institutions." Here we classify human values in tabular form adapted from Speech in *Personal and Public Affairs*, a textbook recently published by myself and my colleague Dr. Ralph T. Eubanks.

These we believe to be typical human values. They are universal life resources, characteristic of those sought for by human beings in all cultures, all civilizations. Says Sumiti Kunai Chatterji, "The mainsprings of human culture are the same—they are universal: and certain ideals, values, attitudes or behaviors, whether good or bad, have always been found to be transmissible. These ideals, values, attitudes or behaviors form patterns comparable to language." Indeed, these values make up human

Abridged from "The Role of Human Values in Communication: The Responsibility of Communicators" by Virgil L. Baker—a speech delivered to the Communications Seminar sponsored by the General Extension Service for Red Cross Volunteer Workers, April 2, 1965, and published in *Vital Speeches of the Day*, May 1, 1965. © 1965 City News Publishing Company. Used by permission.

Human Value System		
Typical Functioning Institution	Typical Value Clusters *Positive/Negative*	
Home	Love/hate	
School	Enlightenment/ ignorance	
Church	Rectitude/immorality	
Library	Literature/trash	
Government	Freedom/bondage	
Court	Justice/impartiality	
Hospital, clinic	Health/illness	
Prison	Reform/punishment	
Occupation	Wealth/poverty	
Social organization	Respect/disgrace	
Leisure organization	Recreation/boredom	
Welfare organization	Charity/miserliness	
Pressure organization	Dissent/conformity	
Museum, gallery	Beauty/ugliness	

nature itself. Let a carpenter from our country meet one in Israel, or India, or Africa, or Mexico, or Japan. He will be able to communicate in large measure with each, and each with him, through the language of universal human values. Erich Fromm makes this doubly clear when he says: "The universal symbol is rooted in the properties of our body, our senses, and our mind, which are common to all men and, therefore, not restricted to individuals or to specific groups. Indeed, the language of the universal symbol is the one common tongue developed by the human race. . ."

How do we, as communicators, speak this universal language? We speak it secondarily by nonverbal symbols of meaning: by our actions, attitudes, and appearance. Others read our values first in the appearance of our possessions: the style, cleanliness, orderliness of our dress, study desk, or interior of our cars or homes. Next they read them in our gestures, facial expressions and body movements. They then hear them in the nuances of vocal tones whether they be tones of joy or anger, love or hate, fear or hope, melancholy or optimism, sympathy or jealousy, pity or envy.

But these are all secondary ways that we communicate our set of values. The primary way, of course, is by our use of words in the sentences we speak or write. By words we express our set of values when we make assertions, demands, requests, pleas, declarations, contracts; when we ask or answer questions or give commands; or when we state opinions, decisions, judgments, and commitments.

Values are the goods of life, without which we cannot be human beings.

Our words are stimuli, standing in or substituting for our values. "The wonderful thing about language," says M. Merleau-Ponty, "is that it promotes its own oblivion." Words are fleeting signs and symbols, as quickly gone as heard or seen, but as they go they probe deep into our set of values, feeding out and feeding back exchanges of value meanings. The ultimate referent of the word is to values. Communication redefined means to exchange values.

It now becomes clear why communications between peoples so easily break down, for no two individuals have precisely the same set of values.

Our value systems differ first of all as we differ in age. The child's set of values shifts as he becomes a teenager; the teenager's values shift as he goes to high school, and again when he goes to college and even during college they may shift, making of him a good student or a dropout; they may change when he leaves college, again when he marries, again when he takes a job, and so on throughout his life as he becomes a father, a grandfather or a great grandfather.

Our value systems differ also according to the particular daily roles we take as afforded by our functional institutions: the home, school, church, library, hospital, occupations, social institutions, and the like. In a single day one may take a dozen or more functional roles, each with its distinctive value patterns. Let me enumerate some of the typical roles taken in a day by an average citizen. He takes the role of a son, a husband, a father, worker, worshiper, student, committeeman, philanthropist, friend, voter, dissenter, writer, speaker, creator of beauty, to mention but a few. And furthermore, we find that every role one takes is hedged about with rules, regulations, customs— communal performance rites—all of which must be observed as one performs the role. As we worship we follow the minute details of the ritual; as we play the role of say a golfer we follow the minute details of the performance rites as set forth in the rules and common practices of that game; and as we take the role given us by our occupation, as a teacher for instance, we follow through the long sequences of communal performance rites and regulations connected with teaching class after class and meeting student after student in conference.

Since each individual's set of values differs from another's, may not such differences account

On Seeing a Policeman

Age 7

Age 14

largely for the breakdowns that occur in communications? Breakdowns occur daily between peoples of different races and colors speaking different languages; between peoples whose forms of government are unlike; between peoples participating in different religious rituals; between individuals belonging to different political parties; between management and labor, teacher and student, executive and subordinate, and even between brother and brother, sister and sister, and husband and wife.

With individual value systems being as varied as they are, it is little wonder that breakdowns occur resulting in speakers shouting hate names: "Nigger," "Wop," "Chink," "Dago"; or writers hoisting hate signs screaming "Whites only," or "Yankee Go Home."

Peoples with highly specialized value clusters find difficulty in communicating with those whose sets of values are less specialized. Individual specialization is highly necessary in our complex industrial society. Yet highly specialized value clusters may stand in the way of effective communications between individuals. For example, teachers may communicate at their best only with teachers, executives with executives, scientists with scientists, doctors with doctors, lawyers with lawyers, and architects with architects.

Probably most breakdowns in communications occur between individuals who have developed extremely lopsided value clusters. As indicated by our chart, the values of life include both the good and the bad—the positive and the negative. Both positive and negative values are found in everyone's set of values, for both are part of our life experiences. We cannot, for instance, know the fuller meanings of love without

having experienced hate, nor enlightenment without being conscious of ignorance, nor rectitude without knowing immorality, nor can we experience freedom to the full without having experienced bondage or servility, nor justice without partiality, health without illness, wealth without poverty, or beauty without ugliness. Thus positive and negative values are counterparts like the two sides of a coin. Love completely divorced from hate, envy, jealousy, and anger, would be a love so thin, anemic, idealistic and lopsided that it would be realistically meaningless. Hate completely divorced from love, trust, pity, and brotherhood would be a monstrous, lopsided figment of the imagination.

What we seek in our sets of values is balance, proportion, harmony, norms. The Greeks brought the concept of The Golden Mean into our Western Communications. Newton in his laws of action-reaction gave us an equa-

tion of equilibrium that is basic in our star and earth sciences. W. B. Cannon noted that the human body had built into its structures a number of energy governors to maintain physical, mental and emotional health. He called this self-governing propensity homeostasis or "The Wisdom of the Body." Homeostasis as we now know is extendable beyond man's physiological and psychological self-governing propensities to a kind of governor in social relationships. There is a tendency toward maintaining relative stability in social conditions among forces with respect to various factors, such as food supply, competing tendencies, and powers within the body politic, and thus to society as a whole and even to culture among men. Only as we succeed in keeping a sane balance between positive and negative values can we find the normal clusters that make for human survival.

The Search for Self-Identity

Kim Giffin and Bobby R. Patton

We all have ideas about who and what we are; taken together these beliefs are our self-image or identity. Some persons, particularly adolescents, seem to be desperately struggling to define themselves. Other persons seem to know what they are, but are most concerned about what they might hope to become.

With respect to this identity-formation, it is useful to note the contribution of G. H. Mead; per-

haps more than any other theorist he viewed the development of self-identity as the product of social interaction. Mead emphasized the importance of face-to-face interpersonal communication—how we respond to others and they in turn respond to us. In this way we learn about ourselves; each interchange gives us cues about how others see us and this shapes our view of ourselves. From the time we are small chil-

Abridged from pp. 22–27, 30–33, 34–37 FUNDAMENTALS OF INTERPERSONAL COMMUNICATION by Kim Giffin and Bobby R. Patton. Copyright © 1971 by Kim Giffin and Bobby R. Patton. Reprinted by permission of Harper & Row, Publishers, Inc.

Age 20

Age 35

Age 50

dren this process goes on; virtually all communication to us gives us indications of our importance, capabilities, and potential, as well as our inadequacies.[1]

The following description of the process of identity formation has been given by another very well-recognized theorist on self-identity, Erik Erikson:

. . . identity formation . . . is a life-long development largely unconscious to the individual and to his society. Its roots go back all the way to the first self-recognition: in the baby's earliest exchange of smiles there is something of a self-realization coupled with a mutual recognition.[2]

Your self-concept develops through contact with others.

The process of identity-formation via interaction with others, suggested by Mead and Erikson, is largely a reflection of the perception of us by others. Cooley coined the phrase "the looking-glass self" and Sullivan spoke of "reflected self-appraisal." These are graphic labels for this process.

Of course, not all beliefs about ourselves are formed by social interaction. Direct sensory perception tells us when we are tired, hungry, or burn our finger. Also, Festinger's social-comparison process tells us when we are as tall as our parents, weigh more than "the average," or work arithmetic problems "faster than most" persons. Even so, *the choice of persons with whom we make such comparisons* is largely shaped by social interaction with persons in close relation to us.[3] There are some indications

Age 70

They, the Jury

Every trial lawyer knows that jurors often start out with prejudices against the defendant or plaintiff. By using his rights to challenge prospective jurors, a lawyer can try to obtain a jury with as little prejudice as possible against his client. To help lawyers assess prospective jurors, a research team working under the auspices of New Jersey's Fairleigh Dickinson University persuaded some 500 persons of varied backgrounds to take an elaborate test designed to reveal prejudices that might affect their judgment as jurors. The test was set up to detect both "overt" and "covert" prejudices. The findings, released this week, include a lot of surprises about who is, or is not, biased toward whom.

RACE.   In view of the national turmoil about discrimination against Negroes, it is remarkable that the study uncovered very little anti-Negro prejudice. Negroes showed detectable biases against the successful and the established—business executives, for example. Negroes also show biases in favor of the young, the poor and the unemployed.

RELIGION.   The people tested revealed, as prospective jurors, almost no prejudice against Roman Catholics, Jews, or any of the old, established Protestant denominations. In contrast, many people in many diverse walks of life showed at least covert prejudice against "Adventists/Jehovah's Witnesses" (the researchers lumped them together as a single category).

OCCUPATION.   The occupational groups against which prejudice is most widespread are government officials and labor union executives. The most prejudiced occupational group among those covered in the study: salesmen, by far. The salesmen, as a group, showed virtually no overt prejudices, but they revealed secret prejudices against the unemployed, people with low incomes and people of Latin or Eastern European origins. The findings also indicate that, as jurors, salesmen tend to be prejudiced in favor of women.

INCOME.   Those with low incomes are often prejudiced against the highly prosperous, and vice versa; so people in the middle, earning from $7,500 to $15,000, are less likely to meet with prejudice than those above or below them in the income scale.

SEX.   Women stand somewhat less chance than men of getting a fair verdict from a jury, because two large groups tend to be biased against women: 1) men earning less than $5,000 a year and 2) women.

AGE.   People in their 30s are less prejudiced than those younger or older. The most prejudice-prone of all the categories covered by the study: the retired.

NATIONAL ORIGINS.   While discovering much less racial and religious prejudice than might have been expected, the study also revealed remarkably pervasive biases against people who trace their origins to Eastern or Southern Europe. Of the 14 nationality groups covered in the test, the one that aroused the most widespread prejudice of all was "Rumanians/Hungarians" (the study grouped them in a single category). It would appear that if a Rumanian-born woman who is a Seventh-Day Adventist gets involved in a damage suit, she would do well to settle out of court.

From "They, the Jury" in TIME, August 9, 1963. Reprinted by permission from TIME, The Weekly Newsmagazine; Copyright Time Inc.

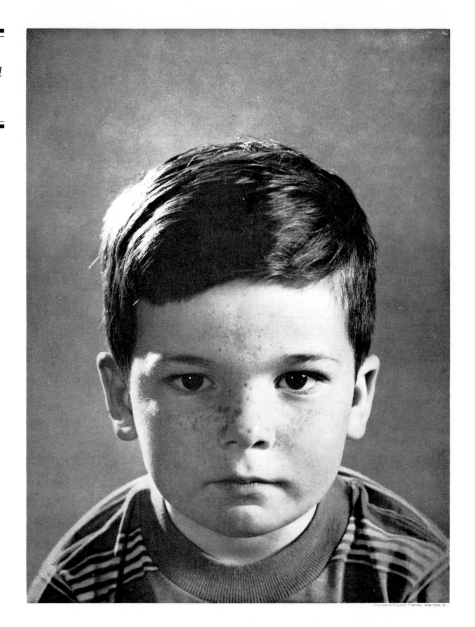

Two unquestioning eyes. Wherever they look, they learn. Whatever they behold, they believe in. Two shining reasons for every father to exercise judgment, wisdom, and moderation in all things...including the use of the products we sell.

Nineteenth in the series of Father's Day messages from THE HOUSE OF SEAGRAM *Fine Whiskies Since 1857*

Reprinted from "Moderation Messages by Seagram." Used by permission of Seagram Distillers Company.

that as we pass from childhood into adulthood, more and more of our beliefs about ourselves are formed through feedback about ourselves from others and employed by us for comparing ourselves with norms, averages, and members of reference groups.[4]

As children we like to have our parents give us things, but most of all we want them to *communicate* with us. We do not know for certain what we are until others (significant to us) tell us. We even prefer mild punishment to total indifference; in later life we can tolerate hate better than we can accept total neglect.[5]

Even in the pain of being hated we can at least know that we really exist. Socrates, condemned to death, faced condemnation with pride and honor; he believed that his death would affect important future acts of his countrymen. But if no one responds to our acts or thoughts, while yet we cannot live without thinking and acting, the incongruity between our needs and our world becomes unbearable. Under such circumstances children aggress against their parents and teenagers test authority by violating rules. In extreme circumstances a person may behave in extreme ways in order to obtain a response —any response— to establish his *existence*, regardless of the degree of antagonism or hostility his behavior will produce.

An unprovoked attack upon another person can never be condoned; however, the terrible sense of loneliness, neglect, and the need for some kind of attention from others which instigates such an attack is pertinent to the study of interpersonal communication. Attempted destruction of oneself may be a call for "help"—attention from and consequential interaction with others; it may also be the despondent conclusion that

Why Communications Falter

Sydney J. Harris

I receive many letters from wistful and well-intentioned correspondents who want to know "why people can't communicate better with one another." Whenever I hear this complaint, it reminds me of the pertinent fact that William James pointed out a half-century ago in one of his psychological texts.

James said that in any dialog between two persons there are six participants; it is not merely a dialog between Jones and Smith, which would be simple, but between three aspects of each personality.

First of all, there is Jones as he appears to himself, Jones as he appears to Smith, and Jones as he really is; the complementary triad, of course, is Smith as he appears to himself, Smith as he appears to Jones, and Smith as he really is.

It is within this multiplicity of identities that the communication gets lost. It is not merely that Jones says one thing, and Smith thinks he means another thing. It is that Jones himself is divided into the man as he appears to himself, and the man he really is. Even before the listener is involved, the communicator himself may be confused, or contradictory, or self-delusive.

We can see the difficulty most clearly in domestic disputes of the sort that happen every day. A wife complains about a certain attitude or activity of her husband—but she is really complaining about something else. Only neither of them is aware of the nature of the true complaint.

Thus, an argument begins on a false basis, and can have no good or final ending. The wife, as she appears to herself, is saying one thing; as she appears to her husband, she is saying another; and as she really is, she is expressing some different and deeper grievance locked within her unconscious and allowed to trickle out only in this distorted form.

Likewise, the generally poor communication between parents and growing children is largely based on differing self-conceptions. The parent, as he appears to himself, is asking only "what is for the child's good." But the child sees it differently; to him the parent is serving his own private needs.

If persons cannot genuinely communicate, how can societies, communities, governments communicate with one another? The answer is that they cannot, except on a formal, superficial level; and even such a communication breaks down in a crisis. Mankind has not even begun to tackle seriously the prime problem of sending, receiving, and decoding messages.

"Strictly Personal" by Sydney J. Harris, Courtesy of Publishers-Hall Syndicate

this need will never be met, that rewarding human interaction for such a person is impossible.

The important point to be understood is that almost every time we initiate communication, even on a nonverbal level, we are making an implied request: "Please confirm my viewpoint." Sometimes this request is actually spoken; usually, however, it is implied on the unspoken, nonverbal level. Sometimes it concerns our understanding of factual data or information; frequently, it involves confirmation of an opinion. Always there is an implicit request for evaluation of us as a person. We can summarize the point thus: *every time we initiate communication or respond to it, we also make this request: "Please validate me—confirm my viewpoint and indicate my value as a person."* In this fashion we use interpersonal communication to form an impression of our self-identity.

The maintenance of a self-image, once it is formed, is a continuing process. Our self-image is confirmed anew whenever another person responds to us. Mutual recognition of such self-image provides confirmation and maintenance.

If there is consistent social confirmation, a strong and integrated self-identity will be developed and sustained. In such a case there is less need to seek confirmatory responses or to shield ourselves from possible disconfirmation. This condition provides greater freedom for the individual to be spontaneous, creative—to live; there is no great need to be concerned about every little criticism or evaluation of one's behavior. Such a person can dare to hear feedback about who and what he is, and can frequently test the validity of his beliefs about himself.

On the other hand, a person whose self-image is frequently disconfirmed will almost continually seek information about it; he will need to hear feedback, but will fear it; he will seek it, and at the same time try to avoid it. His self-image will suffer either way: if he hears negative evaluation no matter how slight, he will likely feel anxiety; if he avoids evaluation he will derogate himself for being a coward—he's "damned if he does and damned if he doesn't" seek self-image confirmation. Someone very wise once said, "To him who hath shall be given, and from him who hath not shall be taken away." This principle very much applies to the maintenance of one's self-image. To a very large extent theories of non-directive counseling developed by Carl Rogers are attempts to break this vicious circle of need, fear, and avoidance of possible image-building feedback.[6]

There is little question of the importance to the individual of the continuing need for interpersonal communication which confirms one's self-image. Once is never enough. Men have developed elaborate social rituals to reduce the probability of disconfirmation. Children are taught to become "tactful," responding to other people in a way that does not challenge the validity of the self-image they present in public. . . .

The Development of Self-Esteem

The self-image one desires must be achieved in his own eyes. Confirmation of this self-image by feedback from others gives a person the feeling that he is entitled to have this image of himself. Continuing confirmation helps him to maintain and to

clarify the image. In this sense the desired self-image is improved—it is perceived as more real, its wearer feels that it fits more comfortably, and the shadows of self-doubt are dispersed.

A desired self-image is the basis of self-esteem. A person acts and in doing so intentionally or unintentionally exposes his view of himself. Another person responds to this behavior; very frequently this response conveys approval or disapproval, acceptance or rejection. This simple unit of interpersonal communication is the basis of self-esteem. We tend to note and to increase our acts that elicit rewarding responses; those actions producing undesired responses are used less and less frequently. To a large extent, the ratio of satisfactory to unsatisfactory responses is the index of our self-esteem.

Communication senders seek to build and defend their self-identities and self-concepts.

Many responses from others are not easily interpreted as clear approval or disapproval. Most of us who are parents set an impossible task for ourselves: we want our children to believe that we love them unconditionally—without reservation; we also want them to behave in a reasonably acceptable way. To accomplish this we must respond approvingly to some of their behavior and disapprovingly to other actions. This will be communicated to them as *approving of them as persons* some of the time, and *disapproving of them as persons* at other times. For a child to interpret our responses as unconditional acceptance of him is almost impos-

sible; therefore, our love will be viewed as conditional. A child learns that certain of his behavior is acceptable and some is not; he will learn to like parts of himself, and parts he will not. His self-esteem will reflect the amount of himself that he likes or accepts; to increase self-esteem he will tend to repress those parts of himself which he does not like.

Interpersonal communication is the hinge upon which this process swings. If a child cannot distinguish between (1) strong approval of himself (and his potential) and (2) disapproval of a few specific behaviors, then his self-esteem will not be congruent with the attitudes expressed by his parents and others toward him. Accurate communication of approval and disapproval of him is imperative to his appropriate development of self-esteem.

The maintenance of self-esteem is as important and complex as its development. Many of our attempts at maintenance are successful; some are self-defeating. *We should look first at those which are least likely to be successful because they are used altogether too much.*

There are three self-defeating approaches to maintenance of self-esteem: (1) trying to hide parts of ourselves from others, (2) acting as if we were something we are not, and (3) following only the "straight and narrow" ritualized patterns of interaction. Our interest in this discussion will center upon the ways in which interpersonal communication is related to the success or failure of such attempts; improving one's own communication habits through new insights should be the reader's goal.

When we perceive that parts of ourselves are eliciting disapproval, we may attempt to hide those parts—if we think it can be done.

We then relate to others as "part-persons" rather than whole persons. For example, we may attempt to hide our anger when aroused. Or we may attempt to show no fear except when we are alone. Generally such attempts are ineffective: people usually see nonverbal signs of tension which are beyond our control; these are communicated to persons close to us despite our efforts to "say nothing." However, there are two considerations which are very important when we are successful at hiding such parts of ourselves. The first is that our anger or fear is stored up inside us, possibly influencing our later responses to communication from others. These feelings may break out in ways we don't understand and which are not understood by others. Such breakouts (or outbreaks) may not even be perceived by us but are easily seen by others.[7] In this fashion, later communication not related to the focus of our anger or fear may be influenced in such a way that others (and we) are confused. At best, such internalized anger and fear contribute to our problem of fighting off an early ulcer.[8] Improved habits of being open and frank in our interpersonal communication can be personally helpful.

A second possibly damaging effect of hiding parts of ourselves is that we cause apprehension in those persons with whom we relate. Suppose as your employer, I must tell you that you have failed to do your job in an adequate manner; suppose I tell you, and you show no reaction—you smile, remain calm, say nothing, and go your way. My interpretation is that you are a cool one, that you maintain your calmness through stiff self-discipline, and do not easily go out of control. But I also wonder if you'll "lay low and stab

me in the back" when I'm not expecting it—I become suspicious of you! I wonder how many emotional stimuli you can take before you react; do you remain calm under stress until at a certain point you "break" and cannot be depended upon at all? The point is this: you have given me no way to assess your emotional behavior—I perceive only part of you and suspect there is more. I have experienced you as only a "part-person," and as such you do not seem to be real. I am confused and will be suspicious until I learn more about you. In the meantime, this attitude will tend to distort my perceptions of even your ordinary, everyday communications which may be totally unrelated to the earlier event. In such fashion interpersonal communications and personal relationships are distorted by attempts to hide part of ourselves.

A second ineffective approach to maintaining our self-esteem is to pretend that we are something we are not. This approach includes attempts to communicate false messages about ourselves—to wear masks or to erect facades. This game can be carried to incredible extremes; we can even put forth a little of that part of ourselves which produces undesired responses and then deride, derogate, or castigate such behavior! . . .

Dishonesty with self and others undermines the self-concept.

A number of points may be made about pretending to be what we are not. In the first place, it takes much energy and concentration—while focusing on our

THEN AS I GREW A LITTLE OLDER AND LEARNED DISAPPOINTMENT I DEVELOPED THE NEW FEELING THAT WHEN I ENTERED A CROWDED ROOM—

—I WAS THE ONLY PERSON WHO WASN'T THERE.

performance, we may miss many clues to the way people are perceiving us. Goffman makes the point that many times people eventually discover that nobody is really watching these performances and in reality could not care less.[9] Such performances, when ignored, can amount to a severe loss of time and effort—time during which a genuinely rewarding interpersonal relationship might have been achieved.

In the second place, such play-acting must be good. Many a television comedy is based upon a character's pretense to be something he is not, with himself being the only member of the group who does not know that all others see through his facade. We may laugh at a comic character in a play, but we hardly want people laughing at our silly performance in real life. We'll mention more damaging effects later, but it seems bad enough to have people meet us and go away saying to themselves, "What an ass!"

A more damaging effect of another person's penetration of our "cover" is that he cannot further depend upon anything we do or say—suspicion haunts his every observation of our behavior—"What a phony!" He may never give us a very *obvious* clue of this suspicion, while his *subtle* show of a clue is lost by us in our concentration on our "performance." But when we need his confidence most—when we very much want his real trust and accurate estimate of our potential, when we ask him sincerely to give us a try—he will try others first, and we may be left alone with our pretenses, a lonely phony.

In our estimation, the most severe consequence of pretending to be something we are not is that it becomes a way of life. The more we pretend, the better we become at "playing a part." And

the better we are at "playing parts," the more we will try to solve our problems of interpersonal relations *by pretense* rather than by honestly facing issues and working out solutions based upon reality. One phony bit of behavior thus produces another, and even if we convince many other people, we will be faced with the problem of trying to find our real self. "Who are you?" is the basic question asked of persons thought to be mentally disturbed. Unlimited pursuit of pretense in life can produce the seeds of madness.[10]

The final disadvantage of pretense which will be mentioned here is that it seldom works for most people. Most of us are incapable of carrying it off on the non-verbal level. By tone of voice, facial expression, modified posture, jerkiness of gesture, and other elements of metacommunication usually beyond our control, we signal our anger, grief, fear, surprise, elation, and other real feelings and attitudes.[11] Few of us are adept at maintaining "poker faces" in our interactions. People may tolerate our pretense but they usually know it for what it is if they care at all to look. . . .

A third ineffective approach to the maintenance of self-esteem is to be very cautious, to pursue only the ritualized, common, "tried and true" forms of interpersonal behavior. "I can't receive negative feedback if I only do as everybody else does." This process is one of deliberate hiding of unique parts of ourselves, responding to the fear that they may be discovered. The effect on the other person is one of appraising you as only a "part-person"—too cautious, unnatural, and somewhat unreal. In some cases the other person becomes somewhat apprehensive, wondering when your real self may show

and what it will be like—and to what extent it may prove to be a threat.[12]

All three ineffective approaches to maintaining self-esteem discussed, hiding, pretending, and cautious adherence to ritualized responses, have been shown in one way or another to be a sham—unnatural, artificial, and to some extent damaging to our interpersonal interactions. Some of the time we may fool other people, and to some extent they may even succeed in helping us to fool ourselves. These approaches project a view of life which is superficial and lacking as to solid foundations, and thus ineffective in maintaining genuine self-esteem. The basis of a strong self-image is eroded.

Effective *maintenance* of self-esteem requires the same kind of behavior that developed it in the first place—exposure, feedback, and honest attempts at desirable change. The cycle must constantly be repeated. Maintaining self-esteem is a lifelong concern for most of us. Few persons appear to receive complete confirmation of perfection. As we expose new parts of ourselves and gain feedback, we see additional need to change; as we try to change, we receive new feedback evaluating these attempted changes. Thus, new exposures produce new change attempts, and so on as the cycle continues.

The Facilitation of Personal Change

Increasing self-esteem requires positive reevaluation of oneself. This reevaluation requires exposure plus awareness and honest responses on the part of another person. As pointed out, it is very difficult for a person to achieve change in interpersonal behavior

IN ALL OF LIFE IT SEEMED TO ME THAT I WAS THE LEAST REAL

BUT OF COURSE GROWTH IS A CONTINUING PROCESS. AS THE YEARS WENT BY I MELLOWED. I NO LONGER LOOKED AT LIFE IN ABSOLUTES.

without interaction with other persons.[13] The helpful relationship is one in which there is unconditional acceptance of a person (or his potential) combined with honest, direct feedback. Some persons achieve this relationship. It begins when people trust themselves and each other enough to start exposing more and more of their thoughts, ideas, and feelings. Each exposure is tentative; it comes in small increments and the response is noted. A disapproving response may stop the interaction temporarily or even permanently. When exposures are met with acceptance, interpersonal trust and self-confidence start to build. Each interacting party is mutually reinforcing: when one person trusts enough to expose himself more, trust is generated in the other person.[14]

In order to establish a relationship in which interpersonal communication of this order can be achieved, we may have to go out of our way to find persons who are open and frank and accepting toward us. There is increasing evidence that such relationships can be obtained if sought, with consequent benefit to both of the interacting persons.[15] Such relationships are to be prized and protected with great care and caring.

We have given extensive consideration to the development of self-image and the achievement of self-esteem. We have done so deliberately because, in all of the areas in which interpersonal communication influences people, we can think of nothing which is more important. We believe that these elements are fundamental to most if not all human interaction.

1. G.H. Mead, *Mind, Self and Society*, Chicago, Univ. of Chicago Press. 1934, pp. 144–64.

2. E. Erikson, "The Problem of Ego Identity," *Psychological Issues*, 1 (1959), 47.

3. B. Latane, "Studies in Social Comparison—Introduction and Overview," *Journal of Experimental Social Psychology Supplement*, 1 (1966), 1–5.

4. R. Radloff, "Social Comparison and Ability Evaluation," *Journal of Experimental Social Psychology Supplement*, 1 (1966), 6–26.

5. H. Duncan, *Communication and Social Order*, New York, Oxford Univ. Press, 1962, pp. 271–73.

6. C. Rogers, *On Becoming a Person*, Boston, Houghton Mifflin, 1961.

7. Ibid., pp. 338–46.

8. S. Jourard, *The Transparent Self*, New York, Van Nostrand Reinhold, 1964, pp. 184–85.

9. E. Goffman, *The Presentation of Self in Everyday Life*, Garden City, N.Y., Doubleday Anchor, 1959.

10. H. Deutsch, "The Imposter: Contribution to Ego Psychology of a Type of Psychopath," *Psychoanalytical Quarterly*, 24 (1955), 483–505.

11. P. Watzlawick, J.H. Beavin, and D.D. Jackson, *Pragmatics of Communication*, New York, Norton, 1967, pp. 62–67.

12. E. Goffman, "On Face-Work: An Analysis of Ritual Elements in Social Interaction," *Psychiatry*, 18 (1955), 213–31.

13. W.G. Bennis, et al., *Interpersonal Dynamics*, rev. ed., Homewood, Ill., Dorsey, 1968, pp. 505–23.

14. J. Gibb, "Defensive Communication," *Journal of Communication*, 11 (1961), 141–48.

15. D. Barnlund, *Interpersonal Communication*, Boston, Houghton Mifflin, 1968, pp. 613–45.

NOWADAYS WHEN I ENTER A CROWDED ROOM—

IM NOT SURE ANY OF US ARE THERE.

Imagination—The First Key to Your Success Mechanism

Maxwell Maltz

Imagination plays a far more important role in our lives than most of us realize.

I have seen this demonstrated many times in my practice. A particularly memorable instance of this fact concerned a patient who was literally forced to visit my office by his family. He was a man of about forty, unmarried, who held down a routine job during the day and kept to himself in his room when the work day was over, never going anywhere, never doing anything. He had had many such jobs and never seemed able to stay with any of them for any great length of time. His problem was that he had a rather large nose and ears that protruded a little more than is normal. He considered himself "ugly" and "funny looking." He imagined that the people he came into contact with during the day were laughing at him and talking about him behind his back because he was so "odd." His imaginings grew so strong that he actually feared going out into the business world and moving among people. He hardly felt "safe" even in his own home. The poor man even imagined that his family was "ashamed" of him because he was "peculiar looking," not like "other people."

Actually, his facial deficiencies were not serious. His nose was of the "classical Roman" type, and his ears, though somewhat large, attracted no more attention than those of thousands of people with similar ears. In desperation, his family brought him to me to see if I could help him. I saw that he did not need surgery . . . only an understanding of the fact that his imagination had wrought such havoc with his self-image that he had lost sight of the truth. He was not really ugly. People did not consider him odd and laugh at him because of his appearance. His imagination alone was responsible for his misery. His imagination had set up an automatic, negative, failure mechanism within him and it was operating full blast, to his extreme misfortune. Fortunately, after several sessions with him, and with the help of his family, he was able gradually to realize that the power of his own imagination was responsible for his plight, and he succeeded in building up a true self-image and achieving the confidence he needed by applying creative imagination rather than destructive imagination.

"Creative imagination" is not something reserved for the poets, the philosophers, the inventors. It enters into our every act. For imagination sets the goal "picture" which our automatic mechanism works on. We act, or fail to act, not because of "will," as is so commonly believed, but because of imagination.

A human being always acts and feels and performs in accordance with what he *imagines* to be *true* about himself and his environment. This is a basic and fundamental law of mind. It is the way we are built. When we see this law of mind graphically and dramatically demonstrated in a hypnotized subject, we are prone to think that there is something occult or supra-normal at work. Actually, what we are witnessing is the normal operating processes of the human brain and nervous system.

Imagination can change your self-concept as you reflect upon your interactions with others.

For example, if a good hypnotic subject is told that he is at the North Pole he will not only shiver and *appear* to be cold, his body will react just as if he were cold and goose pimples will develop. The same phenomenon has been demonstrated on wide-awake college students by asking them to *imagine* that one hand is immersed in ice water. Thermometer readings show that the temperature does drop in the "treated" hand. Tell a hypnotized subject that your finger is a red hot poker and he will not only grimace with pain at your touch, but his cardiovascular and lymphatic systems will react just as if your finger were a red hot poker and produce inflammation and perhaps a blister on the skin. When college students, wide-awake, have been told to *imagine* that a spot on their foreheads was hot, temperature readings have shown an actual increase in skin temperature.

Your nervous system cannot tell the difference between an *imag-*

From the book PSYCHO-CYBERNETICS by Maxwell Maltz, M.D., F.I.C.S. © 1960 by Prentice-Hall, Inc.

ined experience and a "real" experience. In either case, it reacts automatically to information which you give to it from your forebrain. Your nervous system reacts appropriately to what "you" *think* or *imagine* to be *true.*

Why Not Imagine Yourself Successful?

Realizing that our actions, feelings, and behavior are the result of our own images and beliefs gives us the lever that psychology has always needed for changing personality. It opens a new psychologic door to gaining skill, success, and happiness.

Mental pictures offer us an opportunity to "practice" new traits and attitudes, which otherwise we could not do. This is possible because again—your nervous system cannot tell the difference between an actual experience and one that is vividly imagined. If we picture ourselves performing in a certain manner, it is nearly the same as the actual performance. Mental practice helps to make perfect.

In a controlled experiment, psychologist R. A. Vandell proved that mental practice in throwing darts at a target, wherein the person sits for a period each day in front of the target, and imagines throwing darts at it, improves aim as much as actually throwing darts.

Research Quarterly reports an experiment on the effects of mental practice on improving skill in sinking basketball free throws. One group of students actually practiced throwing the ball every day for twenty days, and were scored on the first and last days. A second group was scored on the first and last days, and engaged in no sort of practice in between. A third group was scored on the

Nowhere Man

John Lennon and Paul McCartney

He's a real Nowhere Man,
Sitting in his Nowhere Land,
Making all his nowhere plans for nobody.
Doesn't have a point of view;
Knows not where he's going to.
Isn't he a bit like you and me?

Nowhere Man, please listen,
You don't know what you're missing,
Nowhere Man. The world is at your command.

He's as blind as he can be;
Just sees what he wants to see.
Nowhere Man, can you see me at all?
Doesn't have a point of view;
Knows not where he's going to.
Isn't he a bit like you and me?

Nowhere Man, don't worry.
Take your time; don't hurry.
Leave it all till somebody else lends you a hand.

He's a real Nowhere Man,
Sitting in his Nowhere Land,
Making all his nowhere plans for nobody,
Making all his nowhere plans for nobody,
Making all his nowhere plans for nobody.

first day, then spent twenty minutes a day, imagining that they were throwing the ball at the goal. When they missed they would imagine that they corrected their aim accordingly. The first group, which actually practiced twenty minutes every day, improved in scoring 24 per cent. The second group, which had no sort of practice, showed no improvement. The third group, which practiced in their imagination, improved in scoring 23 per cent!

Practice Exercise

Your present self-image was built upon your own imagination pictures of yourself in the past which grew out of interpretations and evaluations which you placed upon *experience*. Now you are to use the same method to build an adequate self-image that you previously used to build an inadequate one.

Set aside a period of thirty minutes each day when you can be alone and undisturbed. Relax and make yourself as comfortable as possible. Now close your eyes and exercise your imagination.

Many people find they get better results if they imagine themselves sitting before a large motion picture screen—and imagine that they are seeing a motion picture of themselves. The important thing is to make these pictures as *vivid* and as *detailed* as possible. You want your mental pictures to approximate actual experience as much as possible. The way to do this is pay attention to small details, sights, sounds, objects, in your imagined environment. One of my patients was using this exercise to overcome her fear of the dentist. She was unsuccessful, until she began to notice small details in her imagined picture—the smell of the antiseptic

in the office, the feel of the leather on the chair arms, the sight of the dentist's well-manicured nails as his hands approached her mouth, etc. *Details* of the imagined environment are all-important in this exercise, because for all practical purposes, you are creating a *practice experience*. And if the imagination is vivid enough and detailed enough, your imagination practice is equivalent to an actual experience, insofar as your nervous system is concerned.

The next important thing to remember is that during this thirty minutes you see yourself acting and reacting appropriately, successfully, ideally. It doesn't matter how you acted yesterday. You do not need to try to have faith you will act in the ideal way tomorrow. Your nervous system will take care of that in time—if you continue to practice. See yourself acting, feeling, "being," as you want to be. Do not say to yourself, "I am going to act this way tomorrow." Just say to yourself—"I am going to imagine myself acting this way now—for thirty minutes—today." Imagine how you would feel if you were already the sort of personality you want to be. If you have been shy and timid, see yourself moving among people with ease and poise —and *feeling good* because of it. If you have been fearful and anxious in certain situations—see yourself acting calmly and deliberately, acting with confidence and courage—and feeling expansive and confident because you are.

This exercise builds new "memories" or stored data into your mid-brain and central nervous system. It builds a new image of self. After practicing it for a time, you will be surprised to find yourself "acting differently," more or less automatically and sponta-

neously—"without trying." This is as it should be. You do not need to "take thought" or "try" or make an effort now in order to feel ineffective and act inadequately. Your present inadequate feeling and doing is automatic and spontaneous, because of the memories, real and imagined you have built into your automatic mechanism. You will find it will work just as automatically upon positive thoughts and experiences as upon negative ones.

Self-Disclosure

David W. Johnson

How well do I know myself? How well do other people know me? Am I an easy person to get to know? Do I feel free to tell others how I am reacting, feeling, and what I am thinking? These are important questions. To like you, to be involved with you, to be your friend, I must know who you are. In order for me to know you, you must know yourself. In order for you to feel free to disclose yourself to me, you must accept and appreciate yourself.

Without self-disclosure you cannot form a close personal relationship with another person. A relationship between two individuals develops as the two become more open about themselves and more self-disclosing. If you cannot reveal yourself, you cannot become close to others, and you cannot be valued by others for who you are. To become closely involved with another person, you must know him and he must know you. Two people who share how they are reacting to situations and to each other are pulled together; two people who stay silent about their reactions and feelings stay strangers. To like you, to be involved with you, I must know who you are. To like me, to be involved with me, you must know who I am.

Self-disclosure may be defined as revealing how you are reacting to the present situation and giving any information about the past that is relevant to understanding how you are reacting to the present. Reactions to people and events are not facts as much as feelings. To be self-disclosing means to share with another person how you feel about something he has done or said, or how you feel about the events which have just taken place. Self-disclosure does not mean revealing intimate details of your past life. Making highly personal confessions about your past may lead to a temporary feeling of intimacy, but a relationship is built by disclosing your reactions to events you both experience or to what the other person says or does. A person comes to know and understand you not through knowing your past history but through knowing how you react. Past history is only helpful if it clarifies why you are reacting in a certain way.

There has been a considerable amount of research on the effects of self-disclosure upon interpersonal relationships (Johnson, 1972). There is, for example, much evidence that indicates that healthy relationships are based upon self-disclosure. If you

hide how you are reacting to the other person, your concealment can sicken the relationship. The energy you pour into hiding adds to the stress of the relationship and dulls your awareness of your own inner experience, thus decreasing your ability to disclose your reactions even when it is perfectly safe and appropriate to do so. Hiding your reactions from others through fear of rejection and conflict or through feelings of shame and guilt leads to loneliness. Being silent is not being strong; strength is the willingness to take risks in the relationship, to disclose yourself with the intention of building a better relationship.

Several aspects of a relationship influence self-disclosure. The more self-disclosing you are to another person, the more likely that person will like you. You are more likely to self-disclose to a person you know and like than to a person you do not know or do not like. The amount of self-disclosure you engage in will influence the amount of self-disclosure the other person engages in; the more you self-disclose, the more the other person will tend to self-disclose.

Self-disclosure and feedback can help you form close relationships with others.

Willingness to engage in self-disclosure is related to several characteristics. The research done in this field indicates that a person willing to be self-disclosing will likely be a competent, open, and socially extroverted person who feels a strong need to interact with others. He is likely

---

David W. Johnson, REACHING OUT: Interpersonal Effectiveness and Self-Actualization, © 1972. Reprinted by permission of Prentice-Hall, Inc., Englewood Cliffs, New Jersey.

to be flexible, adaptive, and perhaps more intelligent than his less self-revealing peers. He is objectively aware of the realities of the interpersonal situations in which he is involved and perceives a fairly close congruence between the way he is and the way in which he would like to be. Finally, he views his fellowman as generally good rather than evil.

Healthy relationships are based upon self-disclosure.

Communicating intimately with another person, especially in times of stress, seems to be a basic human need. Disclosing yourself to another person builds a relationship which allows for such intimate communication, both by yourself and by the other. If neither you nor the other feels free to engage in self-disclosure, you can be of little or no help to each other during periods of stress.

Being self-disclosing means being "for real." It is important that your self-disclosures are as honest, genuine, and authentic as possible. In this chapter we will focus upon some of the skills involved in effective self-disclosure, but the communication of the sincerity, genuineness, and authenticity of your self-disclosures is one of the most important aspects of building a relationship.

In addition to being *open with* other people, you must be *open to* others to build meaningful relationships. Being open to another person means showing that you are interested in how he feels about what you are saying and doing. It is being receptive to his self-disclosure. This does not mean prying into the intimate areas of another's life. It means being willing to listen to his reactions to the present situation and to what you are doing and saying.

In responding to another's self-disclosure, it is important to accept and support him if possible. Being accepting and supportive will increase the other person's tendency to be open with you. It will strengthen the relationship and help it grow. Even when a person's behavior seriously offends you, it is possible for you to express acceptance of the person and disagreement with the way he behaves. To be open with another person is to risk rejection; to self-disclose is to ask for support and acceptance in trying to build a better relationship. You should be careful, therefore, to give the support and acceptance necessary for the relationship to grow.

Appropriateness of Self-Disclosure

Self-disclosure must be relevant to your relationship with the other person and appropriate to the situation you are in. You can be too self-disclosing. A person who reveals too much of his reactions too fast may scare others away; a relationship is built gradually except in rare and special cases. Certainly being too self-disclosing will create as many relationship problems as disclosing too little. Although you should sometimes take risks with your self-disclosure to others, you should not be blind to the appropriateness of your behavior to the situation. Self-disclosure is appropriate when:

1. It is not a random or isolated act but rather is part of an ongoing relationship.

2. It is reciprocated.

3. It concerns what is going on within and between persons in the present.

4. It creates a reasonable chance of improving the relationship.

5. Account is taken of the effect it will have upon the other person.

6. It is speeded up in a crisis in the relationship.

7. It gradually moves to a deeper level.

While relationships are built through self-disclosure, there are times when you will want to hide your reactions to the present situation from another person. If a person has clearly shown himself to be untrustworthy, it is foolish to be self-disclosing with him. If you know from past experience that the other person will misinterpret or overreact to your self-disclosure, you may wish to keep silent.

Self-Disclosure and Self-Awareness

Your ability to disclose yourself to others depends upon your self-awareness and self-acceptance. You must be aware of your reactions in order to communicate them to others. Without accepting your reactions you cannot feel free to allow other individuals to hear them. In this section we will focus upon self-awareness. In a later chapter in the book we will focus upon self-acceptance.

You should be continually trying to increase your self-awareness in order to be able to engage in self-disclosure. In order to discuss how you may increase your self-awareness, it may be helpful

to look at the models found in Figures 2.1, 2.2, 2.3 (Luft, 1969).

These models are named the Johari Window after its two originators, Joe Luft and Harry Ingham. It illustrates that there are certain things you know about yourself and certain things that you do not know about yourself. Correspondingly, there are certain things other people know about you and certain things they do not know. It is assumed that it takes energy to hide information from yourself and others and that the more information that is known the clearer communication will be. Building a relationship therefore often involves working to enlarge the free area while decreasing the blind and hidden areas. As you become more self-disclosing, you reduce the hidden area. As you encourage others to be self-disclosing with you, your blind area is reduced. Through reducing your hidden area you give other people information to react to, which enables them to help you reduce your blind area. Through reducing your blind area, your self-awareness is increased; this helps you to be even more self-disclosing with others.

Constructive Self-Disclosure[1]

People rarely talk openly about their reactions to each other's behavior. Most of us withhold our feelings about the other person (even in relations that are very important or dear to us) because we are afraid of hurting the other person, making him angry, or being rejected by him. Because we do not know how to be constructively self-disclosing, we say nothing. The other person continues to be totally unaware of our

---

1. The material in this section was originally developed by J.L. Wallen.

	Known to Self	Unknown to Self
Known to Others	1. Free to self and others	2. Blind to self, seen by others
Unknown to Others	3. Hidden area: self hidden from others	4. Unknown self

Fig. 2-1. *Identification of areas of the self*

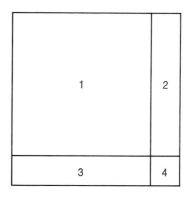

Fig. 2-2. *At the beginning of a relationship*

Fig. 2-3. *After the development of a close relationship*

reaction to his actions. Likewise we continue to be ignorant of the effect our actions produce in him. Consequently, many relations that could be productive and enjoyable gradually deteriorate under the accumulated load of tiny annoyances, hurt feelings, and misunderstandings that were never talked about openly.

The following points increase the chances that self-disclosure will improve a relationship rather than harm it.

1. Self-disclosure must begin with a *desire to improve your relationship with the other person.* Self-disclosure is not an end in itself but a means to an end. We are not open with people when we do not care about them. When you are trying to establish an open sharing of reactions with another person, try to let him know that this means you value your relationship with him and wish to improve it *because* it is important.

2. Try to create a shared understanding of your relationship. You wish to know how the other person perceives and feels about your actions. You want him to know how you perceive and feel about his actions. Each of you will then view the relationship from more nearly the same viewpoint.

3. Realize that self-disclosure involves *risk-taking.* Your willingness to risk being rejected or hurt by the other person depends on how important the relationship is to you. You cannot tell that the other person will not become angry or feel hurt by what you say. The important point is that you are willing to risk his being himself, whatever he

feels, in the effort to make the encounter into a learning situation for both of you.

4. Although the discussion may become intense, spirited, angry, or tearful, it should be *noncoercive* and should not be an attempt to make the other person change. Each person should use the information as he sees fit. The attitude should not be "Who's wrong and who's right?" but "What can each of us learn from this discussion that will make our relationship more productive and more satisfying?" As a result of the discussion one, both, or neither of you may act differently in the future. Each of you, however, will act with fuller awareness of the effect of his actions on the other as well as with more understanding of the other person's intentions. Any change will thus be self-chosen rather than compelled by a desire to please or to submit to the other.

5. Timing is important. Reactions should be shared at a time as close to the behavior that aroused them as possible so that both persons will know exactly what behavior is being discussed. For example, you can comment on behavior during the encounter itself: "What you just said is the kind of remark that makes me feel pushed away."

6. Disturbing situations should be discussed as they happen; hurt feelings and annoyances should not be saved up and dropped on another person all at one time.

7. Paraphrase the other person's comments about you to make sure you understand them as he means them. Check to

make sure the other understands your comments in the way you mean them.

8. Statements are more helpful if they are
   Specific rather than general: "You bumped my plate," rather than "You never watch where you're going."
   Tentative rather than absolute: "You seem unconcerned about Jimmy," rather than "You don't give a damn about Jimmy and never will."
   Informing rather than ordering: "I hadn't finished yet," rather than "Stop interrupting me."

9. Use perception-checking responses to insure that you are not making false assumptions about the other's feelings. "I thought you weren't interested in trying to understand my idea. Was I wrong?" "Did my last statement bother you?"

10. The least helpful kinds of statements are those that sound as if they are information about the other person but are really expressions of your own feelings. Avoid the following:
    Judgments about the other: "You never pay any attention."
    Name-calling, trait labeling: "You're a phony"; "You're too rude."
    Accusations; imputing undesirable motives to the other: "You enjoy putting people down"; "You always have to be the center of attention."
    Commands and orders: "Stop laughing"; "Don't talk so much."
    Sarcasm: "You always look on the bright side of things, don't you?" (when the opposite is meant).

11. The most helpful kinds of

information about yourself and your reactions are:

Behavior descriptions. To develop skills in describing another person's behavior you must sharpen your skills in observing what actually did occur. Let others know what behavior you are responding to by describing it clearly and specifically enough that they know what you saw. To do this you must describe visible evidence, behavior that is open to anybody's observation. Restrict yourself to talking about the things the other person did.

Examples: "Bob, you seem to disagree with whatever Harry suggests today." (*Not* "Bob, you're just trying to show Harry up." This is not a description but an accusation of unworthy motives.)

"Jim, you've talked more than others on this topic. Several times you interrupted others before they had finished." (*Not* "Jim, you're too rude!" which names a trait and gives no evidence. *Not* "Jim, you always want to hog the center of attention" which imputes an unworthy motive or intention.)

"Sam, I had not finished my statement when you interrupted me." (*Not* "Sam, you deliberately didn't let me finish." The word *deliberately* implies that Sam knowingly and intentionally cut you off. All anybody can observe is that he did interrupt you.)

Descriptions of your own feelings. You should attempt to describe your feelings about the other person's actions so that your feelings are seen as temporary and capable of change rather than as permanent. It is better to say, "At this point I'm very annoyed with you," than "I dislike you and I always will."

Reach Out in the Darkness

Jim Post

I think it's so groovy now
That people are finally getting together.
I think it's so wonderful and how that people are finally getting
*   together.*
Reach out in the darkness.
Reach out in the darkness.
Reach out in the darkness and you may find a friend.

I know a man that I did not care for;
And then one day this man gave me a call.
We sat and talked about things on our mind,
And now this man he is a friend of mine.
Don't be afraid of love.
Don't be afraid, don't be afraid to love.
Everybody needs a little love.
Everybody needs somebody that they can be thinking of.

I think it's so groovy now
That people are finally getting together.
I think it's so wonderful and how that people are finally getting
*   together.*
Reach out in the darkness.
Reach out in the darkness.
Reach out in the darkness and you may find a friend.

I WIN AGAIN!

HE **HAS** MADE SOME PROGRESS IN GOAL ORIENTATION.

Perception and Human Understanding

Raymond S. Ross

An understanding of the way people receive, decode, and assign meaning is critical. Listening is much more than hearing acuity. All of our sensory apparatus may be involved in helping us interpret even a primarily oral signal. The perception process is for our purposes identical to the communication process except that the emphasis is on receiving instead of sending. The receiver or perceiver is thought to posit hypotheses which he accepts or rejects. Postman calls this a cycle of hypothesis involving information, trial and check, confirmation or nonconfirmation.[1] The meaning then is supplied primarily by learning and by past experience.

Sensation and Interpretation

Have you ever been on a train which is stopped between other trains in a railroad terminal? Have you then felt, seen, and heard all of the signs indicating movement, only to find that it is the other trains that are moving? Perhaps you discovered this when the other train was actually gone, or perhaps you fixed your gaze on something you *knew* was not moving, such as the ceiling of the station, a roof support, or the ground itself.

The point is that perception involves essentially two acts: (1) the *sensation* caused by the stimulation of a sensory organ, and (2) the *interpretation* of the sensation. . . . It is primarily through our knowledge and experience that we interpret or attach meaning to a symbol.

The complexity of human communication is further indicated by the various levels of perception now thought to exist. We talk of subliminal or subthreshold perception, that is, a receiving below the level of conscious awareness. This is not to be confused with so-called extrasensory perception. Many experiments have been conducted in this field, most of them involving visual projections at speeds above our physiological level of perception, but below our awareness level, or, in some cases, at our awareness level, but below our recognition level. They are complicated by the fact that people vary in their perceptual abilities not only one from another, but also in their own individual range of acuity. The best-known of all subthreshold experiments involved the projection of nonsense syllables.[2] Meaningless combinations of letters were associated with electric shock. When these stimuli were later presented subthresholdly (at speeds too rapid to permit their conscious identification), the subjects' emotional reactions were more intense than their reactions to other nonsense syllables not previously associated with shock. The subjects had been able to identify the stimuli unconsciously before they could do so consciously.

A person's set, expectancy, or preparation to perceive has much to do with his level of perception as well as his individual acceptance of a stimulus.[3] The consciousness defends itself through an apparent refusal to accept certain messages. On the other hand, we may wish or desire so very much to hear something that, regardless of the actual code or words emitted, we attend, interpret, and attach meaning in terms of what we wish to hear. One of the great barriers to good communication is the tendency to hear what we wish to hear, see what we wish to see, and believe what we wish to believe. This kind of behavior is called *autistic thinking*. Piaget defines autism as "thought in which truth is confused with desire."[4] In its extreme form this kind of perception and thinking grows out of an abnormal emotional need for ego-satisfaction, and we actually have a mental disorder known as *paranoia*. The foregoing indicates that perception is a function of *internal* as well as external sources of stimulation. Signals which originate within us also enter into the perceptual act.

Your perceptions may be a prime obstacle to effective communication.

Another closely related perceptual and communication problem arises because of a normal tendency to completeness. In communications which appear to be only partially complete, we often read in the unsaid part or complete the pattern. If we do not arrive at a sense of completeness or closure we often feel upset, ill at ease, confused, and unhappy.

This tendency can be an important factor in motivation. Perhaps you have had a teacher who communicates just enough knowledge in a stimulating way, motivating you to do further reading and research so that you can complete or close the pattern. The problem arises when we close incomplete communication patterns in ways not intended by the speaker. This tendency is illustrated by an incomplete triangle. We find it more reasonable, more comfortable to see figure 1 as a completed triangle.

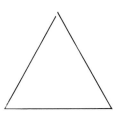

Fig. 1. *Pattern closing tendencies*

Sometimes our habits and previous experience cause us to leave things out. Read the next three messages quickly.

Many people see nothing unusual about these messages even after two or three readings. The good, rapid readers seem to have the most trouble. Why should this be so? A group of second and third graders had no trouble finding the double words in each message. We perceive to a certain extent what our habits, our emotions, and our knowledge and past experiences let us perceive. A good reader has learned to skim and to ignore nonessential words. The beginning reader sees literally one word at a time.

Test your perceptual ability on the next two stimuli. Do you see anything familiar or identifiable? Do you see a message?

You should see the words LEFT and FLY in white on a partial black field. Your experience is typically just the opposite—the area *between* the letters is in black instead of the letters themselves.[5] Even after you see the messages they may escape you momentarily as your longstanding habits and previous experience patterns fight to assert their influence.

Conventionalized Perception

The problem of stereotyped or stylized communication, particularly where gesture and bodily movement are concerned, is also an interesting aspect of perception. Experimental studies of the portrayal and recognition of emotion illustrate this point. Landis performed an experiment designed to discover whether reported emotions are accompanied by definite and easily recognized facial expressions. A series of photographs were taken of his subjects while they were actually undergoing various emotion-producing situations, not simply portraying emotions as an actor would. Landis had a regular torture-chamber experiment,

and after many comparisons he writes: "There is no expression typically associated with any verbal report."[6]

A study similar to the one described above was conducted by Feleky, but with one vital difference: the photographs of emotions were artifically portrayed or acted. The experimenter found in this case a remarkable agreement on the description of the poses, indicating that we may interpret an individual's emotional state with reasonable accuracy from a posed photograph.[7]

A study with more specific conclusions was conducted by Knower and Dusenbury. The design of the study was almost identical to Feleky's. Knower and Dusenbury concluded:

1. Interpretation of the facial expression of emotional tendencies and attitudes may be made with a high degree of reliability.

2. There are significant individual and group differences in ability correctly to interpret facial expressions of the emotions.

3. Women are more accurate in the interpretation of facial expressions of the emotions than men.

4. Patterns of facial expression extended in time, as on a short, moving picture, are judged more accurately than are still photographs of the same emotional tendencies.

5. Accuracy in the interpretation of facial expressions of the emotions is influenced by the conditions under which such expressions are judged.[8]

As far as communication (recognition) is concerned in these experiments, we can say that simulated or stereotyped emotions can be perceived or identified with some reliability. With recognition of real emotions one might just as well leave the judgment to chance.

Good actors and capable speakers appear to communicate emotions with regularity. The actor has the play, the set, the other actors, and the stylized conceptions of the audience to help him. If the cause of whatever emotion the actor is portraying is also perceived (for example, a gun and fear), the communication pattern is easier to follow.

But though certain peripheral patterns or expressions have become stylized, we still have a potential barrier to communication, for these patterns may vary so much from person to person, sender and receiver, that excepting perhaps skilled acting, it remains difficult to communicate the precise emotion intended.

The conclusion of all this research is that the "meaning" is in the eyes, ears, and other senses of the beholder to some extent, but it is more in his previous experience, learning, knowledge, feelings, attitudes, and emotions.

1. L. Postman, "Toward a General Theory of Cognition," in J.H. Rohrer and M. Sherif, eds., *Social Psychology at the Crossroads* (New York: Harper & Row, Publishers, 1951), p. 251.
Also see J.S. Bruner, "Personality Dynamics and the Process of Perceiving," in R.R. Blake and G.V. Ramsey, eds., *Perception: An Approach to Personality* (New York: The Ronald Press Company, 1951).

2. R.S. Lazarus and R.A. McCleary, "Automatic Discrimination Without Awareness: A Study in Subception," *Psychological Review*, 58 (1951), 113–22.

3. Charles M. Solley and Gardner Murphy, *Development of the Perceptual World* (New York: Basic Books, Inc., 1960), p. 239.

4. J. Piaget, *The Child's Conception of Physical Causality* (London: Routledge & Kegan Paul, Ltd., 1930), p. 302.

5. This is referred to as a figure-ground transformation.

6. "Experimental Studies of the Emotions: The Work of Cannon and Others," in Henry E. Garrett, *Great Experiments in Psychology* (New York: Appleton-Century-Crofts, 1941), p. 331.

7. Garrett, *Great Experiments in Psychology*, p. 330.

8. D. Dusenbury and F.H. Knower, "Experimental Studies of the Symbolism of Action and Voice—I: A Study of the Specificity of Meaning in Facial Expression," *Quarterly Journal of Speech* XXIV, No. 3 (1938), 435.

Hi and Lois by Mort Walker and Dik Browne

Problems in Active Listening   Empathic

Carl B. Rogers and Richard E. Farson

Active listening is not an easy skill to acquire. It demands practice. Perhaps more important, it may require changes in our own basic attitudes. These changes come slowly and sometimes with considerable difficulty. Let us look at some of the major problems in active listening and what can be done to overcome them.

The Personal Risk

To be effective at all in active listening, one must have a sincere interest in the speaker. We all live in glass houses as far as our attitudes are concerned. They always show through. And if we are only making a pretense of interest in the speaker, he will quickly pick this up, either consciously or unconsciously. And once he does, he will no longer express himself freely.

Active listening carries a strong element of personal risk. If we manage to accomplish what we are describing here—to sense deeply the feeling of another person, to understand the meaning his experiences have for him, to see the world as he sees it—we risk being changed ourselves. For example, if we permit ourselves to listen our way into the psychological life of a labor leader or agitator—to get the meaning which life has for him—we risk coming to see the world as he sees it. It is threatening to give up, even momentarily, what we believe and start thinking in someone else's terms. It takes a great deal of inner security and courage to be able to risk one's self in understanding another.

For the supervisor, the courage to take another's point of view generally means that he must see *himself* through another's eyes—he must be able to see himself as others see him. To do this may sometimes be unpleasant, but it is far more *difficult* than unpleasant. We are so accustomed to viewing ourselves in certain ways—to seeing and hearing only what we want to see and hear—that it is extremely difficult for a person to free himself from his needs to see things these ways.

Developing an attitude of sincere interest in the speaker is thus no easy task. It can be developed only by being willing to risk seeing the world from the speaker's point of view. If we have a number of such experiences, however, they will shape an attitude which will allow us to be truly genuine in our interest in the speaker.

Hostile Expressions

The listener will often hear negative, hostile expressions directed at himself. Such expressions are always hard to listen to. No one likes to hear hostile words. And it is not easy to get to the point where one is strong enough to permit these attacks without find-

From "Active Listening" by Carl B. Rogers and Richard E. Farson. Reprinted by permission of publisher—Industrial Relations Center, The University of Chicago, Chicago, Illinois 60637.

Invisible Man

Ralph Ellison

I am an invisible man. No, I am not a spook like those who haunted Edgar Allan Poe; nor am I one of your Hollywood-movie ectoplasms. I am a man of substance, of flesh and bone, fiber and liquid—and I might even be said to possess a mind. I am invisible, understand, simply because people refuse to see me. Like the bodiless heads you see sometimes in circus sideshows, it is as though I have been surrounded by mirrors of hard, distorting glass. When they approach me they see only my surroundings, themselves, or figments of their imagination—indeed, everything and anything except me.

ing it necessary to defend oneself or retaliate.

Because we all fear that people will crumble under the attack of genuine negative feelings, we tend to perpetuate an attitude of pseudo peace. It is as if we cannot tolerate conflict at all for fear of the damage it could do to us, to the situation, to the others involved. But of course the real damage is done to all these by the denial and suppression of negative feelings.

Out-of-place Expressions

There is also the problem of out-of-place expressions—expressions dealing with behavior which is not usually acceptable in our society. In the extreme forms that present themselves before psychotherapists, expressions of sexual perversity or homicidal fantasies are often found blocking to the listener because of their obvious threatening quality. At less extreme levels, we all find unnatural or inappropriate behavior difficult to handle. That is, anything from an off-color story told in mixed company to a man weeping is likely to produce a problem situation.

Active listening requires perceiving situations from the point of view of the sender.

In any face-to-face situation, we will find instances of this type which will momentarily, if not permanently, block any communication. In business and industry, any expressions of weakness or incompetency will generally be regarded as unacceptable and therefore will block good two-way communication. For example, it is difficult to listen to a supervisor tell of his feelings of failure in being able to "take charge" of a situation in his department, because *all* administrators are supposed to be able to "take charge."

Accepting Positive Feelings

It is both interesting and perplexing to note that negative or hostile feelings or expressions are much easier to deal with in any face-to-face relationship than are truly and deeply positive feelings. This is especially true for the businessman, because the culture expects him to be independent, bold, clever, and aggressive and manifest no feelings of warmth, gentleness, and intimacy. He therefore comes to regard these feelings as soft and inappropriate. But no matter how they are regarded, they remain a human need. The denial of these feelings in himself and his associates does not get the executive out of the problem of dealing with them. They simply become veiled and confused. If recognized, they would work for the total effort; unrecognized, they work against it.

Emotional Danger Signals

The listener's own emotions are sometimes a barrier to active listening. When emotions are at their height, which is when listening is most necessary, it is most difficult to set aside one's own concerns and be understanding. Our emotions are often our own worst enemies when we try to become listeners. The more involved and invested we are in a particular situation or problem, the less we are likely to be willing or able to listen to the feelings

THE WINDMILLS OF YOUR MIND

(THEME FROM "THE THOMAS CROWN AFFAIR")

Lyric by
MARILYN *and* ALAN BERGMAN

Music by
MICHEL LEGRAND

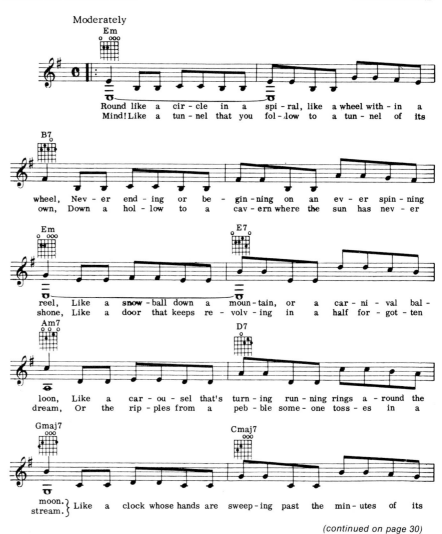

(continued on page 30)

(continued from page 29)

face, And the world is like an ap-ple whirl-ing si-lent-ly in space, Like the cir-cles that you find in The Wind-mills Of Your Mind! Keys that jin-gle in your pock-et, words that jan-gle in your head, Why did sum-mer go so quick-ly? Was it some-thing that you said? Lov-ers walk a-long a shore and leave their foot-prints in the sand. Is the sound of dis-tant drum-ming just the fin-gers of your hand? Pic-tures hang-ing in a hall-way and the frag-ment of a

(continued on page 31)

and attitudes of others. That is, the more we find it necessary to respond to our own needs, the less we are able to respond to the needs of another. Let us look at some of the main danger signals that warn us that our emotions may be interfering with our listening.

Defensiveness

The points about which one is most vocal and dogmatic, the points which one is most anxious to impose on others—these are always the points one is trying to talk oneself into believing. So one danger signal becomes apparent when you find yourself stressing a point or trying to convince another. It is at these times that you are likely to be less secure and consequently less able to listen.

Resentment of Opposition

It is always easier to listen to an idea which is similar to one of your own than to an opposing view. Sometimes, in order to clear the air, it is helpful to pause for a moment when you feel your ideas and position being challenged, reflect on the situation, and express your concern to the speaker.

Clash of Personalities

Here again, our experience has consistently shown us that the genuine expression of feelings on the part of the listener will be more helpful in developing a sound relationship than the suppression of them. This is so whether the feelings be resentment, hostility, threat, or admiration. A basically honest relationship, whatever the nature of it, is the most productive of all. The other party becomes secure when he learns that the listener can express his feelings honestly and openly to him. We should keep this in mind when we begin to fear a clash of personalities in the listening relationship. Otherwise, fear of our own emotions will choke off full expression of feelings.

Listening to Ourselves

To listen to oneself is a prerequisite for listening to others. And it is often an effective means of dealing with the problems we have outlined above. When we are most aroused, excited, and demanding, we are least able to understand our own feelings and attitudes. Yet, in dealing with the problems of others, it becomes most important to be sure of one's own position, values, and needs.

The ability to recognize and understand the meaning which a particular episode has for you, with all the feelings which it stimulates in you, and the ability to express this meaning when you find it getting in the way of active listening will clear the air and enable you once again to be free to listen. That is, if some person or situation touches off feelings within you which tend to block your attempts to listen with understanding, begin listening to yourself. It is much more helpful in developing effective relationships to avoid suppressing these feelings. Speak them out as clearly as you can, and try to enlist the other person as a listener to your feelings. A person's listening ability is limited by his ability to listen to himself.

(continued from page 30)

Are You Listening?

Manuel Escott

"Who me, not listen?" you protest. "I've been listening for years. To my parents, to my teachers, to my boss, sometimes to my kids. And my wife. Man, when she talks, you listen."

The chances are, however, that you don't listen properly. Studies by psychologists who specialize in human behavior show that listening is the least developed of our comprehension skills. Yet we spend 70 per cent of our day communicating with each other; and 45 per cent of that figure is spent in actually listening.

What is even more distressing, researchers have found that we remember only about one-third of what is said to us. And this information loss occurs within eight hours.

Everyone has experienced the situation where the new guy at the cocktail party is introduced as, say, Bill Goodbody. If your host or hostess has the average retention span, by the time old Goodbody has reached the end of the introductions, he's Charlie Goodenough or Joe Goodbye.

Ineffective listening can lead to critical and often frustrating situations. A salesman—it's as important for a salesman to listen properly as to talk well—could lose a big sale because he missed the critical content of what was being said to him. A secretary, if she's an average listener, will retain only one-third of what is said to her.

Take the case of the police officer interviewing witnesses to an accident or a crime. If he's a poor listener and doesn't take notes immediately, statements that are ultimately to become evidence in a court case might be inaccurate or have some vital fact omitted.

We listen more carefully to things we want to hear and tend to blot out things we don't want to hear.

"We're all more fond of articulating than listening," says Brian Mitchell, national sales manager of Xerox of Canada Ltd. Six years ago, Xerox marketed in Canada a course in effective listening. Since that time, Mitchell estimates that some 10,000 people a month from industry, government and police forces, have taken the four-and-a-half hour taped course under the guidance of a moderator.

"Poor listening is the cause of more problems than people imagine," says Mitchell. "It's really incredible that we're taught to read and write properly yet never given instruction on listening when so much of our time is spent doing just that."

The experts tell us that we tend to listen more carefully to the things we want to hear. You'll be all ears if someone phones to tell you that you're a big winner in the Irish Sweepstakes. And you'll be able to pick up the sound of your own name—the sweetest sound of all—across a noisy, crowded room.

Conversely, we tend to blot out or listen poorly to things we don't want to hear. A classic example of this, according to Mitchell, is the confrontation situation in a bargaining session between management and union. Both sides have fixed ideas, fixed positions and a fixed verbal approach in most cases.

"When one speaks the other is not really listening, but waiting until he's finished to rebut the position and put his own views forward," Mitchell says. "Consequently key points are missed by both sides, points that could lead to a settlement. Effective listening avoids situations like this and brings people together more."

Mitchell claims this is one of the added benefits of being a good listener—in a culture where more emphasis is being placed on "togetherness," careful listening can affect a more meaningful association with your peers. "A person always senses when you're listening to him empathetically and sympathetically, and responds to you."

There are four rules of good listening:

Think ahead of the talker and try to anticipate what he's going to say; weigh the evidence used by the talker to support his points and ask yourself if it is valid; mentally review and summarize each point of the talk as it proceeds; watch nonverbal communication or "body language" used by the speaker—facial expressions, gestures—which can be as important as verbal messages.

Everybody's Talkin'

Fred Neil

Everbody's talk'n at me
I don't hear a word they're say'n
Only the echoes of my mind

People stop'n star'n
I can't see their faces
Only the shadows of their eyes

I'm go'n where the sun keeps shin'n
Through the pour'n rain
Go'n where the weather suits my clothes
Begg'n off of the northeast winds
Sail'n on the summer breeze
Skipp'n over the ocean like a storm

Everybody's talk'n at me
Can't hear a word they're say'n
Only the echoes of my mind
I won't let you leave my love behind
I won't let you leave my love behind

Nobody Listens Any More

Hal Boyle

NEW YORK — Are you looking for a profitable hobby or a way to earn post-retirement income? Well, why not become a paid listener? It's a new and wide open field. Hardly anybody in America listens any more. Employees don't listen to their employers. Children don't listen to their parents. Students don't listen to their teachers. Husbands don't listen to their wives. Waiters don't listen to their customers. There are even signs that Congress no longer hears everything that Lyndon B. Johnson says.

The art of listening is about as dead as scrimshaw, which is the art of carving on whalebone.

Won't Listen to Each Other

People will do almost anything for each other except listen to each other. The guy who will gladly give you the shirt off his back balks at merely lending you his ear. Today it's even hard for a minister to recite the marriage ritual without either the bride or the bridegroom interrupting him to ask, "How's that again? What did you say?"

About the only people who do listen are psychiatrists and those who are paid to bug your telephones. And there is considerable suspicion among patients that psychiatrists don't really listen all the time.

The odd thing about it all is: While no one is willing to listen, everybody is more than willing to talk. Everyone has something he wants to get off his chest.

This means there has to be a tremendous market for good listeners. Why not tap it? Why not turn your idle hours to financial advantage by becoming a paid listener? Why not rent your ear?

This is my goal. As soon as I get my pension, I'm going to start a new career as a listener.

(continued on page 35)

Anyone who takes a listening course soon realizes that the skills he is learning can be used to make other people listen to him. Use of key words and visual images for certain points, analysis and review of material are useful aids to effective speaking. "Most good listeners can make the extrapolation that if this is what it takes to be a good listener, then one should learn to speak properly," Mitchell believes.

One behavioral psychologist blames the fantastic efficiency of the human brain for our low listening capacities.

Why are most of us low-grade listeners? Behavioral psychologist Dr. Ralph Nichols, of the University of Minnesota, blames the fantastic *efficiency* of the human brain.

Most of us talk at the rate of about 125 words a minute, but we think very much faster than we talk. Words play a major part in our thinking processes. When we listen we are asking our brains to receive words at a snail-slow pace compared to the brain's capabilities. It could be compared to driving a high-powered sports car at 15 miles an hour.

So, the spoken word arrives slowly and we're thinking at high speed. Hence the lapse in listener concentration. We listen, but have lots of time for idling, mentally dawdling down sidetracks.

Use or misuse of spare thinking time holds the key to effective listening, says Nichols. And he gives this example:

A product manager is telling a salesman about a new program the company is to launch. While the manager talks, the salesman's

Hi and Lois by Mort Walker and Dik Browne

mind slips down a sidetrack. He already knows most of what the manager is going to say.

Psychologists who specialize in human behavior say that listening is the least developed of our comprehension skills.

Unfortunately, he stays too long on the sidetrack. By the time he's back, the manager is ahead of him. Now our salesman finds it harder to understand what's being said. The private sidetracks once more invite him and he slips away again. Slowly, he misses more and more of the manager's plans.

When the manager is through talking, it's a fair assumption that the salesman will have received and understood less than half of what was said to him.

Nichols, who's been preaching the benefits of effective listening since the 1950s, knocked down several long-held assumptions about the skill: That intelligent people listen better than unintelligent ones and that reading will automatically teach you how to listen.

Because of these widely accepted assumptions, little attention has been paid to aural communication in our schools and colleges. Reading ability has been upgraded and listening ability left on its own has degenerated, Nichols claims.

The objective of the Xerox course is to double listening effectiveness. Mitchell says that validation studies show that this is achieved along with long and high retention. Refresher courses are seldom necessary.

(continued from page 34)

Earn Living by Listening

Whenever anyone grabs me by the lapels and starts wagging his jawbone, I'll silently hand him a printed folder which says:

"You are speaking to a man who earns his living by listening. So, please button your mouth unless you are willing to pay my rates, which are as follows:

"Listening to comments on the weather, baseball and politics: 50 cents an hour.

"Listening to husbands complain about their wives: 75 cents an hour.

"Listening to wives complain about their husbands: Ditto.

"Listening to campaign speeches and periodically breaking into loud cheers: $1 an hour.

"Listening at cocktail parties: $2 an hour before midnight, $4 after midnight, plus two free drinks for the road.

"Listening to views on Vietnam and other international problems: $5 for 15 minutes.

"Listening to gossip: No charge—if it's about anyone I know. Otherwise, $1 an hour.

"Listening over the telephone: Double usual rates, payable in advance.

"Listening to your troubles: $15 a morning, money to be refunded if you spend all afternoon listening to my troubles.

"Standby rate for waiting while you make up your mind what you want to talk about: 10 cents a minute.

"Pay up or shut up!"

What do you think of the idea? What, you didn't hear a word I said? See what I mean?

Nobody listens.

35

The value of effective listening in business need hardly be emphasized. Failure to pass on verbal messages accurately can mean costly mistakes. There's even some evidence to support the fact that better oral communication leads to fewer memos. And any scheme that could cut down on the paper war is worth hearing about.

Behavioral psychologists like to talk about upward communication, which merely means getting the boss's ear. There are lots of avenues for downward communication. Bad listeners in middle management, whose job it is to pass information up the line, can cause all kinds of morale problems.

Says Mitchell: "A man who knows he is listened to properly and whose beefs or ideas are getting to the right place is likely to be happy where he works. And if his wife is listening to him too, this could be Utopia."

Prods

1. Personality varies from person to person. What causes us to have differing personalities? Do we always see our personalities as others see them?
2. As no two personalities are alike, no two sets of human values are identical. What effects can these differing values have on our success as communicators?
3. Self-esteem is developed through contact with others. As we communicate with other people, what approaches are effective in developing our self-esteem? What kinds of behavior must we exhibit to maintain our self-esteem?
4. How can creative imagination help us build and maintain positive self-concepts? How can creative imagination make us a success?
5. Self-disclosure can create a strong relationship between you and another person. When is self-disclosure appropriate?
6. The way we perceive each other can be a prime obstacle to effective communication. How can active listening change our perceptions of one another and help us communicate effectively?

Appropriate verbal and non-verbal symbols are essential to effective communication.

The words you use should adequately represent what you want to say.

Nonverbal cues can help you read messages.

You can communicate with plants and animals.

Component

2

The Message

The Message Symbolized

Gordon Wiseman and Larry Barker

Appropriate verbal and nonverbal symbols are essential to effective communication.

Symbolic formulation involves the selection of appropriate symbols and is vital to any communication situation. Symbols clothe ideas and make them understandable. In everyday communication, both verbal and nonverbal symbols are the means by which you express your ideas, endeavor to understand what others are trying to say, and attempt to understand what you mean. Symbols are the medium which enables you to conduct your business affairs, form friendships, worship, learn new ideas, develop new formuli, explore new areas, and express your likes and dislikes. Symbols also help you to respond correctly, establish the appropriate mood, and make interaction with others possible. In other words, symbols enable you to adapt to and change your environment.

Symbolization

The symbolic process is the means by which you, as a human being, are able to let symbols stand for ideas, events, places, and things. Although most of the time words are the primary concern in communication, the symbolic process includes nonverbal as well as verbal symbols. If a fellow squeezes his girlfriend's hand and she squeezes back, communication occurs through a nonverbal symbol, a symbol that has been given meaning by our culture. Communication takes place even if he squeezes her hand and she does not return the squeeze. Most human reactions, both present and future, are controlled by symbols. Life often seems to be a process to obtain and accumulate symbols that provide feelings of accomplishment and success. Good clothes, ornaments, new homes are symbols of wealth. Rags and shacks seem to symbolize poverty. Since symbols are an integral part of your life orientation, they need to be studied and understood.

Symbols need to be controlled so that they do not control you and determine your daily life. A girl who assumes that a person with freckles is homely and then considers herself homely because she has freckles is letting herself be controlled by the symbol. The mature individual differentiates between *structural reality* and symbols and reacts to symbols as only representations of events in the real world. At the present time a military command in the form of a few symbols could cause the destruction of civilization. Perhaps even more important is the knowledge that a few poorly chosen symbols can disintegrate a human spirit. Many a G.I. felt his world give way not so much by the shelling and the dangers of combat as by the words "Dear John." Personal destruction is always more real to the individual. Even though reactions to the symbolic process are

Dennis the Menace by Hank Ketchum

often incorrect, the process is still basic to human communication. The first step involved in the control of symbols is to understand and to recognize the symbolic process. Once this has been achieved then you are ready to implement this knowledge into your communication patterns.

Keeping in touch with *structural reality* is basic to control over the symbolic process, and symbolic control is basic to effective communication. The relationship between symbols and reality should be the same as the relationship between a map and the territory it represents. Alfred Korzybski used this analogy and suggested that the relationship should be considered in three ways: (1) the map is not the territory (the symbol is not the thing symbolized); (2) the map does not represent all the territory (symbols cannot say all there is to be said about a thing); (3) the ideal map would have to include a map of itself (symbols are self-reflective).[1] Korzybski based many of his theories of general semantics on these ideas. These theories expanded semantics to include the behavioral aspects of language and meaning.

The Triangle of Meaning

Ogden and Richards in their book, *The Meaning of Meaning*, have helped to clarify meaning.[2] Of particular interest in the understanding of communication is their triangle of meaning, which illustrates the relationship between language and symbols. The triangle presented in Fig. 1 is an adaptation on theirs.

Meaning usually starts with a thought. A person thinks of an object with four legs, a wagging tail, and a moist nose. He thinks of this object in relationship to

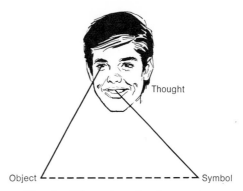

Fig. 1. The triangle of meaning

other objects and the mind sorts out the symbol *dog*. The thought, object, and symbol form the parts of the triangle. Each point of the triangle could be discussed at length, but in communication the important concepts to remember are these: There are definite relationships between thought and object, and between thought and symbol; however, the relationship between object and symbol is only inferred and the inference must be recognized. The symbol and the object symbolized are never exactly the same, just as a map and the territory it represents are independent of each other. The thought (perception) can even cause your concept of an object to be different from that of someone else.

The triangle of meaning aids in the understanding of other concepts about language. It illustrates the risk you often take in communicating when you assume that the other person thinks of the same object you have in mind when you use a symbol to represent that object. When you use the symbol *rose*, a variety of ideas immediately come to the minds of your responding communicators: petals, thorns, colors, scents, four, "mighty-lak-a," compass, war of the, long-stemmed, American Beauty, of Picardy,

climb up to her window, Billy, and the ring, dew on the, the yellow of Texas, or any of thousands of others. In word-association tests when the word *rose* is used, the word most commonly associated with it is red. Similarly many people think only of orange juice when the word *juice* is mentioned. They know there are other kinds of roses and juices, but the immediate response is one of red or orange.

Your life orientation determines your response to a certain symbol. This is best illustrated by the responses of two students in a class. When asked what came to their minds when the symbol *rose* was used, a girl replied, "I think of a beautiful little white cottage with a thatched roof on the hilltop surrounded by a beautiful blue sky with fleecy white clouds. All around the cottage are beautiful beds of flowers which are encircled by a white picket fence. Over the gateway of the picket fence is an archway that is covered by beautiful red roses." In the same class a fellow replied to the word *rose* by saying that he thought of dirt. Life orientations, philosophies, and other patterns are reflected in these two replies. As a communicator you cannot take for granted that your audience will have the same referent (ob-

ject) in their minds when you use a specific symbol, or that they will even associate the proper referent with your symbol. The learning of language is a complicated process. It is not sufficient to say that the symbol and the thing symbolized are not the same thing. A knowledge of the way you have learned symbols and the structure of language will give you insights into communication.

The Structure of Language

Learning Words and Symbols

Few stop to consider how they learned a word or the way in which they are learning new words and symbols now. Yet this process is so basic to understanding communication that you must be constantly aware of it. A word or symbol is usually learned in context rather than in isolation. This context is not always verbal, but may take the form of feelings, hopes, and aspirations. The meaning you attach to a word learned in this way is usually referred to as the connotative meaning. The connotative meaning of a word is the relationship between a word, an object, and a person. The connotative meaning is personalized; you attach personal meaning to the word as a result of past experiences. The denotative meaning of a word is the relationship between a word and an object and is concerned with structural reality. Sometimes this is called the historical or dictionary meaning of a word.

The establishment of connotative meanings for symbols may have lifelong effects. On the way home from school a boy learned a new word from his friends. The boy used this word at home. His parents, however, did not share

his enthusiasm and promptly suggested that if the word were used again, he would be punished by having his mouth washed out with soap. As the boy grew older that word carried many connotations with it that dated back to this incident. Although its effect is not always discernible, the setting in which a word is learned often colors the word. Therefore, the learning of words or symbols must be considered an individual matter. This is another example of the importance of understanding your life orientation in order to communicate effectively.

Word Meanings

A word is not a container like a glass. Words do not contain meaning within themselves, but are sounds in the air or marks on paper. One general semantics concept is that the meaning of words is not within the words, but within the individual. Since individuals have learned the same word in slightly different contexts, they have different meanings for the word. There are words which are frightful to some people and yet do not produce fear in others. To the individual who has had tuberculosis, the mention of "T.B." can bring reactions which would not be present in another individual who has not had the disease. The word *dead* might produce certain emotional responses within an individual who has just lost a loved one and yet not produce the same reaction two or three years later. Individuals are usually thought of as being different yet uniqueness in terms of reactions is not often comprehended. A communicator must be sensitive to feedback and constantly check the reactions of others as well as his own reactions, or as a student put it, "you need to put your antenna up."

Hidden Assumptions in Language

Communication is made more difficult, if not impossible at times, because of the silent or hidden assumptions that lie buried in language. In communicating, it is not enough to reason well; your reasoning must begin with correct premises. The connotative associations that are learned with a word, or a symbol, are disguised as premises or assumptions upon which you base your communication. The feeling that snakes are fearful, awful, and to be despised becomes attached to the symbol snake until you may react to the word *snake* as to a snake itself. These feelings are often generalized to an assumption that suggests all snakes are frightening and dangerous, while in reality many snakes are harmless.

Many times reactions are transformed into assumptions about racial and color characteristics. Some people's ideas about foreigners, Jews, Negroes, or Christians are based upon prejudices associated with the word, or symbol. One of the difficulties with these assumptions is that they are often below the threshold of consciousness and are not brought to the conscious level without a great effort. These hidden assumptions are ingrained in the nervous system and control the communication process, which in turn affects the nervous system. Language has conditioned your nervous system for the most part, which will control your reactions to the language of others. As you think, so you speak; as you speak, so you think.

Language and Your Nervous System

An analysis of language does not reveal all the characteristics of the nervous system, but it is dif-

ficult to discuss, shape, mold, change, or interpret your nervous system without language. Since language is the medium of interpretation, you should be constantly aware of the role it plays in your life. Also, understanding the way in which your nervous system operates will help you to understand your reactions to language. A bit of criticism given at one time will not have the same effect as a bit of criticism at another time. There are some areas within individuals in which a certain stimulus will generally evoke the same response. However, the connotative meaning in language will often alter the response when the time or circumstance changes.

A study of your life orientation should include the effect words, symbols, hidden assumptions, and language concepts have on you. An understanding of your life orientation will often give you a clue to the reason you react in a particular manner. More than half the battle is to recognize the reason for a reaction, even if the reaction cannot be altered. There are areas in which it is possible for a communicator to choose language that is appropriate to the responding communicator's nervous system. Listen to a boy who talks with his sister before he leaves the house and then listen to the same boy as he talks to his girlfriend on a date. He probably has altered his language to fit the nervous system of his date to produce the desired effect.

As you gain an understanding of language and its effect on your nervous system you will realize that words are only symbols and that to discover meaning you must properly interpret the symbol. This understanding will enable you to have symbol reactions to language and not signal reactions. If, in the course of a conversation, someone talks about "dirty labor leaders" and your father is a labor leader, you will not have a breakdown in your communication if you will realize that (1) the other individual is speaking from his nervous system, his background; (2) you are interpreting from your nervous system, your background; and (3) both of you may be correct to some extent. Communicators must recognize their sensitive areas and understand how they affect symbolization for them if they are to communicate successfully. They must also know and understand the sensitive areas of the responding communicator's life orientation if they are to move or change his nervous system.

You learn to interpret your world and yourself through language. This interpretation starts as you begin to learn words, their meanings and associations. Assumptions and concepts are soon built deeply into your nervous system. Communication is like the waters of a river; the flow of language controlled by past patterns forms new patterns for other language to flow over, as the river follows and enlarges its bed. Many rough places could be taken out of the flow of communication if you realized that it was your nervous system which created the rough place and not the language.

---

1. Alfred Korzybski, *Science and Sanity*, 4th ed. (Lakeville, Conn.: Institute of General Semantics, 1958), p. 58.

2. Charles K. Ogden and I. A. Richards, *The Meaning of Meaning* (New York: Harcourt, Brace and Company, 1946), p. 11.

Your Verbal Maps

Kenneth S. Keyes, Jr.

Clear thinking helps you to predict the future. It enables you to make plans that will get you what you want out of life.

Suppose you are starting out on a weekend trip to your favorite lake. You get one of the latest road maps and pick the best-looking route. But when you are a little beyond Plankerville, you find that road repairs make you detour through thirty miles of the dustiest dirt road you've ever breathed. You feel hot and grimy and the polish job on the car is shot.

Why did you get fouled up? *The map on which you relied did not represent the territory adequately.* Last week it may have represented the territory quite well, but that does not help get the dust out of your ears now. At the time you used it, your map lacked *predictability.*

Whenever you use maps that do not adequately represent the territory—maps that have poor predictability—you will not get what you want. Bad maps will lead you to anything from minor annoyance to sudden death, depending on the nature of the situation.

A verbal map is simply a map or a "picture" drawn with words. A reliable verbal map represents the territory adequately; a bad verbal map lies to you about the territory. For example, if I say, "Mosquitoes breed in standing water," I have made a verbal map that represents the territory.

If someone tells you, "Female canaries sing," he has given you an incorrect map that will mislead you if you rely upon it.

The words you use should adequately represent what you want to say.

Every time you open your mouth to let out words, you are making a verbal map. If you tell Junior "George Washington was the first President of the United States," you are making a map of territory that existed over a century ago. If Henry Brown says, "Beginning next year, I will definitely cut out smoking," he is making a verbal map of future territory. If he stops smoking, as the map says, it represents the actual territory. Otherwise, no. When I say, "My big toe hurts," I am making a verbal map of some territory that I, alone, am able to survey. I am mapping territory within my own body. If I say, "I am very disappointed," I am again mapping territory within me—my feelings.

All the knowledge and memories we have filed away in our heads may be regarded as "mental maps." All the thousands of words we shoot at each other every day may be regarded as

Abridged from HOW TO DEVELOP YOUR THINKING ABILITY by Kenneth S. Keyes, Jr. Copyright 1950 By Kenneth S. Keyes, Jr. Used with permission of McGraw-Hill Book Co.

verbal maps representing past, present, or future territory.

Inadequate Maps Put Us in Hot Water

Tim McCarthy was hit by a truck, and the first report of the doctor was discouraging. "I'm afraid your husband hasn't long to live," he told Tim's wife. "I'll come again tomorrow."

The next day, the doctor's report was still gloomy. But when the doctor called a third time, the patient was rallying, and on the fourth day he was out of danger.

"Well, missus," the doctor said. "Tim is going to pull through all right."

"Puts me in a bit of a hole, though," said the woman. "I've gone and sold all his clothes for funeral expenses."

Whenever we act on maps that do not adequately represent the territory, it puts us in a "bit of a hole."

In everything we do, we need adequate verbal maps. If we make a mistake in our checking account and think the balance is $352 when it is only $241.50, some of our checks are going to bounce. The map in our checkbook must adequately represent the funds in our account if we are to avoid trouble. If the gas gauge in our car says half full when our tank is about empty, it does not map the territory very well. If we rely on it, our blood pressure is going up—especially if we want to get somewhere in a hurry.

Why Accurate Maps May Not Be Good Enough

You may have wondered why so much emphasis has been put upon "adequate" verbal maps. The word *adequate* has been carefully chosen. A verbal map may be considered strictly accurate and yet, *for our purposes*, be quite inadequate and misleading!

For example, Bob had fished all day without any luck. On his way home he went to Captain Tom's Fish Market and said:

"Tom, pick out five of your biggest fish and toss them to me."

"You mean throw them?"

"Yes, just throw them over to me one at a time so I can tell the family I caught them. I may be a poor fisherman, but I'm no liar."

Some people might say our fisherman was making an accurate verbal map if he said he caught the fish. But no one would insist it was an adequate verbal map. We see readily that however accurate that map is, it is thoroughly misleading and has nothing to do with the actual territory.

I am writing to the Welfare Department to say that my baby was born two years old. When can I get my money?

I am forwarding my marriage certificate and six children. I have seven but one died which was baptized on a half sheet of paper.

I cannot get sick pay. I have six children. Can you tell me why?

Getting Along with People

Kenneth S. Keyes, Jr.

The tools of clear thinking can help you get along with people.

If you are not a hermit or a little dictator surrounded by "yes men," you will find the tools for thinking useful in helping you get along with people as you find them in this scrambled world of ours.

Tool No. 1: So Far As I Know

No argument can be settled when one or both parties blow up emotionally. One of the best ways I have ever found to turn aside wrath is to add "so far as I know" to my verbal maps. Most people will not mind your expressing an opinion that is different from theirs as long as you use "so far as I know" to indicate that your opinion is based upon your experiences and your evidence, and that you are not pretending to be God's mouthpiece. You have not weakened your position at all by saying "so far as I know." After all, who has a right to say more? In a changing world about which our knowledge is incomplete, no one is able to say the final word.

Look at the results Benjamin Franklin achieved when he dropped the dogmatic attitude. In his *Autobiography*, he attributes much of his success to his adoption of the "so far as I know" attitude:

I made it a rule to forbear all direct contradiction to the sentiments of others, and all positive assertion of my own. I even forbid myself the use of every word or expression in the language that imported a fixed opinion, such as *certainly, undoubtedly,* etc., and I adopted, instead of them, *I conceive, I apprehend,* or *I imagine* a thing to be so or so, or *it so appears to me at present.*

When another asserted something that I thought an error, I denied myself the pleasure of contradicting him abruptly and of showing immediately some absurdity in his proposition; and in answering, I began by observing that in certain cases or circumstances his opinion would be right, but in the present case there *appeared* or *seemed* to me some difference, etc. I soon found the advantage of this change in my manner; the conversations I engaged in went on more pleasantly. The modest way in which I proposed my opinions procured them a readier reception and less contradiction; I had less mortification when I was found to be in the wrong, and I more easily prevailed with others to give up their mistakes and join with me when I happened to be in the right.

And this mode, which I at first put on with some violence to natural inclination, became at length so easy, and so habitual to me, that perhaps for these fifty years past no one has ever heard a dogmatical expression escape me. And to this habit (after my character of integrity) I think it principally owing that I had early so much weight with my fellow-citizens when I proposed new institutions, or alterations in the old, and so much influence in public councils when I became a member; for I was but a bad speaker, never eloquent, subject to much hesitation in my choice of words, hardly correct in language, and yet I generally carried my points.

Abridged from HOW TO DEVELOP YOUR THINKING ABILITY by Kenneth S. Keyes, Jr. Copyright 1950 Kenneth S. Keyes, Jr. Used with permission of McGraw-Hill Book Co.

Tool No. 2: Up to a Point

When we criticize people it is important to tell up to what point that criticism is appropriate. Suppose, for example, someone complains that doctors are mercenary and think more of the long green lining their pockets than of the Hippocratic ideal of helping suffering humanity. Such a one-sided verbal map will needlessly antagonize the very doctors he would like to change. He has not told up to what point his verbal map represents the territory. His map implies that all doctors, everywhere, are that way in every respect.

But if he tries to make his verbal maps represent the territory and indicate, for example, that *certain doctors in certain places* accept "kickbacks" or "bonuses" from medical laboratories and supply houses that sometimes amount to from 25 to 50 percent of the money their patients pay for eyeglasses, X rays, medical appliances, Wassermann and other tests, then he will find that open-minded members of the medical profession will agree with him. Overstating one's case only causes antagonism. One should be careful not to let his assertions outstrip his facts.

Tool No. 3: To Me

A Chinese delegate to the United Nations was just leaving the gangplank of his ship at a New York dock. He was immediately surrounded by reporters. One of the questions shot at him was, "What strikes you as the oddest thing about Americans?"

The delegate thought seriously for a moment, then smiled. "I think," he said, "it is the peculiar slant of their eyes."

Intra-campus MEMORANDUM

State University

July 31, 1972

FROM: Acting Chairperson, Speech Communication
TO: Academic Deans and Department Chairpersons

Please be advised that effective September 1, 1972, official correspondence and material associated with the Department of Speech Communication will carry the terms "Acting Chairperson" or "Chairperson" instead of "Acting Chairman" or "Chairman."

This change is an attempt to reflect cultural change and avoid sex bias associated with the department and the university.

Intra-campus MEMORANDUM

State University

August 1, 1972

FROM: Dean, College of Arts and Sciences
TO: Acting Chairman, Speech Communication

I am against your intended change for the following reasons:

1. We have "chairmen"—not "chairpersons"— on the university records.
2. *Man* can be interpreted as "mankind" as well as "male."
3. We have no chairwomen.

Intra-campus MEMORANDUM

State University

August 4, 1972

FROM: Chairman, Department of English
TO: Acting Chairman, Speech Communication
RE: Your July 31 memo addressed to Academic Deans and Department Chair-persons

Dick, please don't give in to this women's lib nonsense. I am all for the desir-able aspects of the movement, but the linguistic gobbledygook is more than I can take. When I accepted the job of Chairman of the English Department, I accepted the job of *Chairman*—not Chair*person*. If we go this route, we may as well start talking about *flagperson, personkind, policeperson, personful, person-hole, personhood, person-hour, personhunt, person-in-the-street, person of the street, every person jack, person-made, person of God, person of letters, person of straw, person of the world, person-of-war, person-of-war bird, personpower, personservant, person slayer*. We may even have to talk about *personing the ship, personing the capstan, personing the production lines*. And then we run into *personish, person of the house*, and finally *persons' room*. Now, surely we do want to be able to tell what is behind the door labeled "Persons' Room," don't we? So, we will have to start talking about *persons' room* in contrast to *wopersons' room*. Then we can distinguish *person of the house* from *woperson of the house*. Next we can go to *person* and *woperson kind*, to *flagperson* and *flagwoperson*, to *policeperson* and *policewoperson*, et cetera, et cetera. Surely, wopersons—or fepersons—would want to distinguish *woperson power* from *person power, woperson suffrage* from *person suffrage*, and most of all *woper-sons' lib* from *persons' lib!*

We live in a world made up of five major skin colors, thousands of religions and philosophies, and a range of customs and mores of amazing diversity. If we are to get along with any people except those in our own group, we learn to add "to me" to our verbal maps. We must recognize that what seems "right" to us may not seem "right" to other people.

When the British movie film *The Wicked Lady* was sent to the United States, the American cen-sors objected to the necklines of some of the dresses—there was too much "cleavage." For Ameri-cans, the censors said, the neck-lines are immoral. J. Arthur Rank, England's leading film pro-ducer, was unable to understand the situation, "In England," he said, "bosoms aren't sexy!"

A little later Hollywood sent *Her Husband's Affairs* over to England. In this movie, twin beds were shown touching each other. The flabbergasted producers in Hollywood could hardly believe their ears when the English ex-plained that they just couldn't show the picture with the twin beds right together. It was neces-sary to reshoot that scene with the beds placed one foot apart in order to make it in good moral taste for English audiences.

The only way we can get along with people who have a contrast-ing background is to add "to me" to our verbal maps. We must admit we are fallible humans trying to do the best we can. We must not act as if we alone have the key to the treasury of truth.

Our Judgments Are Self-Reflective

When we say, "Jane is an inter-esting girl," we're talking about ourselves just as much as we are talking about Jane. The way we react to things is partly deter-mined by what is outside us and partly by what is inside us. When we say, "Jane is an interesting girl," we really mean that we find Jane interesting for one or more reasons. That statement gives other people very little information about Jane—it only expresses the way *we feel about her.*

If we hear someone say, "That building is hideous," we must remember that he is expressing his standards and his ideas of architecture just as much as he is talking about the building. That statement simply means he doesn't like the building.

The tool "to me" will help us become conscious of the way our own nervous system abstracts differently from other nervous systems. All we have the right to say is, "To me this is beautiful. To me this is bad. To me this is fun. To me this tastes wonderful. To me this is interesting. To me this is dull," and so on. We can speak only for ourselves.

Tool No. 4: The What Index

A retired judge once remarked to one of his friends that during his career on the bench, he had *on the average* done a pretty good job. "Of course," he admitted, "I have sent to the gallows a good many innocent people and have set free a good many guilty people, but I feel on the whole my errors of leniency have been pretty well offset by the times when I was too severe."

From a *statistical* point of view the judge may have averaged out all right—but from an *individual human* point of view there is no such thing as averaging out. It is small comfort to an innocent man about to be hanged to realize that his execution will be balanced out by the mistake of setting a murderer free!

Cutting Words

A man of true science uses but few hard words, and those only when none other will answer his purpose; whereas the smatterer in science . . . thinks that by mouthing hard words he proves that he understands hard things.

"Dr. Cuticle"
in Herman Melville's White Jacket

By Melville's criterion, suggests Dr. Lois DeBakey in the *New England Journal of Medicine*, medicine must be full of "smatterers in science." Hospital records, casual conversations and technical reports "are loaded with shoptalk, incomprehensible to nonphysicians and often confusing even to physicians from other regions." A member of a notable family of surgeons—one brother is Houston Surgeon Michael DeBakey (Time cover, May 28), another brother, Ernest, is also a surgeon—Dr. Lois, who has a Ph.D. in English and is an associate professor in scientific communication at Tulane University, is a surgeon of language. She advises medical writers to concentrate on cutting out the "learned" words and using the simple substitutes in the following list of choices:

Agrypnia	Insomnia
Cephalalgia	Headache
Cholelithiasis	Gallstones
Deglutition	Swallowing
Emesis	Vomiting
Hemorrhage	Bleeding
Obese	Fat
Pyrexia	Fever
Respire	Breathe

Carrying her criticism right to the end (not "termination") of life, Dr. DeBakey thinks *"in extremis* is a pretentious expression for dying."

Gobbledygook Must Go

Webster's defines *gobbledygook* as "wordy and generally unintelligible jargon." Others have described it as a conglomeration of flossy, pompous, abstract, complex, jargonistic words which we too frequently try to pass off as communications. Gobbledygook is almost always loaded with jargon of the writer's own professional interest—words seldom used by persons outside the writer's little word-world. It seems to stem from an ingrown (perhaps subconscious) professional desire to impress rather than to communicate, to be "proper" rather than personal and direct.

To show how easy it is to get balled up in the jargon of our own trade or profession, let's look at a little game we recently heard about. You play it with three groups of buzzwords numbered from zero to nine:

Group 1	Group 2	Group 3
0. evaluate	0. educational	0. competencies
1. coordinate	1. diffusion	1. research
2. upgrade	2. program	2. implications
3. formalize	3. professional	3. planning
4. total	4. leadership	4. subject matter
5. balanced	5. clientele	5. role
6. finalize	6. differential	6. image
7. systematized	7. decision-making	7. focal point
8. ongoing	8. innovative	8. flexibility
9. responsive	9. policy	9. programming

Now think of any three-digit number, and then, from each of the above groups, select the numbered word corresponding to each digit in the number you picked. For example, take the number 220, and you come up with "upgrade program competencies," or use 359 and your phrase turns out to be "formalize clientele programming." Your resulting phrases may lack real meaning, but most of them will have a ring of familiarity.

Abridged from "Gobbledygook Must Go" in *Inside Information*, July 1966. © 1966 *Inside Information*. Used by permission of Information and Publications Dept., University of Maryland.

What Is Prejudice?

Prejudice arises when people take a statistical approach to man₁ or thing₁. We are prejudiced when we react to labels instead of looking at man₁ or thing₁. We are prejudiced when we are content with "averaging out."

All of us carry around in our heads a pack of prejudices. We may be prejudiced against certain races and certain classes. We may be prejudiced against certain races and certain classes. We may be prejudiced against people with immigrant heritages. We have political prejudices, religious prejudices, prejudices against people in other parts of the world and in other parts of our own country, and we can even be prejudiced against people in the next town or in another part of our own town. We can have prejudices about newfangled contraptions, red automobiles, or modern art.

We get an unfavorable picture in our heads and then proceed blindly as though that picture were an adequate map to represent all people or things that are included under the label. Or we can get a favorable picture in our heads and then blind ourselves to all sorts of unfavorable aspects of man₁ or thing₁. We ask what a person or thing "is." Then we react to the label. Why bother getting acquainted with the territory—it's too much trouble.

Regardless of whether few, many, or most of the people are covered by a generalization, we will meet some who are not. We must observe man₁ who stands before us in order to act intelligently and fairly toward him.

The index numbers can remind us that we do not deal with people-in-general. We deal with individual people and an individual person may or may not fit the

"Are you a—quote—'Vivacious female, intellectual, bored with companions, like soft music, canoeing, laughter, wishes to cut loose from surroundings?'"

average map we have. We must remember that man$_1$ is not man$_2$, Democrat$_1$ is not Democrat$_2$, Republican$_1$ is not Republican$_2$, Southerner$_1$ is not Southerner$_2$, New Englander$_1$ is not New Englander$_2$, Catholic$_1$ is not Catholic$_2$, etc. As Henry van Dyke said, "There is one point in which all men are exactly alike and that is that they are all different." By using index numbers we can avoid being misled by the stereotyped notions we carry around in our heads.

Tool No. 5: The When Index

In dealing with people, we must remember that although their names do not change, they may act differently with the passing of time. Susie $^{(1960)}$ may have had many habits that made people call her selfish. Susie $^{(today)}$ may not have those habits. You cannot simply meet Susie $^{(1960)}$ and decide she is selfish, then for the rest of your life assume that's the way she is because that's the way she was. Susie may have changed (and, of course, Susie may not have changed). The point is, again, to survey the Susie-territory before you hang a 1960 label on her today.

If we want to react to people as they *are* (rather than to people as they *were*), we must recognize the process factor in knowledge. We must remember with Whitehead that "Knowledge keeps no better than fish."

All of us make missteps. All of us have done mean, selfish, illegal, unworthy, and terrible things. If people make verbal maps of us at such unfortunate times, and then set them in concrete in their minds and refuse to reevaluate us at later times, then we're sunk. When that happens, a person may feel there is no need to try to act

better or improve himself. He may feel that his reputation is established, and no matter how he changes, it will not help him because people are not openminded enough to revise their verbal maps when the territory changes. You can see what unhappiness poor thinking habits can cause. Clear thinking demands that we use the when index to attune ourselves to the possibilities of change.

Tool No. 6: The Where Index

According to words, Mary Williams is Mary Williams. But according to facts, Mary Williams $_{(married\ to\ Roger\ Brown\ in\ Boston,\ Mass.)}$ is not the same as Mary Williams $^{(married\ to\ Tom\ Smith\ in\ Miami,\ Fla.)}$. We act differently in different environments and with different people. For example, with some people you usually feel lighthearted and gay, and you get known to them as a clever and witty person. With others, the serious aspect of your personality is brought out.

Suppose two friends of Mary Williams get together:

"Mary is certainly full of the devil. She doesn't have a serious thought in her head."

"We must not be talking about the same person. The Mary I know is quite serious. Her grasp of current affairs is amazing."

"Well, that's not the Mary I'm talking about."

"Mary Williams?"

"Yes, Mary Williams. Lives at the Wingate Apartments."

"I don't know what's the matter. You must not know her very well."

"Why, I've known her for years."

"Well, you certainly aren't much of a judge of character then."

"Well, I like that. I think you're

the batty one." (At this point they stop talking about Mary Williams entirely, and inferences and judgments are exchanged that have no relation to the territory.)

To get along in this world, we need to develop a deep feeling for the way different situations, circumstances, or surroundings bring out different aspects of people and things. The where index can help us understand where we might otherwise misunderstand.

To Sum Up

The tools for thinking can do a great deal to help you get along with other people. When you say so far as I know, you can keep from antagonizing people by your dogmatic assertions. The tool "up to a point" can help you to avoid irritating people needlessly by keeping you from implying "all" when "some" is more in accordance with the facts. The tool "to me" tells you that your reactions are determined both by what is outside you and your own nervous system. When you use "to me" you admit you're a human being and are not pretending to see things from the cosmic aspect of eternity. By using index numbers, you will remember to discriminate *between* individuals and not *against* individuals. No matter how accurate your generalizations and averages are, they do not put the finger on any individual. You must survey the territory to find out if a generalization applies to the man$_1$ or thing$_1$ you are dealing with. The when index will remind you that two verbal maps may seem to contradict each other, but when the date is added both may be found adequate. The where index will remind you that people and things act differently in different places.

"Remember the kid brother we used to throw quarters to?"

Nonverbal Communication: Basic Perspectives

Mark Knapp

Those of us who keep our eyes open can read volumes into what we see going on around us. E. Hall

Herr von Osten purchased a horse in Berlin, Germany in 1900. When von Osten began training his horse, Hans, to count by tapping his front hoof, he had no idea that Hans was soon to become one of the most celebrated horses in history. Hans was a rapid learner and soon progressed from counting to addition, multiplication, division, subtraction, and eventually the solution of problems involving factors and fractions. As if this were not enough, von Osten exhibited Hans to public audiences where he counted the number in the audience or simply the number of people wearing eye glasses. Still responding only with taps, Hans could tell time, use a calendar, display an ability to recall musical pitch, and perform numerous other seemingly fantastic feats. After von Osten taught Hans an alphabet which could be coded into hoofbeats, the horse could answer virtually any question—oral or written. It seemed that Hans, a common horse, had complete comprehension of the German language, the ability to produce the equivalent of words and numerals, and an intelligence beyond that of many human beings.

Even without the promotion of Madison Avenue, the word spread quickly and soon Hans was known throughout the world. He was soon dubbed "Clever Hans." Because of the obviously profound implications for several scientific fields and because some skeptics thought there was a "gimmick" involved, an investigating committee was established to decide, once and for all, whether there was any deceit involved in Hans' performances. Professors of psychology, physiology, the director of the Berlin Zoological Garden, a director of a circus, veterinarians, and cavalry officers were appointed to this commission of horse experts. An experiment with Hans from which von Osten was absent demonstrated no change in the apparent intelligence of Hans. This was sufficient proof for the commission to announce there was no trickery involved.

The appointment of a second commission was the beginning of the end for Clever Hans. Von Osten was asked to whisper a number into the horse's left ear while another experimenter whispered a number into the horse's right ear. Hans was told to add the two numbers—an answer none of the onlookers, von Osten, or the experimenter knew. Hans failed. And with further tests he continued to fail. The experiment-er, Pfungst, discovered on further experimentation that Hans could only answer a question if someone in his visual field knew the answer.[1] When Hans was given the question, the onlookers assumed an expectant posture and increased their body tension. When Hans reached the correct number of taps, the onlookers would relax and make a slight movement of the head—which was Hans' cue to stop tapping.

The story of Clever Hans is frequently used in discussions concerning the capacity of an animal to learn verbal language. It also seems well suited to an introduction to the field of nonverbal communication. Hans' cleverness was not in his ability to verbalize or understand verbal commands, but in his ability to respond to almost imperceptible and unconscious movements on the part of those surrounding him. It is not unlike that perceptiveness or sensitivity to nonverbal cues exhibited by a Clever Carl, Charles, Frank, or Harold when picking up a girl, closing a business deal, giving an intelligent and industrious image to a professor, knowing when to leave a party, and in a multitude of other common situations.

Perspectives on Defining Nonverbal Communication

Conceptually, the term *nonverbal* is subject to a variety of interpretations—just like the term *communication*. The basic issue seems to be whether the events traditionally studied under the heading *nonverbal* are literally *non* verbal. Ray Birdwhistell, a pioneer in nonverbal research, is reported to have said that studying *nonverbal* communication is like studying *noncardiac* physiology. His point is well taken. It is

---

Nonverbal cues can help you read messages.

not easy to dissect human interaction and make one diagnosis which concerns only verbal behavior and another which concerns only nonverbal behavior. The verbal dimension is so intimately woven and so subtly represented in so much of what we have previously labeled *nonverbal* that the term does not always adequately describe the behavior under study. Some of the most noteworthy scholars associated with nonverbal study refuse to segregate words from gestures and hence, work under the broader terms *communication* or *face-to-face interaction*.

The theoretical position taken by Dance concerning the whole process of communication goes even further in order to call to our attention that perhaps not everything labeled nonverbal is literally nonverbal. Dance might even argue that there is no such thing as uniquely human communication that is nonverbal. He takes the position that all symbols are verbal and that human communication is defined as the eliciting of a response through verbal symbols. He does not deny the fact that we may engage in nonverbal behaviors, but the instant these behaviors are interpreted by another in terms of words, they become verbal phenomena.

While many researchers recognize this theoretical and conceptual problem with the term *nonverbal*, their research proceeds. Most of this research is based on the premise that if words are not spoken or written, they become nonverbal in nature. Also included in the term *nonverbal* under this definition are all those nuances which surround words—e.g., tone of voice or type of print. This is frequently called paralanguage. In their early classic, *Nonverbal Communication: Notes on the Visual Perception*

Every Human Being Is a Separate Language

Pat Hardman
IN Correspondent

Sometimes silence is best.

Words are curious things, at best approximations. And every human being is a separate language.

If the knowledge of that paralyzes you, withdraw for a little. Silence is best.

And even if you accept the awkwardness of language and try to work with it, you can have times when you agonize over your inability to make the phrase empathetic with the moment.

Maybe silence is best, for a little while.

Conflict over abstract ideas, the fact that man is a finite being and has no omniscient knowledge and no answers to metaphysical questions—that can paralyze, too. You start wondering: What is reality?

So hold your tongue, turn your back and be silent.

If there are no words, or no right words, choose quiet. Better to be silent than communicate on a mediocre level. Better to be quiet than uneasy over what you have said.

You can still smile or frown or laugh or cry, can't you? And in turning your back, you do not lose your eyes. You are always looking at something. You have simply changed your view for awhile. Restraint is not rejection.

Problems From People

The problem comes from the people around you. Who can ask for privacy and have others watching their aloneness? Demand time by yourself and people—know. They don't understand, they just know and that destroys all chance of being really alone and quiet.

A friend's knowledge of you is an increase and sharing. For a stranger to hold knowledge of you is an invasion and violation.

So don't tell anyone, don't ask for anything, just take what you need. Follow the demands of your confusion and find your place. Don't worry about consequences of opinion. If you do, you have forgotten who you want to listen to you.

Impulse to Silence

There are times when nothing is more important that your own impulses, the impulse to silence or isolation among them. The call of a friend: "Come here." The call of a moment: "Experience me." The call of yourself: "Go and find me."

High points and low points, too deep for words. Indecision and conflict that cannot be voiced. Doubt of your own tongue.

Very well, then, choose silence. If you cannot be great with words, be great in quiet.

---

of *Human Relations*, Ruesch and Kees took essentially this point of view. But, in addition, the authors outlined what they considered to be the primary elements in the study of nonverbal communication. This classification system has been highly influential in providing a basis for most of the work done in this field to date.

In broad terms, nonverbal forms of codification fall into three distinct categories:

Sign Language includes all those forms of codification in which words, numbers, and punctuation signs have been supplanted by gestures; these vary from the "monosyllabic" gesture of the hitchhiker to such complete systems as the language of the deaf.

Action Language embraces all movements that are not used exclusively as signals. Such acts as walking and drinking, for example, have a dual function: on one hand they serve personal needs, and on the other they constitute statements to those who may perceive them.

Object Language comprises all intentional and nonintentional display of material things, such as implements, machines, art objects, architectural structures, and—last but not least—the human body and whatever clothes or covers it. The embodiment of letters as they occur in books and on signs has a material substance, and this aspect of words also has to be considered as object language.[2]

Another way of defining a field of study is to examine the work that has been done to see if any common directions have been followed. As previously mentioned, one common trend is the assumption that nonverbal communication encompasses those events in which words are not spoken or written. Other recurring trends are exemplified by the following classification system which represents a definition of the field of nonverbal human communication as evidenced in the writing and research available.

Nonverbal Dimensions of Human Communication

Body Motion or Kinesic Behavior

Body motion, or kinesic behavior, typically includes gestures, movements of the body, limbs, hands, head, feet and legs, facial expressions (smiles), eye behavior (blinking, direction and length of gaze, and pupil dilation) and posture. The furrow of the brow, the slump of a shoulder and the tilt of a head—all are within the purview of kinesics. Obviously, there are different types of nonverbal behavior just as there are different types of verbal behavior. Some nonverbal cues are very specific, some more general; some intended to communicate, some expressive only; some provide information about emotions, others carry information about personality traits or attitudes. In an effort to sort through the relatively unknown world of nonverbal behavior, Ekman and Friesen developed a system for classifying nonverbal behavioral acts.[3] These categories include:

Emblems. These are nonverbal acts which have a direct verbal translation or dictionary definition—usually consisting of a word or two or a phrase. There is high agreement among members of a culture or subculture on the verbal definition. The gestures used to represent "A-OK" or "Peace" are examples of emblems for a large part of our culture. Toffler notes in his bestseller, *Future Shock,* that some emblems which were perceived as semi-obscene are now becoming more respectable with changing sexual values. He uses the example of the upraised finger—designating "up yours." Emblems are frequently used when verbal channels are blocked (or fail) and are usually

used to communicate. The sign language of the deaf, nonverbal gestures used by television production personnel, signals used by two underwater swimmers, or motions made by two people who are too far apart to make audible signals practical—all these are emblems. Our own awareness of emblem usage is about the same as our awareness of word choice.

Nonverbal messages come from body motions, physical characteristics, touching behavior, vocal cues, social and personal space, objects, and environmental factors.

Illustrators. These are nonverbal acts which are directly tied to, or accompany, speech—serving to illustrate what is being said verbally. These may be movements which accent or emphasize a word or phrase; movements which sketch a path of thought; movements pointing to present objects; movements depicting a spatial relationship; or movements which depict a bodily action. Illustrators seem to be within our awareness, but not as explicitly as emblems. They are used intentionally to help communicate, but not as deliberately as emblems. They are probably learned by watching others.

Affect Displays. These are simply facial configurations which display affective states. They can repeat, augment, contradict, or be unrelated to, verbal affective statements. Once the display has occurred, there is usually a high degree of awareness, but it can occur without any awareness. Often, affect displays are not intended to communicate, but they can be intentional.

United Press International Photos

Regulators. These are nonverbal acts which maintain and regulate the back and forth nature of speaking and listening between two or more interactants. They tell the speaker to continue, repeat, elaborate, hurry up, become more interesting, give the other a chance to talk, etc. They consist mainly of head nods and eye movements, and there seem to be class and cultural differences in usage—improper usage connoting rudeness. These acts are not tied to specific spoken behavior. They seem to be on the periphery of our awareness and are generally difficult to inhibit. They are like overlearned habits and are almost involuntary, but we are very much aware of these signals sent by others. Probably the most familiar regulator is the head nod— the equivalent of the verbal mm-hmm.

Adaptors. These nonverbal behaviors are perhaps the most difficult to define and involve the most speculation. They are labeled adaptors because they are thought to develop in childhood as adaptive efforts to satisfy needs, perform actions, manage emotions, develop social contacts, or perform a host of other functions. They are not really coded; they are fragments of actual aggressive, sexual or intimate behavior and often reveal personal orientations or characteristics covered by verbal messages. Leg movements can often be adaptors, showing residues of kicking aggression, sexual invitation, or flight. Many of the restless movements of the hands and feet which have typically been considered indicators of anxiety may be residues of adaptors necessary for flight from the interaction. Adaptors are possibly triggered by verbal behavior in a given situation which is associated with condi-

What Your Tongue May Really Be Saying

On a conscious level, the human tongue is regularly put to a wide variety of useful purposes: it licks postage stamps, demolishes ice-cream cones and also performs a major function in the delivery of that staccato sputter of derision known as the Bronx cheer, or raspberry. In Tibet, when one hill tribesman encounters another, the two exchange greetings by protruding their tongues, much as two Westerners might wave or shake hands.

Now, however, a team of evolutionary biologists at the University of Pennsylvania has completed a five-year study of how people use their tongues at the unconscious level. Their major finding seems to be that the unconscious display of the tongue is a universal sign of aversion to social encounter—a sign that is used alike by all races, and also by such other primates as orangutans and gorillas.

Drs. W. John Smith and Julia Chase, assisted by graduate student Anna Katz Lieblich, first studied tongue displays at Philadelphia's Mulberry Tree Nursery School. There, they noted that toddlers tend to show their tongues when they are engrossed in difficult tasks, such as finger painting or climbing over obstacles, and also when they are involved in awkward social situations, such as receiving a scolding for misbehavior. This suggested to Smith that the action indicated a desire to be left alone, so he decided to test the hypothesis by trying to provoke tongue showing.

Adults: Smith stationed himself in the path of a 4-year-old girl who was running a repeated route from room to room, and caught her eye as she approached him. The girl averted her eyes and protruded her tongue. She repeated this behavior four times. But on the sixth circuit, now sure that Smith would not grab her, the girl showed no hint of her tongue.

The biologists then made unobtrusive observations of tongue-showing among the general public in Philadelphia and in Panama. They found that it occurred among adults in exactly the same settings as with children. Adults show their tongues during tasks requiring intense concentration—when making a tricky shot at pool, for example, or backing into a small parking space—and also in socially threatening situations, such as being interrupted in conversation. Extending the study further, Smith and his colleagues watched a number of gorillas and orangutans at close quarters, with identical results. For although the apes tended to show their tongues more prominently than did humans, the circumstances involved either complex tasks such as peeling bananas with their toes, or unpleasant situations in which the apes were scolded for fighting. On a conscious level, apes also use their tongues to eat ice-cream cones.

tions occurring when the adaptive habit was first learned. We are typically unaware of adaptors.

Physical Characteristics

Whereas the previous section was concerned with movement and motion, this category covers things which remain relatively unchanged during the period of interaction. They are influential nonverbal cues which are not movement-bound. Included are such things as: physique or body shape, general attractiveness, body or breath odors, height, weight, hair, and skin color or tone.

Touching Behavior

For some, kinesic study includes touch behavior; for others, however, actual physical contact constitutes a separate class of events. Some researchers are concerned with touching behavior as an important factor in the child's early development; some are concerned with adult touching behavior. Subcategories may include stroking, hitting, greetings and farewells, holding, guiding another's movements, and other, more specific instances.

Paralanguage

Simply put, paralanguage deals with how something is said and not what is said. It deals with the range of nonverbal vocal cues surrounding common speech behavior. Trager felt paralanguage had the following components:[4]

Voice Qualities. This includes such things as pitch range, pitch control, rhythm control, tempo, articulation control, resonance,
glottis control, and vocal lip control.

Vocalizations. *Vocal characterizers* include such things as laughing, crying, sighing, yawning, belching, swallowing, heavily marked inhaling or exhaling, coughing, clearing of the throat, hiccupping, moaning, groaning, whining, yelling, whispering, sneezing, snoring, stretching, etc. *Vocal qualifiers* include intensity (overloud to oversoft), pitch height (overhigh to overlow), and extent (extreme drawl to extreme clipping). *Vocal segregates* are such things as "uh-huh," "um," "uh," "ah," and variants thereof.

Related work on such topics as silent pauses (beyond junctures), intruding sounds, speech errors, and latency would probably be included in this category.

Proxemics

Proxemics is generally considered to be the study of man's use and perception of his social and personal space. Under this heading, we find a body of work called small group ecology which concerns itself with how people use and respond to spatial relationships in formal and informal group settings. Such studies deal with seating arrangements, and spatial arrangements as related to leadership, communication flow, and the task at hand. The influence of architectural features on residential living units and even on communities is also of concern to those who study man's proxemic behavior. On an even broader level, some attention has been given to spatial relationships in crowds and densely populated situations. Man's personal space orientation is sometimes studied in the context of conversational distance—and how
it varies according to sex, status, roles, cultural orientation, etc. The term "territoriality" is also frequently used in the study of proxemics to denote the human tendency to stake out personal territory—or untouchable space— much as wild animals and birds do.

Artifacts

Artifacts include the manipulation of objects in contact with the interacting persons which may act as nonverbal stimuli. These artifacts include perfume, clothes, lipstick, eyeglasses, wigs and other hairpieces, false eyelashes, eyeliners, and the whole repertoire of falsies and "beauty" aids.

Environmental Factors

Up to this point we have been concerned with the appearance and behavior of the persons involved in communicating. This category concerns those elements which impinge on the human relationship, but which are not directly a part of it. Environmental factors include the furniture, architectural style, interior decorating, lighting conditions, smells, colors, temperature, additional noises or music, etc. within which the interaction occurs. Variations in arrangements, materials, shapes, or surfaces of objects in the interacting environment can be extremely influential on the outcome of an interpersonal relationship. This category also includes what might be called traces of action. For instance, as you observe cigarette butts, orange peels, and waste paper left by the person you will soon interact with, you are forming an impression which will eventually influence your meeting.

Summary

The term *nonverbal* is commonly used to describe all human communication events which transcend spoken or written words. At the same time we should realize that many of these nonverbal events and behaviors are interpreted through verbal symbols. In this sense, then, they are not truly *non*verbal. The theoretical writings and research on nonverbal communication can be broken down into the following seven areas: (1) body motion or kinesics (emblems, illustrators, affect displays, regulators, and adaptors), (2) physical characteristics, (3) touching behavior, (4) paralanguage (vocal qualities and vocalizations), (5) proxemics, (6) artifacts, (7) environment. Nonverbal communication should not be studied as an isolated unit, but as an inseparable part of the total communication process. Nonverbal communication may serve to repeat, contradict, substitute, complement, accent, or regulate verbal communication. Nonverbal communication is important because of the role it plays in the total communication system, the tremendous quantity of informational cues it gives in any particular situation, and because of its use in fundamental areas of our daily life. Nonverbal behavior is partly taught, partly imitative, and partly instinctive. There is a growing body of evidence which suggests a pancultural (or universal) element in emotional facial behavior, but this does not suggest there are not cultural differences in such things as the circumstances which elicit an emotion, the display rules which govern the management of facial behavior in certain settings, and the action consequences of an emotion.

1. O. Pfungst, *Clever Hans, The Horse of Mr. Von Osten* (New York: Holt, Rinehart and Winston, 1911).

2. J. Ruesch and W. Kees, *Nonverbal Communication: Notes on the Visual Perception of Human Relations* (Berkeley and Los Angeles: University of California Press, 1956): 189. Originally published by the University of California Press; reprinted by permission of The Regents of the University of California.

3. P. Ekman and W. V. Friesen. "The Repertoire of Nonverbal Behavior: Categories, Origins, Usage, and Coding," *Semiotica* 1 (1969): 49–98.

4. G. L. Trager, "Paralanguage: A First Approximation," *Studies in Linguistics* 13 (1958): 1–12.

In the Business World Every Body Talks

Barry Fishler

The man across the desk appears relaxed. He leans back comfortably, folds his arms across his chest and stares quietly into space as he evaluates your proposal.

One leg is thrust casually across the corner of the desk. At intervals, he touches his nose in contemplation.

Your own posture is that of business-like confidence. Sitting erect, legs crossed, jacket neatly buttoned, you make point after point, driving each one home with an emphatic finger.

Two gentlemen on the verge of an agreement?

Hardly.

More likely, you will leave in eventual frustration – without sale, contract or raise. And even worse, you won't have the slightest idea why.

Gerard I. Nierenberg knows why. He pinpoints the defensiveness in the folded arms, the doubt in the lightly touched nose, the arrogant claims of territoriality made by the outstretched leg. All were indicators for a "body talk" expert like Nierenberg, who has trained himself to recognize the hidden meanings behind everyday gestures.

Your own body actions were no less revealing. The crossed legs and buttoned jacket were a failure to open yourself up and communicate. Coupled with the pointing finger – a highly antagonistic, rude and degrading gesture to the person on the receiving end – they virtually insured the rupture of a line of communication that was never really open to begin with.

As a New York City attorney for the past 25 years (senior partner in Nierenberg, Zeif and Weinstein), the 48-year-old Nierenberg long ago realized that the practice of law – or anything else, for that matter – is as much the art of reading people as it is digesting facts and theories. And reading people, in turn, involves a great deal more than listening to what they say.

Nierenberg's authored three books on the way people communicate . . . or don't . . . and is president of The Negotiation Institute.

Twenty to 25 per cent of our communication is nonverbal. By

neglecting it, we do ourselves a great injustice, he explains. "How can a person afford to miss—not even *look for*—a quarter of what is going on?

"And people get only 40 per cent of those gestures, anyway. We start out by looking at each other, then look away, then come back on the periods and commas. It's important to catch that 40; you're missing 60 per cent to begin with."

Nierenberg's message—that successful business negotiation hinges on mutual recognition of a cooperative human process, in which there need be only winners and no losers—is finding increasing acceptance among top-level American executives. More than 100,000 have paid about $300 apiece to sit through two-day seminars on the art of negotiating, offered under the sponsorship of Nierenberg's institute and *Journal of Advanced Management*.

"In every human relationship," says Nierenberg, "a negotiation occurs. People meet with the intention of changing the relationship in some way.

"My basic philosophy is that everyone wins in a successful negotiation. It's only common sense that you leave the other fellow something of his own. If you don't, you've planted dragon seeds for the future. What we're trying to do is replace the outdated win/lose approach with a creative approach that will be in the best interests of both parties."

In this type of approach, of course, you get nowhere unless you recognize the needs of the other person. To do this, you have to make use of feedback. Which is where nonverbal communication comes in.

Nierenberg cites numerous situations where an inability to recognize nonverbal feedback works to the disadvantage of one or both parties.

There is the employee who asks his boss for a raise or initiates an important conversation when the boss' bodily indicators—perhaps he has his hand on his brow or his feet on the desk—are saying, "Stay away. I'm upset. Don't bother me."

Or, the boss might have one leg over the arm of his chair, showing a position of dominance and unconcern for the other person's needs. Possibly he is leaning back, hands behind his head, indicating he considers himself in the driver's seat.

The raise, of course, is refused, and whatever matter it was that deserved full consideration is dealt with brusquely, because the boss' body language was not heeded.

And there is the attorney who goes through jury selection with complete disregard for the attitudes and prejudgments being broadcast by the prospective jurors. The sharp courtroom technician will "read" the jurors with as much tenacity as he does his witnesses. For, as Nierenberg points out, "once that jury is selected, you're stuck with it."

Not to mention the salesman who plods along with his prestructured pitch, sailing right by the moment when all signals—if he would only read them—are virtually screaming, "Close now; I'm receptive." What he does do, of course, is attempt to close at the end of his pitch, ignoring the signals then that tell him, quite frankly, to get lost.

It does not, of course, have to be this way. And, if Nierenberg has his way, everyone eventually will be making use of the tremendous means of communication available on a nonverbal level— not for purposes of keeping a competitive scorecard of success-

Photos by Andrew Schneider

ful negotiations, but as a means to more effective interaction between people.

"I only 'read' to relate to people, not to go 'one up.' You have to realize that it's difficult for anyone, even a trained actor, to be another person—someone he's not—and that this is not a study in manipulation."

Nierenberg's assurances notwithstanding, sitting opposite him in The Negotiation Institute's plush Park Avenue offices can be a disconcerting experience. Not through any fault of his, because he communicates a relaxed, friendly attitude. His unbottoned jacket, slightly cocked head, alert posture, as he leans toward you on the edge of his seat, hand on his hip, are all sure signs of interest and cooperation.

It's you that's the problem, wondering whether or not to cross your legs, adjust your glasses, scratch that itch, smile, frown, fidget. Is nothing safe from his subtle inspection?

It takes awhile, but eventually you relax, your sensibilities softened by Nierenberg's manner, perhaps proof-positive of what he is trying to convey. The arrangement of his office also works its spell, for its living room decor is designed to create a physical environment conducive to relaxation, cooperation and, hence, successful negotiation.

Nierenberg's understanding of the methods by which people communicate nonverbally grew out of seminars in which more than 2,500 negotiating situations were put on video tape. The tapes were played back to the participants, who were asked to give their reactions to gestures shown on the screen.

What, in other words, was this man thinking when he did that?

One mistake often made, Nierenberg points out, is to seize upon a single gesture in an attempt to find meanings.

"A gesture doesn't necessarily mean something in and of itself, any more than a word does. You have to appreciate them in context, in what we call gesture clusters."

Nierenberg believes most people adopt two or three gestures early in life, but don't really develop any perception about them. An exception is the woman who has raised a child—having to understand a baby's every need on a nonverbal basis puts her ahead of the game.

Still, it's a language anyone can learn: "If a man can gain an awareness, he can build on it. But it's like any other language. You have to practice to become proficient."

One method of practicing is to keep your eyes open in places where people are likely to gather—at parties, restaurants and, one of Nierenberg's favorite spots, the airport.

In the opening pages of his *How to Read a Person Like a Book*, Nierenberg offers a row of telephone booths at the airport as a small example of what you can gather from simple observation.

A man who stands almost at attention, jacket buttoned, might be talking to someone very important to him, perhaps a client or his boss. In the next booth, a caller will be slouched casually against the wall, nodding his head, perhaps talking to his wife or a friend. The third, who is likely talking to his girl friend, has his back turned, his face hidden, his head tilted to one side, and is holding the telephone almost caressingly.

The next time you're at a party, keep your eyes on the various groups. See which are formed into closed circles, which are open. Note clusters of signals

being flashed to members of the opposite sex, the preening gestures of adjusting clothing or hair, or the signals indicating boredom, disinterest or discomfort.

Two people in a closed discussion will sit with legs crossed and bodies turned toward each other, indicating interest. Protected from interruption, they will communicate well. On the other extreme, two people with arms crossed defensively, legs crossed *away* from each other, have not established communication.

Also, remember that the signals you transmit can be instinctively picked up by someone else, whose own mood can be influenced—if not determined—by them. Too often, says Nierenberg, we project a negative attitude picked up and returned by the other person.

Body talk—suddenly it's a whole new language.

Yet, it's far from new. As Nierenberg points out, people have been using nonverbal communication since before they became "people," that is, before they became civilized.

What is new is the world of information awaiting those of us who will learn this old/new language.

The Man Who Reads Nature's Secret Signals

Thorn Bacon

Sweet Talking Soothes Pullets

BELLEVUE, Wash. (AP)—Scientists say hysteria in chicken flocks is caused by some of the same things that might trigger hysteria in humans—social pressures, pain and fear. Besides being noisy, hysterical chickens often kill themselves and one another.

Speakers at the Washington State University Poultrymen's Institute recommend the combination of diet supplements and soft talk to pacify pullets which might otherwise take a cackling, clawing, flying leap off the deep end.

Suppose you were to be told that the philodendron plant resting on the window sill above your kitchen sink screams silently when you break a breakfast egg in the frying pan, or that the potted dracaena on the sun porch grows apprehensive whenever your dog goes by? Finally, would you dare believe that when you accidentally cut your finger the dying cells in the drying blood transmit signals to the philodendron, the dracaena and the parsley in your refrigerator?

Provocative questions? Indeed, yes, but ones which are being seriously, soberly and quietly investigated by scientists at several major American universities as a result of some bizarre findings by the Backster Research Foundation of New York City.

The object: To discover if there is an unknown communication link between the cells of plants and animals through which distress signals are transmitted that broadcast threats against any member of the living community!

These staggering implications were reported in an abstract published on September 7, 1967, by Cleve Backster, a former interrogation specialist with the Central Intelligence Agency, who operates a New York school for training law enforcement officers in the techniques of using the polygraph—commonly known as the lie detector.

Backster was one of a four-man panel of experts called to testify before the 1964 Congressional Hearings on the Use of Polygraphs by the federal government. Following duty with the CIA as an interrogation specialist, he became director of the Leonarde Keeler Polygraph Institute of

You can communicate with plants and animals.

Chicago. Since 1949, he has acted as a consultant to almost every government agency which makes use of the polygraph. He introduced the Backster Zone Comparison polygraph procedure, which is the technique standard at the U. S. Army Polygraph School.

Changed His Life

Teaching polygraph, however, became a secondary interest to Backster on a February morning in 1966 when he made the discovery which changed his life.

These are the words he used to describe what happened in his laboratory that morning:

"Immediately following the watering of an office plant, I wondered if it would be possible to measure the rate at which water rose in a plant from the root area into the leaf. I chose the psychogalvanic reflex (PGR) index as a possible means of measuring the rate of moisture ascent. The pair of PGR electrodes could be attached to a leaf of the plant. Hopefully, by using the Wheatstone bridge circuitry involved, I could measure the increase in the plant leaf's moisture content onto the polygraph tape.

"Deciding to pursue the idea, I placed a psychogalvanic reflex electrode on each side of the same leaf of the nearby *Dracaena massangeana* plant with a rubber band. The plant leaf was successfully balanced into the PGR circuitry, its electrical resistance falling within the resistance limit of the instrumentation.

"Contrary to my expectation, from the outset the plant leaf tracing exhibited a downward trend. Then, after about one minute of chart time, the tracing exhibited a contour similar to a PGR reaction pattern typically demonstrated by a human subject experienc-

Egg Comunication

Observant biologists have long known that among such game birds as quail, partridge, pheasant and grouse, all the eggs in a nest tend to hatch at about the same time—even though they were laid several hours apart. The value of the phenomenon seems obvious: it enables the mother bird to leave the nest for food and protect her brood without worrying about any unhatched eggs. But how is the hatching synchronization achieved? No one has known. Now it appears that scientists were simply not listening hard enough to hear the obvious answer.

Working with nests of quail eggs, Cambridge University Research Psychologist Margaret Vince used sensitive instruments to record the movements and sounds of quail embryos during the last three days of their incubation period. Some twelve to 18 hours before hatching, she discovered, the eggs began to emit faint and intermittent clicks in time with the breathing of the embryo. The clicking gradually became louder and more regular, drowning out the sound of breathing, until it suddenly stopped only minutes before the eggs hatched.

Psychologist Vince is not sure what causes the clicking, but she thinks it is associated with lung ventilation and serves as a form of communication between the eggs. As more mature embryos move toward the hatching stage, she says, their clicking stimulates faster development of younger embryos in adjacent eggs, so that all of the eggs hatch around the same time. To check her theory, she shortened the normal incubation period of a quail egg by placing it in a nest of other quail eggs that began incubation at least 24 hours earlier. Stimulated by the surrounding clicks, the newer quail egg hatched at the same time as the more mature ones.

The quail-egg experiments also demonstrate that the communication between eggs works only when they are in actual contact. When Psychologist Vince separated the eggs, placing them four inches apart, the embryos could not sense the clicks made by their siblings. As a result, they hatched independently—as much as two days apart.

The Man Who Reads Nature's Secret Signals

Editor's Note

Dick Kirkpatrick

The editors of *National Wildlife* were as doubtful as you may be after reading Thorn Bacon's account of "Backster's Phenomenon," so we visited and photographed him in his offices, just off Times Square in New York City.

We found a quiet, polite, serious and successful student of the psychology of interrogation, working almost full time on the exploration of his discovery in an office cluttered with extremely sophisticated electronic gear and decorated with thumbtacked records of plant—and other cell life—reactions.

He showed us the original tape from his first discovery of the phenomenon, and yard after yard of tapes from succeeding experiments. One thing impressed us immediately: First, Cleve Backster is not some kind of a nut. He really knows his business, and is pursuing his investigations with great care to avoid any chance of criticism from the doubting scientific community, though he admits that seems inevitable.

As we talked, Backster set up his specially modified polygraph with a fairly ordinary philodendron leaf clamped in position for reading the psychogalvanic reflex index. He mentioned that he no longer handles his plants with anything but great care, since they seem to be attached to him as their owner and caretaker. When a plant must be handled or stimulated to produce a reaction, that is done by his assistant, Bob Henson, who "plays the heavy."

As we sat, chatting, the pen traced a graph of normal repose for the plant, until Bob walked in the room. The graph turned suddenly to one of agitation, and bobbed markedly until he left. Then it calmed down again to a normal tracing.

Later, we talked about ways to stimulate the plant for a photograph, and Backster explained that he preferred not to "hurt" the plant. I remarked that

(continued on page 61)

ing an emotional stimulation of short duration. Even though its tracing had failed to reflect the effect of the watering, the plant leaf did offer itself as a possibly unique source of data.

"Staggering as it may be to contemplate, a life signal may connect all creation . . ."

"As I watched the PGR tracing continue, I wondered if there could be a similarity between the tracing from the plant and a PGR tracing from a human. I decided to try to apply some equivalent to the threat-to-well-being principle, a well-established method of triggering emotionality in humans. I first tried to arouse the plant by immersing a plant leaf in a cup of hot coffee. But there was no measurable reaction.

"After a nine minute interim, I decided to obtain a match and burn the plant leaf being tested. At the instant of this decision, at thirteen minutes fifty-five seconds of chart time, there was a dramatic change in the PGR tracing pattern in the form of an abrupt and prolonged upward sweep of the recording pen. I had not moved, or touched the plant, so the timing of the PGR pen activity suggested to me that the tracing might have been triggered by the mere thought of the harm I intended to inflict upon the plant. This occurrence, if repeatable, would tend to indicate the possible existence of some undefined perception in the plant."

Backster began to explore how the suffering of other species affected his plants. He bought some brine shrimp, ordinarily used as live food for tropical fish, and killed them by dumping them into boiling water. As he saw the polygraph recording needle leap frantically, he was awed by a startling and apparently new concept: "Could it be that when cell life dies, it broadcasts a signal to other living cells?" If this was so, he would have to completely automate his experiments, removing all human elements which might consciously or unconsciously contaminate the results.

Space Age Lab

In the three years since, Backster has spent many thousands of dollars in transforming his offices into a space-age assembly of mechanized shrimp-dump dishes, a sophisticated electronic randomizer and programmer circuitry and multiple PGR monitoring devices. But the results continue to point to a capability for perception in all living cells—a perception that Backster calls "primary." I asked him for more details:

Q. What do you mean by primary?

A. I mean primary in the sense that this perception applies to all cells that we have monitored, without regard to their assigned biological function.

Q. What types of cells have you tested?

A. We have found this same phenomenon in the amoeba, the paramecium, and other single-cell organisms, in fact, in every kind of cell we have tested: fresh fruits and vegetables, mold cultures, yeasts, scrapings from the roof of the mouth of a human, blood samples, even spermatozoa.

Q. Do you mean that all of these cells have a sensing capacity?

A. It seems so. Incidentally, we have tried unsuccessfully to block

(continued from page 60)

perhaps I could do it, and reached for a match, watching in astonishment as the plant produced a violently agitated reaction even as I began to speak.

Still later, the plant's readings became calmer and calmer, and Backster explained that after an extended time, they seemed to become accustomed to stimuli and their reactions became less marked. At that point I blew a cloud of cigarette smoke over the plant without warning, and it produced a jagged little graph that Backster didn't try to interpret but which I proclaimed to be a reaction of annoyance.

While George Harrison was shooting a photograph, Backster suddenly asked him if anything was wrong; the plant was showing something like a sympathetic reaction to consternation, but was not being stimulated in any way. George admitted that he had just discovered that one lens was not working properly, and had been worrying about the photographs he had already made.

Altogether, we ran the machine on that plant for two hours, and produced a dozen very interesting reactions, some of which Backster recognized (though he is very reluctant to try to interpret them in human terms) and some others that made no particular sense at all, like the up-and-down reading yielded from a telephone conversation Backster held in a neighboring office. The plant reacted differently to the periods of Backster's talking and listening for some reason. But it *did* react.

So the reactions continue, and Cleve Backster's work continues, as he attempts to analyze the nature of the plants' graphs. Some of the possible applications of the phenomenon, in medical diagnosis, criminal investigation and other fields, are so fantastic that he asked me not to repeat them here. His first serious paper on the phenomenon, titled *Evidence of a Primary Perception in Plant Life*, is scheduled for publication in the *International Journal of Parapsychology* in January 1969. He awaits the reaction of the scientific community; we await the reaction of *National Wildlife* readers. What do you suppose he has discovered?

whatever signal is being received by using a Faraday screen, screen cage, and even leadlined containers. Still the communication continues. It seems that the signal may not even fall within our electrodynamic spectrum. If not, this would certainly have profound implications.

Q. What kind of a signal is it?

A. I can answer your question better by telling you what we think the signal is *not*. We know it is not within the different known frequencies, AM, FM, or any form of signal which we can shield by ordinary means. Distance seems to impose no limitation. For example, we are conducting research that would tend to indicate that this signal can traverse hundreds of miles.

Q. Are plants attuned to stress?

A. Perhaps. I used to have a Doberman Pincher in my office. He slept in the back room where I had an electric timer hooked to a loud pulsating alarm, which was located directly above his bed. Actuation of the timing mechanism was accompanied by a barely audible click which preceded the alarm by approximately five seconds. The dog would invariably hear the click, and would leave the room before the bell, which he disliked intensely, started to ring. Although in a different room, with the plants, I knew exactly when the dog was leaving his room, even though I could not hear the click, because the plants acknowledged his movements by showing reaction coincidental to the click, reflecting the Doberman's anxiety.

Q. In the final analysis, aren't you saying that we must reassess our definitions of sensory perception and intelligence?

A. Who can say at this point? There are certainly implications here that could have profound effects on those concepts. Our

observations show that the signal leaps across distances, as I said before. I have been as far away as New Jersey—about fifteen miles from Manhattan—and have merely thought about returning to my office, only to learn when I returned that at the precise moment I had had the thought—checked against a stop watch—there was a coincidental reaction by the plants to the thought of coming back. Relief? Welcome? We aren't sure, but evidence indicates something like relief. It isn't fear.

Do Plants Have Emotions?

The trend of Backster's research results does indeed embrace profound implications. Do plants have emotions? Do they make strange signals of awareness beyond our own abilities to comprehend? It seems so. Personally, I cannot imagine a world so dull, so satiated, that it should reject out of hand arresting new ideas which may be as old as the first amino acid in the chain of life on our earth. Inexplicable has never meant miraculous. Nor does it necessarily mean spiritual. In this case, it may simply prove to mean another extension of our natural laws.

Let me leave you to ponder a question Backster asked me. Many hunters have observed that game animals somehow sense the exact moment of the opening of the hunting season. We can perhaps ascribe this to the noise of the first gunshots. But, how can we explain the similar observation of game's apparent awareness of the exact moment of the season's close? Cleve Backster may be approaching the answer to that question, and a lot of others.

Prods

1. Verbal maps are maps or pictures drawn with words. Why is it important that our verbal maps represent the territory they describe?
2. Appropriate verbal and nonverbal symbols are essential to effective communication. How can we develop the skill to send and interpret symbols properly?
3. What are some of the tools of clear thinking? How can they help us communicate more effectively?
4. What are nonverbal messages? What are their special characteristics?
5. Animals, plants, eggs, and other nonhuman organisms appear to send and respond to messages. Do you think plants can communicate?

Social trends and technological advancements influence your life.

The conflict between what you want and the environment in which you live produces stress in your life.

Component

3

The Environment

Communication Shock

Alvin Toffler

Time and Change

How do we *know* that change is accelerating? There is, after all, no absolute way to measure change. In the awesome complexity of the universe, even within any given society, a virtually infinite number of streams of change occur simultaneously. All "things"—from the tiniest virus to the greatest galaxy—are, in reality, not things at all, but processes. There is no static point, no nirvana-like un-change, against which to measure change. Change is, therefore, necessarily relative.

It is also uneven. If all processes occurred at the same speed, or even if they accelerated or decelerated in unison, it would be impossible to observe change. The future, however, invades the present at differing speeds. Thus it becomes possible to compare the speed of different processes as they unfold. We know, for example, that compared with the biological evolution of the species, cultural and social evolution is extremely rapid. We know that some societies transform themselves technologically or economically more rapidly than others. We also know that different sectors within the same society exhibit different rates of change— the disparity that William Ogburn labeled "cultural lag." It is precisely the unevenness of change that makes it measurable.

We need, however, a yardstick that makes it possible to compare highly diverse processes, and this yardstick is time. Without time, change has no meaning. And without change, time would stop. Time can be conceived as the intervals during which events occur. Just as money permits us to place a value on both apples and oranges, time permits us to compare unlike processes. When we say that it takes three years to build a dam, we are really saying it takes three times as long as it takes the earth to circle the sun or 31,000,000 times as long as it takes to sharpen a pencil. Time is the currency of exchange that makes it possible to compare the rates at which very different processes play themselves out.

Given the unevenness of change and armed with this yardstick, we still face exhausting difficulties in measuring change. When we speak of the rate of change, we refer to the number of events crowded into an arbitrarily fixed interval of time. Thus we need to define the "events." We need to select our intervals with precision. We need to be careful about the conclusions we draw from the differences we observe. Moreover, in the measurement of change, we are today far more advanced with respect to physical processes than social processes. We know far better, for example, how to measure the rate at which blood flows through the

Social trends and technological advancements influence your life.

body than the rate at which a rumor flows through society.

Even with all these qualifications, however, there is widespread agreement, reaching from historians and archaeologists all across the spectrum to scientists, sociologists, economists and psychologists, that many social processes are speeding up—strikingly, even spectacularly.

Psychophysiologists studying the impact of change on various organisms have shown that successful adaptation can occur only when the level of stimulation—the amount of change and novelty in the environment—is neither too low nor too high. "The central nervous system of a higher animal," says Professor D. E. Berlyne of the University of Toronto, "is designed to cope with environments that produce a certain rate of . . . stimulation . . . It will naturally not perform at its best in an environment that over-stresses or overloads it." He makes the same point about environments that understimulate it. Indeed, experiments with deer, dogs, mice and men all point unequivocally to the existence of what might be called an "adaptive range" below which and above which the individual's ability to cope simply falls apart.

Future shock is the response to overstimulation. It occurs when the individual is forced to operate above his adaptive range. Considerable research has been devoted to studying the impact of inadequate change and novelty on human performance. Studies of men in isolated Antarctic outposts, experiments in sensory deprivation, investigations into on-the-job performance in factories, all show a falling off of mental and physical abilities in response to understimulation. We have less direct data on the impact of overstimulation, but such evidence as does exist is dramatic and unsettling.

Bombardment of the Senses

We still know too little about this phenomenon to explain authoritatively why overstimulation seems to produce maladaptive behavior. Yet we pick up important clues if we recognize that overstimulation can occur on at least three different levels: the sensory, the cognitive and the decisional.[1]

The easiest to understand is the sensory level. Experiments in sensory deprivation, during which volunteers are cut off from normal stimulation of their senses, have shown that the absence of novel sensory stimuli can lead to bewilderment and impaired mental functioning. By the same token, the input of too much disorganized, patternless or chaotic sensory stimuli can have similar effects. It is for this reason that practitioners of political or religious brainwashing make use not only of sensory deprivation (solitary confinement, for example) but of sensory bombardment involving flashing lights, rapidly shifting patterns of color, chaotic sound effects—the whole arsenal of psychedelic kaleidoscopy.

The religious fervor and bizarre behavior of certain hippie cultists may arise not merely from drug abuse, but from group experimentation with both sensory deprivation and bombardment. The chanting of monotonous mantras, the attempt to focus the individual's attention on interior, bodily sensation to the exclusion of outside stimuli, are efforts to induce the weird and sometimes hallucinatory effects of understimulation.

At the other end of the scale, we note the glazed stares and numb, expressionless faces of

A Chicken in Every Pot

The Forgotten Man

Blood, Sweat, and Tears

All the Way with L. B. J.

Peace in Our Time

The Full Dinner Pail

You Never Had It So Good

I Like Ike

The Slogan Society

In politics, it seems, bad times make good slogans. Herbert Hoover's promise of "a chicken in every pot" did not get him re-elected in 1932, but it was a far more ingenious catch phrase than the Republicans' 1944 theme, "Time for a change," or "I like Ike" in 1952. And for all John F. Kennedy's eloquence, no Democratic orator since the Depression has matched Franklin D. Roosevelt's phrasemaking prowess on behalf of "the forgotten man." Lyndon Johnson's vision of "the Great Society" is not only vague, but *vieille vague* as well; the term was the title of a 1914 book by British Political Psychologist Graham Wallas, and the idea is as old as Plato's *Republic*. Equally lackluster is Barry Goldwater's "In your heart you know he is right"—which L.B.J. could not resist parodying in his speech before the Steelworkers Union last month ("You know in your heart that I am telling you the truth").

"Word Magic"

To many scholars, all slogans are bad slogans. George Mowry, dean of social sciences at U.C.L.A., argues that they "compress a lot of truth into what is basically an untruth." Indeed, for the majority of voters not inclined to analyze issues for themselves, slogans are a welcome substitute for logical argument. "Most people would rather die than think," says Bertrand Russell. "In fact, some do." Russell's own ban-the-bomb marchers, mindlessly chanting "Better Red than dead," prove his point.

Phrases such as "Peace in our time" and "Prosperity is just around the corner" invoke "word magic," as linguists call verbal formulas that promise to make dreams come true through sheer repetition. On the other hand, observes San Francisco State College's S. I. Hayakawa, a pioneering U.S. semanticist, "You don't move a mass society with a volume by Galbraith." Particularly in the U.S., as Cambridge Historian Denis Brogan has pointed out, "the evocative power of verbal symbols must not be despised, for these are and have been one of the chief means of uniting the United States and keeping it united."

The most effective political slogans are timely, yet live long beyond their time. Passing into the language, they help crystallize great issues of the past for future generations: "Give me liberty or give me death"; "*Lebenstraum*"; "The world must be made safe for democracy"; "There'll always be an England"; "unconditional surrender"; "the Great Leap Forward"; "We shall overcome." In an increasingly complex society, as Hayakawa points out, such coinages are essential "short cuts to a consensus."

(continued on page 67)

youthful dancers at the great rock music auditoriums where light shows, split-screen movies, high decibel screams, shouts and moans, grotesque costumes and writhing, painted bodies create a sensory environment characterized by high input and extreme unpredictability and novelty.

An organism's ability to cope with sensory input is dependent upon its physiological structure. The nature of its sense organs and the speed with which impulses flow through its neural system set biological bounds on the quantity of sensory data it can accept. If we examine the speed of signal transmission within various organisms, we find that the lower the evolutionary level, the slower the movement. Thus, for example, in a sea urchin egg, lacking a nervous system as such, a signal moves along a membrane at a rate of about a centimeter an hour. Clearly, at such a rate, the organism can respond to only a very limited part of its environment. By the time we move up the ladder to a jellyfish, which already has a primitive nervous system, the signal travels 36,000 times faster: ten centimeters per second. In a worm, the rate leaps to 100 cps. Among insects and crustaceans, neural pulses race along at 1000 cps. Among anthropoids the rate reaches 10,000 cps. Crude as these figures no doubt are, they help explain why man is unquestionably among the most adaptable of creatures.

Yet even in man, with a neural transmission rate of about 30,000 cps, the boundaries of the system are imposing. (Electrical signals in a computer, by contrast, travel billions of times faster.) The limitations of the sense organs and nervous system mean that many environmental events occur at rates too fast for us to follow, and we are reduced to sampling experience at best. When the signals reaching us are regular and repetitive, this sampling process can yield a fairly good mental representation of reality. But when it is highly disorganized, when it is novel and unpredictable, the accuracy of our imagery is necessarily reduced. Our image of reality is distorted. This may explain why, when we experience sensory overstimulation, we suffer confusion, a blurring of the line between illusion and reality.

Information Overload

If overstimulation at the sensory level increases the distortion with which we perceive reality, cognitive overstimulation interferes with our ability to "think." While some human responses to novelty are involuntary, others are preceded by conscious thought, and this depends upon our ability to absorb, manipulate, evaluate and retain information.

Rational behavior, in particular, depends upon a ceaseless flow of data from the environment. It depends upon the power of the individual to predict, with at least fair success, the outcome of his own actions. To do this, he must be able to predict how the environment will respond to his acts. Sanity, itself, thus hinges on man's ability to predict his immediate, personal future on the basis of information fed him by the environment.

When the individual is plunged into a fast and irregularly changing situation, or a novelty-loaded context, however, his predictive accuracy plummets. He can no longer make the reasonably correct assessments on which rational behavior is dependent.

To compensate for this, to bring his accuracy up to the normal level again, he must scoop up and

(continued from page 66)

Seven Is Tops

The word "slogan," from the Gaelic *sluagh* (army) and *gairm* (a call), originally meant a call to arms—and some of history's most stirring slogans, from "Erin go bragh" to "Remember Pearl Harbor" have been just that. In peacetime, argues Hayakawa, electorates respond more readily to slogans that promise change, since people are rarely satisfied with things as they are. One notable exception was the catch phrase that helped return Britain's Tory Party to power in 1959: "You never had it so good." In general, though, Democrats, like detergent manufactures, favor slogans that offer a new and better product ("New deal," "New Frontier"). The Grand Old Party, like whisky distillers, prefers to emphasize aged-in-the-wood reliability, from Abraham Lincoln's "Don't swap horses in the middle of the stream" to 1924's "Keep cool with Coolidge."

To be fully effective, say psychologists, a slogan should express a single idea in seven words or less. "It is a psychological fact," says Harvard's Gordon Allport, "that seven is the normal limit of rote memory." (Example: telephone numbers.) Whether plugging cat food or a candidate, sloganeers lean heavily on such verbal devices as alliteration ("Korea, Communism, Corruption"), rhyme ("All the way with L.B.J."), or a combination of both ("Tippecanoe and Tyler Too").* Other familiar standbys are paradox ("We have nothing to fear but fear itself"), metaphor ("Just

the kiss of the hops"), metonymy ("The full dinner pail"), parody (a Norwegian travel folder promises "a Fjord in Your Future"), and punning ("Every litter bit helps"). By using what semanticists call "affective" language, many slogans deliberately exploit chauvinism ("Made in Texas by Texans"), xenophobia ("Yankee go home"), insecurity ("Even your best friends won't tell you"), narcissism ("Next to myself I like B.V.D. best"), escapism ("I dreamed I barged down the Nile in my Maidenform bra").

Long before Poet T. S. Eliot expounded his theory of the "auditory imagination," Pioneer Adman Earnest Elmo Calkins used pocket poetry to make "Phoebe Snow" glamorize passenger service on the coal-burning Delaware, Lackawanna & Western Railroad. Slogans nearly always overload the language and often debase it ("coffee-er coffee"). English teachers curse Madison Avenue for institutionalizing bad grammar with such calculated lapses as "us Tareyton smokers" and "like a cigarette should." By contrast, some of history's most enduring slogans were plucked from literature. Winston Churchill's call to "blood, sweat and tears"—boiled down from his first statement as Prime Minister in 1940, "I have nothing to offer but blood, toil, tears and sweat"—was adapted from a passage in a 1931 book by Churchill; but strikingly similar words were used in previous centuries by the British poets John Donne, Byron and Lord Alfred Douglas.

*Tyler was the Whig vice-presidential candidate in 1840. "Tippecanoe" was used to glamorize Gentleman Farmer William Henry Harrison, who had scored a dubious victory over the Indians in a skirmish at Tippecanoe Creek twenty-nine years earlier, but routed Martin Van Buren in the election. A more forgettable Whig slogan affirmed: "With Tip and Tyler we'll bust Van's biler."

process far more information than before. And he must do this at extremely high rates of speed. In short, the more rapidly changing and novel the environment, the more information the individual needs to process in order to make effective, rational decisions.

Yet just as there are limits on how much sensory input we can accept, there are in-built constraints on our ability to process information. In the words of psychologist George A. Miller of Rockefeller University, there are "severe limitations on the amount of information that we are able to receive, process, and remember." By classifying information, by abstracting and "coding" it in various ways, we manage to stretch these limits, yet ample evidence demonstrates that our capabilities are finite.

The acceleration of change, overstimulation from the environment, and information overload result in communication shock.

To discover these outer limits, psychologists and communications theorists have set about testing what they call the "channel capacity" of the human organism. For the purpose of these experiments, they regard man as a "channel." Information enters from the outside. It is processed. It exits in the form of actions based on decisions. The speed and accuracy of human information processing can be measured by comparing the speed of information input with the speed and accuracy of output.

Information has been defined technically and measured in terms of units called "bits."[2] By

now, experiments have established rates for the processing involved in a wide variety of tasks from reading, typing, and playing the piano to manipulating dials or doing mental arithmetic. And while researchers differ as to the exact figures, they strongly agree on two basic principles: first, that man has limited capacity; and second, that overloading the system leads to serious breakdown of performance. . . .

Managers plagued by demands for rapid, incessant and complex decisions; pupils deluged with facts and hit with repeated tests; housewives confronted with squalling children, jangling telephones, broken washing machines, the wail of rock and roll from the teenager's living room and the whine of the television set in the parlor—may well find their ability to think and act clearly impaired by the waves of information crashing into their senses. It is more than possible that some of the symptoms noted among battle-stressed soldiers, disaster victims, and culture shocked travelers are related to this kind of information overload.

One of the men who has pioneered in information studies, Dr. James G. Miller, director of the Mental Health Research Institute at the University of Michigan, states flatly that "Glutting a person with more information than he can process may . . . lead to disturbance." He suggests, in fact, that information overload may be related to various forms of mental illness.

One of the striking features of schizophrenia, for example, is "incorrect associative response." Ideas and words that ought to be linked in the subject's mind are not, and vice versa. The schizophrenic tends to think in arbitrary or highly personalized categories. Confronted with a set of blocks of

various kinds—triangles, cubes, cones, etc.—the normal person is likely to categorize them in terms of geometric shape. The schizophrenic asked to classify them is just as likely to say "They are all soldiers," or "They all make me feel sad."

In the volume *Disorders of Communication*, Miller describes experiments using word association tests to compare normals and schizophrenics. Normal subjects were divided into two groups, and asked to associate various words with other words or concepts. One group worked at its own pace. The other worked under time pressure—i.e., under conditions of rapid information input. The time-pressed subjects came up with responses more like those of schizophrenics than of self-paced normals.

Similar experiments conducted by psychologists G. Usdansky and L. J. Chapman made possible a more refined analysis of the types of errors made by subjects working under forced-pace, high information-input rates. They, too, concluded that increasing the speed of response brought out a pattern of errors among normals that is peculiarly characteristic of schizophrenics.

"One might speculate," Miller suggests, ". . . that schizophrenia (by some as-yet-unknown process, perhaps a metabolic fault which increases neural 'noise') lowers the capacities of channels involved in cognitive information processing. Schizophrenics consequently . . . have difficulties in coping with information inputs at standard rates like the difficulties experienced by normals at rapid rates. As a result, schizophrenics make errors at standard rates like those made by normals under fast, forced-input rates."

In short, Miller argues, the breakdown of human performance under heavy information loads may be related to psychopathology in ways we have not yet begun to explore. Yet, even without understanding its potential impact, we are accelerating the generalized rate of change in society. We are forcing people to adapt to a new life pace, to confront novel situations and master them in ever shorter intervals. We are forcing them to choose among fast-multiplying options. We are, in other words, forcing them to process information at a far more rapid pace than was necessary in slowly evolving societies. There can be little doubt that we are subjecting at least some of them to cognitive overstimulation. What consequences this may have for mental health in the technosocieties has yet to be determined.

---

1. The line between each of these is not completely clear, even to psychologists, but if we simply, in commonsense fashion, equate the sensory level with perceiving, the cognitive with thinking, and the decisional with deciding, we will not go too far astray.

2. A bit is the amount of information needed to make a decision between two equally likely alternatives. The number of bits needed increases by one as the number of such alternatives doubles.

WHEN I MET MY GURU WHO KNEW EVERYTHING IN MY HEAD, I REALIZED THAT HE KNEW EVERYTHING IN MY HEAD WHETHER "I" LIKED IT OR NOT. HE KNEW IT.

Excerpted from *Remember: Be Here Now* by Richard Alpert. © Lama Foundation, 1971, Year of the Earth Monkey, Box 444, San Cristobal, New Mexico. Distributed by Crown Publishing, 419 Park Ave. S., New York, N.Y. 10016. Used by permission of the Lama Foundation.

AND THERE WOULD BE TIMES AFTER A PARTICULARLY BEAUTIFUL DARSHAN WITH HIM WHEN HE'D SAY TO ME: "OH! YOU GAVE MUCH MONEY TO A LAMA," AND I'D SAY YES AND HE'D SAY: "YOU'RE VERY GOOD. YOU'RE COMING ALONG WITH YOUR SADHANA," AND I FELT SO GOOD AND THEN I'D GO BACK TO THE TEMPLE AND THINK "BOY! I'M GOING TO BE A GREAT YOGI. I'LL HAVE GREAT POWERS. WHAT AM I GOING TO DO WITH THEM?"...AND I'D START TO HAVE THESE HORRIBLE THOUGHTS AND ALL MY IMPURITIES WOULD RISE TO THE SURFACE AND THEY WOULD REALLY BE...AND THEN I'D GO TO BED AND HAVE ALL KINDS OF SEXUAL FANTASIES AND I'D THINK "LOOK YOU'RE BEING A YOGI AND YOU SEE THE ABSURDITY OF THAT SITUATION YOU'RE IN..." BUT I'D STILL HAVE THE THOUGHT. AND THEN, IN THE COURSE OF IT, I'D HAVE A THOUGHT (I'D BE GOING THROUGH MY SHOULDER BAG AND COME ACROSS A NOTE I'D WRITTEN TO MYSELF: "REMEMBER TO VISIT LAMA GOVINDA") AND I'D THINK, "I MUST VISIT LAMA GOVINDA WHILE I'M IN INDIA."

AND THE NEXT MORNING AT 8 O'CLOCK THERE IS THE MES-SENGER WITH INSTRUCTIONS: "THE GURU SAID YOU'RE TO GO VISIT LAMA GOVINDA."

NOW! THERE ISN'T A MESSAGE SAYING: "CUT OUT THOSE SEXUAL THOUGHTS," BUT HE MUST OBVIOUSLY KNOW THEM. DO YOU THINK HE JUST PICKED UP ON THE LAMA GOVINDA THING?

CAN I ASSUME THE PROBABILITIES ARE HE ONLY TUNES IN EVERY TIME I HAVE A POSITIVE THOUGHT?

AND THEN I COME BEFORE HIM AND NOW I'M FREAKED BECAUSE I KNOW HE KNOWS IT ALL; AND I WALK IN, AND HE

LOOKS AT ME WITH TOTAL
LOVE

AND I THINK: HOW CAN HE DO IT?
THIS GUY MUST BE NUTS! HE'S LOVING
THIS CORRUPT... WHY ISN'T HE...?
YOU SEE THE PREDICAMENT I WAS IN?
AND THEN! WHAT I UNDERSTOOD WAS:
HE WAS LOVING THAT IN ME WHICH WAS
BEHIND MY PERSONALITY AND BEHIND
MY BODY.
NOT: "I REALLY LOVE RAM DASS"
IT WASN'T INTERPERSONAL LOVE
IT WASN'T POSSESSIVE LOVE
IT WASN'T NEEDFUL LOVE
IT WAS THE FACT THAT

HE IS  LOVE

The Components of a Communication Situation

Person

Message

Environment

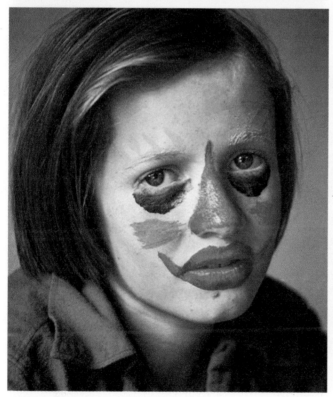

upper left: Burke Uzzle/Magnum
lower left and right: Ron Partridge/BBM Associates

Elliot Landy/Magnum
Elihu Blotnick/BBM Associates

Jeffrey Blankfort/BBM Associates
BBM Associates

upper and lower left: Elihu Blotnick/BBM Associates
right: Burke Uzzle/Magnum

Mass Media and Social Trends

Ithiel de Sola Pool

The impending technical changes that make up the communications revolution raise some very big questions. Perhaps the biggest and most fundamental one is this:

Is society being pushed toward increased conformity by these changes or toward more diversity? That is the biggest question, but there are many more. For instance:

How fast can society absorb the new kinds of communication it is being offered?

Where will the changes come first?

What will they do to present communications media?

How—in sum—will *people* be affected? What will this revolution do to the ways people live and think and associate with each other?

End of the Mass Media?

Until now, the effect of the technology of communication has been to encourage growth of mass media. And the effect of the mass media, so social critics have argued, has been to make for a homogenized society. Technology made it cheap to reach large numbers of people by mass-produced messages on the printed page and later by mass-produced radio and television.

Great economies of scale could be achieved by standardizing the information output. The number of different newspapers published in the United States has declined from 2042 in 1920 to about 1750 today—and they get most of their nonlocal news from two wire services. A dozen magazines with circulations of 4.5 million to 16 million dominate the popular field. Any evening, in prime time when as many as 60% of the families have their TV sets turned on, the only choice most of them have is to view the entertainment offered by one of three networks—all of which offer fairly similar programs.

There can be no doubt that this standardized fare is a powerful force toward conformity. Wherever one goes in the United States, the same fads, the same styles, the same scandal of the week, the same ball scores, the same entertainments are on people's lips.

However, the effects which technology has had over the past hundred years may be quite different from what is to come. There is a new technology of communication emerging and the effect of this new technology could be to individualize people rather than to homogenize them.

We are at the beginning of an era in which the preferred communications devices need no longer have the quality of mass communications. Increasingly, communications devices will be adapted to individualized use by the consumer where and when he wants, on his own, without the cooperation of others; he will use machines as an extension of his own capabilities and personality, talking and listening world-wide, picking up whatever information he wants.

One simple example of this sort of thing is the evolution of text reproduction from a technology of mass production toward devices that produce exactly the text the user wants.

The printing press made text available to the millions, while the photographic and electrostatic copiers now found everywhere enable each reader among the millions to acquire just the pages he wants when he wants them at a cost hardly greater than printing.

In the future, it seems likely, television will undergo a similar transformation. TV now is what it is mostly because only a few channels are available in any one place, and so each channel must compete for the central mass of the audience. That median group wants light entertainment so that is what is offered. The technology requires the user to take what TV offers when it chooses, not when he chooses. Busy men simply will not collect their information in that way.

Your life style is being revolutionized by electronic media.

But the technology of TV is changing. Many more channels will be coming into each home, probably by wire, making it possible to serve minority audiences. Videotape will make it possible for the viewer to watch at his own convenience. Devices will undoubtedly be marketed allowing the consumer to skip and scan, finding that which he wishes and nothing else. More distant but even more important is the availability in each household of computer help in searching the whole file of available material and retrieving just what is wanted.

In fantasy, I visualize the evening at home which these developments suggest. Suppose the family would like to watch a musical. Perhaps someone dials a number on the telephone and asks by voice or code for a list of available musicals that are set in the present, have a satirical tone, and are musically jazzy. A list appears on the TV screen; someone asks who the singers are in one of them and gets an answer; somehow everyone agrees on a choice, and they settle down to watch.

The newspaper might work the same way. A reader starts by asking for a digest of the news, which appears on a screen or is printed out on a console. He can ask for details on any story that interests him. Perhaps he can ask specific questions about a story—such as the previous votes of a congressman referred to in the news item.

But First at the Office

Long before even the prosperous American has a reactive information service like that available to him at home, he is likely to be using one in his professional work. The technology can pay off most immediately in file management for institutions that are swamped with data of a fairly standard sort. For example, the State Department receives about 2000 telegrams a day from its posts all over the world and reproduces an average 70 copies of each. That file should be—and is now being—made computer-stor-

able and retrievable. And there are comparable flows of information in most of our large business or research organizations.

If you use census data a lot and have regular access to a computer, you can now buy from the Bureau a computer tape carrying a one-in-a-thousand sample of all the census replies, with identifying information removed. So it is just now becoming possible for some well-equipped students to browse fruitfully in the data.

When the reactive computer-aided communications network which the technology is now moving toward has emerged, it will be unnecessary to print all those thick volumes of census data. The 200-million replies will be stored in some bulky memory, and any table anybody wants will be computed whenever he wants it. Today that would be horrendously expensive—but economic trends are working in favor of that approach as the cost of computation goes steadily downward and the cost of shelving hard-copy material goes steadily upward. In future it may well be cheaper as well as more convenient to give everyone access to the raw information, with identification removed. Since the data will be on-line in a reactive way, an individual can explore to any depth he wants. He can get the three-sentence answer; or, if he needs it, he can get the 300-page answer by constantly asking "why?" to each preliminary answer, the way a child does.

The author is currently engaged in development of an on-line, computerized system of file management, the ADMINS system, to allow a social researcher to work in a total library of raw data. The system keeps track of where each file is, the relations among them, how the user has modified the files, and similar clerical mat-

ters—so that the user can think about his substantive problem instead of about mechanics.

Possibilities of this kind suggest that the revolution in communication will change our working lives as much as or more than it changes our personal lives. And certainly sooner. We are already at the point where for many scientific purposes retrieval systems stumblingly meet the test of usefulness.

How Fast Can We Take It?

But let us not be too hasty in prediction.

One of the easiest traps in technological prediction is to predict from single items of technology. To change society—and that is what we are talking about when we talk of a communications revolution—takes whole systems of mutually reinforcing technological opportunities. The possibilities inherent in any one invention are likely to be bypassed if supporting technologies fail to come in at the same time.

Moreover, if a technology is to affect a society deeply, it must be compatible with the desires and the habits of the people in the society—which may not be the same thing as meeting their needs.

New technologies are adopted more rapidly when they can be adopted piecemeal, more slowly when an entire system must come into use all at once. This is why television arrived so slowly. TV sets were available back in the thirties, and yet few people had ever watched one except over a drink in a bar until television became a universal thing in one great rush between 1950 and 1954. Television had to come in all at once as a system. Not just because the signal had to be

How to be fully understood without talking too much...

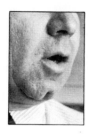

IN TEACHING

An Iowa school superintendent put it this way: "We're convinced that sound movies increase learning efficiency by 20% to 30%. Even slow learners grasp meanings quickly when they *see* a subject in context."

Movies add to the learning experience only so long as the projector does not intrude. It's important that mechanical troubles do not snap the tenuous thread of attention. This is one of the reasons why we transistorized the sound amplifier of the KODAK PAGEANT 16mm Sound Projector, Model AV-126-TR. To make it more of a *teaching* projector.

There are no tubes in this projector to interrupt showings. None to burn out. None to keep classes waiting while they warm up. There are none of the irritating hissing or popping sounds sometimes found in vacuum tube amplifiers. We use the same type of relied-upon circuitry used in space satellites. The sound you hear is as pure as can be recorded on 16mm film. At low volumes, at peak volumes, this projector speaks clearly and with authority the instant you push a button.

Pictures start the instant you move a lever. Comfortable pictures with edge-to-edge brilliance.

There's so much to be said about this projector, we'd like to say it in person. May we?

IN TRAINING

A man concerned with industrial training programs told us: "Movies communicate in minutes what would otherwise take hours or days to learn. They can create an understanding vitally needed among engineering teams widely separated by place, time or technology."

Interruptions interfere with the effectiveness of communication. The projector must take every distraction out of screened instructional material. It must contribute continuity. We make a projector that contributes superbly. It's the KODAK PAGEANT 16mm Sound Projector, Model AV-126-TR.

If you've budgeted 40 minutes to a film, a PAGEANT Projector gives you the full 40 minutes worth. No seconds lost for a warm-up. No minutes squandered on a breakdown.

If your film is highly sophisticated, still no worry. Every word, every meaning comes through loud and clear. No muffled basses, no sibilant-ridden trebles. This is projected sound-on-film at its very best.

No matter how you use it, this projector can make your training activities more fruitful to trainees and more rewarding to management.

May we demonstrate this in person?

IN SELLING

A real estate promoter says it this way: "...28 minutes after I flip a switch, I can count on 25% of my audience becoming buyers. Because our sales story is filmed, the presentation is never diluted, always perfectly duplicated, always successfully the same."

But that wasn't all this man had to say. He makes the point that salesmen aren't mechanics. A *selling* projector must be easy to set up and operate. It must *never* get in the way of the presentation. We make one like that. It's the KODAK PAGEANT 16mm Sound Projector, Model AV-126-TR.

The transistorized sound system of this projector should never need servicing—even when subjected to the bumps and jars of travel in the trunk of a car.

Setting up is as easy as opening a sample case and just about as fast. Speaker and power cords are permanently attached. And they're long enough to reach anywhere in rooms of a size salesmen are likely to be using.

There's ample power in the 12-watt amplifier to drive extra speakers or feed a PA system without distortion.

May we give you a salesman-to-salesman demonstration? You can begin by sending the coupon.

Send this:

. . . And Now a Word about Commercials

Commercials are infuriating. They are also irresistible. Commercials are an outrageous nuisance. They are also apt to be better than the programs they interrupt. Commercials are the heavy tribute that the viewer must pay to the sponsor in exchange for often dubious pleasure. They are also an American art form. A minor art form, but the ultimate in mixed media: sight, sound and sell.

Commercials—or a great many of them—are better than ever. How and why this came about is one of the more fascinating phenomena in television. They are part of the background music, as it were, of the American scene. Hardly anybody pays total attention to them; hardly anybody totally ignores them. Many, the very good and the very bad, force or insinuate themselves into the imagination. Even a reluctant viewer cannot quite resist the euphoria induced by airline ads that waft him up up and away, or travel spots, island-hopping in a wink of quick cuts, that drop him on a sun-splashed beach. Even while grumbling, he marvels at the dexterity, not to say ludicrous imagery, of a white tornado suddenly swirling through an untidy kitchen. He wakes up singing "You can take Salem out of the *country*, BUT . . . " His kids, riding shotgun on the shopping cart, may not know a stanza of *The Star-Spangled Banner*, but they can rap out several verses of "To a Smoker, It's a Kent."

With their vast and relentless power of amplification, the writers of commercials sprinkle more tag lines and catch phrases into the conversation than the poets, fettered to their paper and print, can ever hope to put into the American idiom. "A little dab'll do ya," "Fly the friendly skies" and "Leave the driving to us" are in fact a kind of pop poetry.

The money alone that goes into commercial production is stupefying. Film Director Stanley Kubrick, himself something of a big spender (*2001: A Space Odyssey* cost $11 million), observed recently that "a feature film made with the same kind of care as a commercial would have to cost $50 million." As it is, the

(continued on page 81)

standardized but because no one wants to buy a set unless there are attractive programs; advertisers won't finance programs until there are many sets turned on.

Many of these new interactive services are the sort that *can* come gradually. Many of them can use the voice-grade telephone lines that already reach into just about every home and office. And meanwhile, lines with very high channel capacity are being brought into more and more homes just in the effort to improve TV service. Telephone and TV together provide the routes by which newer services can spread.

The great *social* fact that technological prediction must take into account is this: If a new technology is to come rapidly into wide use it must be easy to use— very easy to use.

Here's an example of the errors one can get into by predicting from technical capability alone. From a technical viewpoint, the now widely available videotape recorder should make it possible to avoid many of the worst limitations of TV entertainment, the necessity to accept what is offered from a very limited choice. Actually, the technology for doing this same thing has been available for decades in the form of the home movie projector—offering better definition and a wider choice than TV offers. Why is it that we don't find 60 percent of American households watching motion pictures every night?

Essentially, the reason is that it puts too much of a burden on the user if he has to select the home movies he wants. Purchase of films one only wants to see once is uneconomic, of course, but library systems have not proved popular either. The real problem is that one cannot know what one would enjoy borrowing from a large store unless social communication has identified it. It is easier just to tune in on an evening's offerings, which at least have been professionally selected to be as popular as possible. It would take planning and research for the viewer to make a similar selection on his own. Retrieving information from any large file system has always required a high order of professional training. Accountants, librarians, archivists, scholars, all take years to educate. Even among those of us who are professional researchers, the job of looking up library materials is so unrewarding that most of us do less and less of it as we get older.

That is where the computer comes into our thinking about future communications systems. For the computer promises to make it possible to interrogate an inanimate data base with the same ease and success with which we can now ask questions of a friend or colleague, face to face or over the telephone. The communications system which I find is likely to make the mass media archaic is a combination of the telephone, the computer, and a variety of print, visual, and audio outputs. Its difference from contemporary mass communication modes is that—potentially, at least—it is easily interactive and responsive to the requests of the consumer. Computers are not now that easy to use. The problem technical men face is to create systems which will be responsive enough, convenient enough, and inexpensive enough, so that an untutored user can make retrievals that will be more satisfactory—to him—than *Life* or the *New Yorker* or Channel 9. It will not be easy, but it does not seem impossible.

It illuminates the problem if one looks at the history of communication methods. The two

(continued from page 80)

cost of a one-minute commercial—rehearsals, filming, reshooting, dubbing, scoring, animation, printing—runs to an average of $22,000 or about five times more than a minute of TV entertainment. . . .

While a TV series films an average of ten minutes' worth of script in one day, the shooting of a 60-second commercial often takes two or three days and can run through 25,000 ft. of film to get the final, worthy 90 ft. For an ad introducing Mattel Toys' new Bathhouse Brass line, a film crew covered 1,000 miles to shoot in eight different locations. The spot shows a parade of kids cavorting across sand dunes and careering down slides while madly blasting away on their plastic "brassoons," "toobas" and "flooglehorns." A kind of psychedelic version of the Pied Piper, the ad is typical of the wild, hyped-up pitches aired in the "Saturday morning jungle". . . .

Humorist Stan Freberg, a freelance commercial producer who created the Sunsweet prune and Jeno's pizza ads for TV, is pushing . . . "The Freberg Part-Time Television Plan: A Startling but Perfectly Reasonable Proposal for the De-escalation of Television in a Free Society, Mass Media-wise." The plan calls for a week like this:

Monday. Television as usual.

Tuesday. The set goes black, but one word shines in the center of the screen: Read!

Wednesday. Television as usual.

Thursday. The set goes black again, but this time we see the word Talk!

Friday. Television as usual.

Saturday. The words Unsupervised Activity.

And Sunday? Says Freberg: "We have to have somewhere to lump all those leftover commercials, don't we? Think of it! Twenty-four glorious, uninterrupted hours of advertising!"

It might just work—and it could be worse.

Pay for Sports on TV?

The goal of cable TV is to siphon away all of your favorite sports programming (and all other top entertainment) and charge you on a separate basis for every good program you watch.

$60.00 a year for television you now get free is more than a lot of Albuquerqueans can afford and the cost will go up and up and up.

Don't Be Fooled—Cable TV Is Pay TV

Abridged from an ad by KOB-TV in *Albuquerque Journal*, July 9, 1972. Used by permission of KOB-TV.

To the Citizens of Albuquerque,

Thank you for your patience and confidence!

LVO Cable, parent corporation of General Communications and Entertainment, cable franchise holder for Albuquerque, regrets that you have recently been subjected to a barrage of irrational propaganda disseminated by local broadcasters.

Cable service is voluntary. Nonsubscribers will not lose their present service. Subscribers will pay five dollars per month, with no contract and the right to cancel on 24-hour notice.

Cable TV is no more "pay" TV than is commercial TV "free." "Free" TV is paid for by you every time you buy a box of cereal or bar of soap or any other product advertised on commercial TV.

The rules and regulations of FCC, controlling both commercial and cable TV, combined with regulatory powers of your local elected city officials, insure that special sports and entertainment events will not be siphoned off the network channels and that GenCoE will live up to its commitments to serve this community with expanded communications services.

Cable TV is a clean, privately owned, tax-paying industry, dedicated to improving the quality of life for the citizens of Albuquerque. We are an independent medium. We feel cable can contribute significantly to the moral, educational and multi-cultural welfare of the population.

Abridged from an ad by LVO Cable TV in *Albuquerque Journal*, July 15, 1972. Used by permission of LVO Cable, Inc.

oldest, of course, are speech and writing, and both of them are very difficult. It takes about ten years of a person's life—ten of his most effective learning years—to get command of these arts and of arithmetic. Hardly anyone ever again in his lifetime puts such effort into learning a skill. The effect of the difficulty is evident. No one knows by what steps speech entered the human repertoire, but the process most likely extended over hundreds of thousands of years. After the discovery of writing, it took about 4000 years for literacy to become a nearly universal thing. And all other communication techniques which require special skills are still handled by specialists or assistants: the 2000-year-old art of storing and retrieving information in archives is still done by specialists with college training.

The technique of reproducing text dates back 400 years to the invention of printing. It was for centuries handled by skilled craftsmen, and even in this day of the mimeograph only a few people in any office have yet learned to run off copies.

Similarly, the typewriter, though it requires only a modest amount of training to use it, is still, after 100 years, a tool that an assistant to a communicator uses.

The new communication tools that are universally used directly by the communicator himself are the telephone, the radio, and the television, none of which require any skill that can't be acquired in ten minutes.

It is interesting to note that the communications technologies which require professional assistants were the ones introduced in the 2000 years between the emergence of urban civilization and the later nineteenth century—the period of complex class societies

B.C. *by Johnny Hart*

MANKIND WILL NEVER MASTER THE ART OF COMMUNICATION!

in which a small elite functioned at a high cultural level with the help of lots of low-cost labor. In the twentieth century, labor has become so expensive and white-collar aspirations so widespread that we increasingly develop devices such as the electrostatic copier and the telephone that people can use employing only their own labor.

Introduction of a computer into the communications network raises a new need for specialized skills. But it is getting easier and easier to gain access to a computer. Before it realizes its full potential for use in information management, it must become nearly as easy to use a computer as it now is to query a human informant or to utilize the complex digital equipment that backs up the telephone dial. The computer can and must take over the really difficult archival skills needed if people are to make free use of the wide choice among sources offered by an individualized responsive information network.

Will It Change Our Lives?

On both technical and social grounds, then, it seems clear that individualized information and communications systems are coming. It remains to consider some of the social consequences of that revolution in communications.

Popular commentators sometimes exaggerate and sometimes understate the influence on society that communication media can have. Vance Packard, for example, would have us believe that "hidden persuaders" controlling the mass media are able to shape our desires and beliefs. And yet anyone who has ever run a campaign on behalf of a good cause must be aware how painfully slight are the results of massive efforts at persuasion. Where does the truth lie?

Social-science studies of the effect of communication demonstrate that significant changes in beliefs result only rarely from propaganda campaigns; few soldiers are ever converted against their side by psychological warfare. Yet by other criteria than conversion, propaganda can be very effective indeed. The effect of an election campaign, for example, is to focus public attention on one set of issues or another. A candidate may stress war or peace, medical care, employment, dams and post offices—and he will probably have little influence upon the public view about any of these issues. But if he can focus the debate on those particular issues where his is the popular view, he may well win.

The communications that most often change people's minds in the long run are not arguments, as such, but new information and new images which are not originally seen as partisan. The mere presentation of a great deal of additional material because of improved communication can have profound effects. In general, the most striking results of a new communications system arise out of the fact that the system exists at all rather than out of any particular things that are said over it. For example, one of the major effects of TV on children is to enlarge their vocabularies. No one on TV set out to expand vocabulary, but the medium was trying to attract a combined audience of children and adults, and the impact on the children's vocabularies followed. Marshall McLuhan, in his often brilliant though seldom coherent com-

ments on communication, has made much of this point; the medium itself is part of the message, and the message may be much more than what the communicator thinks he is saying.

ABSURD!   RIDICULOUS!   TOMMYROT!   HOGWASH!

Patterns of Swearing

Helen E. Ross

The conflict between what you want and the environment in which you live produces stress in your life.

Swearing is a subject which seems to have received very little attention from psychologists. It is seldom mentioned, except in the course of some other study, and only the psychoanalysts offer theories about its origin and purpose. Fenichel,[1] for example, regards obscene swearing as a substitute sex activity which gives the swearer a sense of power over the sex demon. This theory may help explain obscene swearing, but does not account for blasphemous swearing which often occurs in the same breath. Moreover, for many, especially among the industrial working classes, swearing is a habit no more meaningful than a difference in dialect.

Upbringing and temperament play a large part in determining the swearing habits of an individual, but I was especially interested in the way group morale can encourage or discourage swearing in its members.

Since swearing is often thought to be a sign of annoyance or stress, I kept records of swearing rates as an indication of group morale during three weeks of a university expedition to Arctic Norway. The group consisted of five men and three women between nineteen and twenty-four years of age, all of whom were zoologists, except myself, a psychologist.

The main purpose of the expedition was to study the diurnal rhythms of birds during continuous daylight. As the work entailed considerable interruption or loss of sleep, most members had good cause for becoming irritable and swearing.

I recorded the swearing rates for each member on different colored knitting counters which I kept in my pocket. Records were only kept for a few hours at the beginning and end of each day when most of the group were together, but these scores were sufficient to show general trends. Unfortunately, the group soon discovered I was keeping records, but after the initial reactions of anger or amusement had died down this seemed to have no effect on the scores (apart from one day when the two heaviest swearers engaged in a deliberate competition).

Each individual had his own vocabulary and habitual level of swearing, and tended to keep to the same rank order in the group however much the total swearing-level rose or fell.

The words used were blasphemous rather than obscene, as is to be expected among the middle classes. Unlike the working classes, however, their use of obscene words was deliberate rather than habitual, and they took a delight in using them in their correct biological sense. The heavier swearers used the more violent language. No new expressions were coined apart from the word "Click!" which arose in connection with my knitting counters. Hence such phrases as "That clicking psychologist!"

The relationship between swearing and stress was slightly

ATLAS, World Press Review, reprinted from *Discovery*, London.

unexpected. The amount of swearing increased noticeably when people were relaxed and happy and, though it also increased under slight stress, it decreased when they were really annoyed or tried. In fact there seemed to be two types of swearing: "social" swearing and "annoyance" swearing. Social swearing was intended to be friendly and a sign of being "one of the gang"; it depended upon an audience for its effect, while annoyance swearing was a reaction to stress regardless of the audience. Social swearing was by far the commoner.

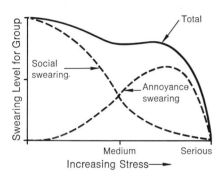

The total amount of swearing varied as shown on the chart given above. Under conditions of very low stress it was almost entirely social, but with increasing stress it diminished and annoyance swearing increased. The drop-off of the one was more rapid than the rise of the other, resulting in a dip in the total under conditions of medium stress. Under higher stress, social swearing almost entirely disappeared and annoyance swearing increased until it too reached a peak and began to drop. Under conditions of serious stress, there was silence.

Social swearing was easily inhibited by the lack of an appreciative audience or the presence of non-swearers. The men who had

Police-State Terror at State University

The president insists that he is not stupid. He is not only immoral, but also criminally insane.

A man that can manipulate the law to his satisfaction and bring on the police-state terror that existed at the university union this morning is a dangerous monster. How thoroughly he and his administration have become creatures of the oppressive forces in this state is now completely exposed.

State university has again sold out the principles of peaceful assembly and protest.

Why? Because state university is an arm of the corporations. It does not exist for the students. State university, as a part of the military-industrial complex, is under orders to produce docile engineers, technicians, and teachers who will follow the commands of the Establishment.

Students are being guided into the "correct" thought patterns and into the "correct jobs" by their overseer, the president. If they do not perform correctly, they are flunked and drafted. If they object to their circumstances, they are terrorized by the police-state tactics of the early morning arrest.

These things we have seen in action. We know them to be true. We are inmates of an asylum at which the lunatics are the guards.

The president must be destroyed.

From a student bulletin handed out during a campus crisis.

Editorial

Well, last week some of the tiny minds on the Penn State campus decided to defy a restraining order and have a demonstration. So they gathered their playthings together and held a demonstration. But they tried to smash a bus and they only hurt about nine state policemen when they threw their little playthings. (Point of law: when someone carries a stone or bottle to one of these little play sessions with intent to throw it, why isn't that object then classed as a weapon and punishable as such?)

It's one heck of a good thing I'm not in charge of some of the troops when these idiots are around doing their thing, because if I were there would be some dead ones! And what a blessing that would be. Just think of the favor to the taxpayer. He wouldn't have to pay for that person's education. (They call it education—not me!) He wouldn't have to pay to remove him from the campus any more. He wouldn't have to pay for their unwanted children any more. He wouldn't have to pay for his court costs.

Now look, you stupid educators. If these kids wanted to get an education, they would go there and get an education. As it is now they are there only. They should be smart enough to know that a public place must have rules to live by. If you don't like those rules, get out! That's the freedom within our nation—if you don't like it, get out.

THE PROSECUTION RESTS.

CREDO
for
Free and Responsible Communication
in a Democratic Society

Recognizing the essential place of free and responsible communication in a democratic society, and recognizing the distinction between the freedoms our legal system should respect and the responsibilities our educational system should cultivate, we members of the Speech Communication Association endorse the following statement of principles:

We Believe that freedom of speech and assembly must hold a central position among American constitutional principles, and we express our determined support for the right of peaceful expression by any communicative means available to man.

We Support the proposition that a free society can absorb with equanimity speech which exceeds the boundaries of generally accepted beliefs and mores; that much good and little harm can ensue if we err on the side of freedom, whereas much harm and little good may follow if we err on the side of suppression.

We Criticize as misguided those who believe that the justice of their cause confers license to interfere physically and coercively with the speech of others, and we condemn intimidation, whether by powerful majorities or strident minorities, which attempts to restrict free expression.

We Accept the responsibility of cultivating by precept and example, in our classrooms and in our communities, enlightened uses of communication; of developing in our students a respect for precision and accuracy in communication, and for reasoning based upon evidence and a judicious discrimination among values.

We Encourage our students to accept the role of well-informed and articulate citizens, to defend the communication rights of those with whom they may disagree, and to expose abuses of the communication process.

We Dedicate ourselves fully to these principles, confident in the belief that reason will ultimately prevail in a free marketplace of ideas.

been in camp for a week without the women said they felt it necessary to watch their tongues once the women arrived. When half the group, including the only three non-swearers, left on a separate expedition, the swearing rate immediately doubled and remained very high. This may have been due to a deliberate attempt to compensate for lost numbers by an increase in solidarity. Similarly, when a medium swearer (female) spent two days alone with a heavy swearer (male), all swearing rates of both increased, but when she spent a fortnight with a medium swearer (male), all swearing soon stopped, probably because the latter two needed the facilitative effect of a heavy swearer or a larger audience. Other subjects might not be so easily influenced by the moods of their companions, but unless they are affected to some degree their swearing cannot be classed as "social" and must be merely a verbal habit.

The fact that the usual reaction to serious stress is silence suggests that swearing is a sign that a disagreeable situation is bearable; indeed, the verbal expression of discomfort may even help to reduce stress. There is some experimental evidence which seems to lend support to the hypothesis that, in a given situation, subjects who swear or complain are likely to be under less stress than those who keep silent. For example, Reiser *et al.*,[2] when examining the effects of different laboratory procedures on the physiological reactions to stress of enlisted soldiers, found that those subjects who felt free to "gripe" about army life with their interviewer were much less likely to show a rise in blood pressure than those who did not complain. King and Henry[3] have shown that subjects who direct their anger against the

Beetle Bailey by Mort Walker

© King Features Syndicate, Inc.

experimenter when under stress show a less tense physiological reaction than those who control their anger (a norepinephrine cardiovascular pattern as opposed to epinephrine). A similar difference was found by MacKinnon[4] among subjects taking a written test where it was possible to cheat; those who swore and blamed the questions were liable to cheat without compunction whereas those who kept silent or blamed their own stupidity felt guilty at the very idea of cheating and were more anxious and tense during the test.

The scientific study of swearing is complicated by the difficulty of deciding what is to count as swearing. The same words may be habitual for one individual and very rare for another. In future studies it would probably be best to discount habitually heavy swearers and concentrate on medium swearers. More light might be thrown on social swearing by studying the same individual in similar experimental situations but among different sizes and types of groups. More direct experiments could also be made on the effects of swearing on reducing tension, and on the differences in upbringing and personality which encourage such swearing; using Eysenck's[5] extraversion-introversion scale I should expect heavy swearing to correlate with extraversion and light swearing with introversion.

The potential for communication shock in an environment of stress and change necessitates responsible understanding of others.

1. Fenichel, O., "The Psychoanalytic Theory of Neurosis," p. 350, Routledge & Kegan Paul Ltd.

2. Reiser, M. F., et al., 1955, "Effects of Variation in Laboratory Procedure and Experimenter on Cardiac Data in Subjects," *Psychosomatic Medicine*, vol. 17, pp. 185–99.

3. King, S. H., and Henry, A. F., 1955, "Aggression and Cardiovascular Reactions Related to Parental Control Over Behaviour," *J. Abnorm. Soc. Psychol.*, vol. 50, pp. 206–10.

4. MacKinnon, D. W., 1937, "Violation of Prohibition," in H. A. Murray's "Exploration in Personality" (pp. 491–501), New York, O.U.P.

5. Eysenck, H. J., 1947, "Dimensions of Personality," Kegan Paul.

"Grin and Bear It" by George Lichty
Courtesy of Publishers-Hall Syndicate

"Flunking in grammar again! . . How are you going to express a grievance or make a wage demand if you lack communication skills?"

Prods

1. What effect do social trends such as popular interest in Eastern religions have on our lives?
2. In what ways have electronic media changed our lives in the last ten years?
3. List several of your desires that are thwarted by your environment.
4. How does communication shock develop? How can we maintain free and responsible communication in an environment of constant change and massive individual stress?

Meaningful dialogue requires a depth of understanding of others and maximum involvement.

Intimate communication requires that the partners make explicit what they expect of each other.

You can improve your communication skills by practicing several techniques and watching out for certain pitfalls.

Relationship

1

Dyadic

From Monologue to Dialogue

Charles T. Brown and Paul W. Keller

If you and I were to change places, I could talk like you . . .   The Book of Job

A girl amused the other students in one of our classes by telling about meeting a "guy" at a folk festival who was the best conversationalist she had ever known. It turned out that she couldn't remember anything in particular that he had said or that in fact he had even talked very much. She had been the one who talked and she really didn't remember what she had talked about. But she yearned to meet this person again and feared that she would not as it was one of those events where people came from long distances. "I have never been as free and as exhilarated in my talk with anyone. And you are wrong, I only had one drink all night. I ranged free and easy. I was so fluent and said things that were meaningful. My life seemed just right that night. There was no show-off—and that's not me. I knew he understood and that we understood much together. There was a strange intimacy—and yet there was no intimacy at all. This is one of the most beautiful and most precious memories of my life."

It turns out that occasionally complete strangers quickly develop openness and intense relationships, largely perhaps because they know that they will not meet again and thus entanglements and commitments are not endangered. This may be what happened here. But it is well that the girl remembers the incident cited for she will know that moment when she is met, confirmed, and listened to in depth only a few times, even if she lives to be an ancient lady. Many many times she will talk to impress and her auditor will indulge her, especially if he is male. (She is an extremely attractive female.) Many times she will argue and be caustic. (She is an aggressive female too.) How much of her verbal demand is the consequence of hungering for a person who understands her, one can only speculate. How many people never know what it is to be listened to at all and spend their lives talking to themselves in the presence of other people?

Meaningful dialogue requires a depth of understanding of others and maximum involvement.

The levels of interpersonal communication exist on a continuum between self-talk, at the one end, and a depth of understanding of others—real dialogue—at the other. . . .

Charles T. Brown and Paul W. Keller, MONOLOGUE TO DIALOGUE: An Exploration of Interpersonal Communication, © 1973. Reprinted by permission of Prentice-Hall, Inc., Englewood Cliffs, New Jersey.

feiffer by Jules Feiffer

Monologue

Communication marked by indifference for the other person results in a speech in which the intended receiver is the self. The other person serves almost exclusively as a stimulant. Just as an amputated leg or arm can be experienced as a phantom limb, so another person can be experienced as a part of one's own communication system—a kind of phantom.[1] And this is what happens in monologue, a kind of communication we learn early in life.

The Russian psychologist A. R. Luria found that children talk six times as much in the presence of others as when alone. Apparently, internal speech is excited by the presence of another child. Internal speech, or *verbal thought*, if you like, develops as the child internalizes the partner who is not present, a feat which depends upon, as a first stage, imagining he is talking to another person— best done when he has somebody present. In this way a child turns himself into the recipient of his own message. Recently we asked a four-year-old girl to repeat a comment that was unclear. She looked startled for a moment and then replied, "Oh, I was talking to myself."

But children are not the only ones who do this. Professors, the better ones, who are essentially our more mature children, behave similarly quite often in their lectures. Their faces may go vacant, eyes lose focus, perhaps the head will tilt back while they explore some thought just at the edge of awareness. All creative people have this self-orientation. While monologue, by definition, means a minimum of involvement with the other, the self-listening is at a maximum and it is extremely valuable as above suggested.

Narcissistic Monologue

However, the listening of monologue may be for the purpose of self-adoration, rather than for the exploration of one's thoughts. When this happens a self-reflective smile (the dead giveaway) dominates the speech, especially at the end of sentences. The articulation of such speech, almost always unduly precise, expresses language to match, likely ornate. This behavior is all highly infuriating to others, often arousing caustic response.

However, we all do this "face work," and when it is half hidden it is socially acceptable.[2] Indeed one's feelings about himself, his position with his conversants, and his status at large, are always involved in his communication. One may lapse into silence, over-respond, joke, mimic, argue, ignore, belittle, bitch, praise, blame, or laugh in order to draw attention to himself. It is inevitable, for we are all self-conscious, one of the chief accomplishments of language. The laws of human interaction do not rule out "face work"; they can and do order it into the background.

Yet some people insist upon talking openly for their own amusement and amazement, and it is this that is infuriating. If one does this in most of his interaction he gradually evolves into a socialized isolate, that is, he spends much of his time with people, actually alone. Any honest emotional exchange initiated by another causes him to grow silent or flippant, in some way to evade the relationship suggested by conversation.

Narcissistic monologue is largely self-destructive, but exploratory monologue has its important value for both the individual and society, as noted above. . . .

Dialogue

In a day when we lean so heavily on attack and denunciation in social interaction, let us make clear at the onset of an examination of dialogue that dialogue is not some ideal that belongs to a nonexistent peaceful world. Even the gentle Martin Buber said that he often struggled with his partner in order to alter his view.[3] Dialogue goes directly and honestly to the difference between "me and thee," and this requires an immense toughness of self— for it does combat without going on the defensive. And so there is considerable difference between the struggle of dialogue and that of confrontation. In confrontation the purpose is the humiliation of the other person. When, however, conflict develops between people in dialogue the other person is confirmed. He is looked upon as responsible and competent though he may not be persuaded.[4] Even downright rejection of a view can still stay within the framework of dialogue. To reject ideas or behavior in another while confirming him as a person is, of course, difficult, requiring a deep faith in self. And yet this is the true test of one's ability to carry on dialogue. It is one thing to feel in such a way as to say, "I don't like you" and quite another thing to say, "I am getting angry with you." The former judges you and excludes you and initiates the termination of dialogue—the work of anxiety. To say, "I am getting angry," however, makes an authentic statement about one's feelings, recognizes the status of the relationship, and musters the courage to continue in dialogue. It does not cover up as in the distortion "I like you" (when actually I don't), nor does it polarize the feelings of the two conversants, as is likely, when

one openly attacks the other. The upshot is this, that the deepest level of human interaction has a profound faith in the intentions, and the ideal self-concept of the other person—attained when things and events are seen as he sees them.

Why is this empathy difficult to achieve in the face of conflict?

Above all else the need of every person is to be confirmed as he is. How else can we hope to be more? Without a future what is hope? And what is life without hope? But no person is capable of doing his own confirming. Indeed his confirmation rests in his impact upon others; again, a human self is a social satellite, not an independent planet. In our search for confirmation, however, we deceive ourselves if we dare not differ with others, for we are different. Only as we are confirmed in our uniqueness are we confirmed at all. Thus our greatest assurance depends upon support for what we are when we dissent from the other's opinion. But as Buber points out this is probably the Achilles' heel of the human race.[5] Almost all humans are stingy with support except when they are agreed with—when they themselves are confirmed. So the great moments in dialogue are not those nice exchanges between people when they agree with each other. We are talking about the nature of talk where the listening senses the deep differences with the other and yet trusts the other implicitly. Let it be clear we are not saying that people have to be in conflict with each other in order to have dialogue. Good exchange can take place when there is no conflict to threaten the listening. What we are saying is this: (1) we really have no test of the ability to carry on dialogue if the talk has no threat in it, and (2) that actually one does not

know the deepest level of dialogue except when he is comfortably related to a person from whom he differs greatly.

The first point should be obvious. The test of anything is its ability to endure under stress. The second point is not so obvious. Let us approach it with a comment on the command of the ages, "To love thine enemy." This command is not basically a moral injunction but an invitation to know the deepest experiences in relationship—drawing heavily on one's courage. The ultimate in *self-confirmation*, thus, takes place when one trusts his enemy —an "untrustworthy" person. The Western movie has much of its appeal in the fact that it melodramatically explores this relationship when it pictures the hero talking calmly to an enraged man who has him covered with a cocked pistol. We, the audience, are entranced because we know the hero is saying to himself, "Circumstances call for me to calm this man. If I panic he will fire. If I put my trust in his stability and this I can do so long as I do not threaten him I have a good chance of surviving this encounter. I could be wrong. He may fire without provocation. That's the chance I take. Everything considered I choose to take the chance." If one can command himself to do this he learns several remarkable things at once:

1. That he has the capacity to face death calmly—and death is a reality each person must one day experience.

2. That, as a consequence he can probably face any experience calmly.

3. That he has attained a maximum command of himself.

4. That he has also attained the maximum in human free-

dom—for freedom is that internal state which permits choice among the choices made available by conditions.

5. That he has achieved the ultimate in self-confidence for he has achieved the minimum in self-hate, therefore the minimum in self-doubt.

In the end there is not hate except hate of the self; no anger, except anger with the self. All *our responses* toward other people are proofs of our potentials which others have but stimulated. All feelings are self-reflexive. Whether one panics or remains calm in the face of danger, the stimuli are the same. It is the self that is different.

Thus most talk and listening between nations in conflict—to illustrate the view—is not dialogue because the parties do not have the courage to experience dialogue. By definition the defensive posture is the acceptance of self-doubt. The political leader who insists "we shall bargain only from a position of strength" reflects his fears, not his strength. The perception of the self as strong when one is weak is a deception that comes because one blames the other for his feelings. He conceives of the enemy as wholly distrustful, thus freeing himself from responsibility for his own feelings. If he really wants to talk openly and defenselessly with his enemy he must develop sufficient trust in himself to stir responsible behavior in the other —which means he faces possible treachery, having dropped his guard. Conversely, by maintaining his guard, he excites the defensiveness of his enemy and thus insures the failure of dialogue—unless the enemy is actually the stronger person of the two, and creates the conditions for dialogue.

Perhaps the hardest of all lessons to learn is that defensive listening (which, as we all know, establishes pseudo dialogue) is irresponsible behavior. Defensive behavior insists that the responsibility for one's feelings is in the other person. Let it be clear. The lowering of our defense, especially once mutual defense has developed, may be a miscalculation. But then the escalating of our defenses may be, too. There is no guaranteed safe path for people in conflict. The question is, shall we depend upon our capacity to survive in dialogue or in defense? Defense and dialogue are mutually exclusive behaviors, and there is danger in either course because no person has complete control over the other person.

In dialogue you risk more than in monologue.

We have cast this discussion, by our example, in the frame of the international conflict in order to highlight the mutually exclusive differences between dialogue and defense. But we should not limit ourselves to that frame of reference. The basic character trait of the effective psychotherapist, for instance, is his ability to trust his own health while listening to his sick patient. And this he can do only if he believes the relationship will stir the potential health of his patient. Two swim as one only as each gives up one swimming arm to embrace the other. Yes, the therapist confirms the sick man and thus initiates the healing, but this is not achieved without risk. And so the great test of the professional listener is his capacity to maintain the rela-

tionship when his partner is sinking.

In similar fashion, the great test of a marriage is the ability of partners to listen to each other when in conflict. Can the one embrace the other when differences arise? Each is tested. "Do I have enough tolerance for myself to embrace a person whose very being I learn stimulates my awareness of those qualities I dislike in myself?"

The capacity of a person to carry on a dialogue with a politician, a policeman, a teacher, a teenager, a foreigner, a whore, a homosexual, a thief, a murderer, or an insane man is the capacity to tolerate the feelings about the self aroused when we identify with that other person—to understand life from his point of view. After all, life can be lived in his way. It is the fear aroused by contemplating that prospect that cuts off the dialogue.

Abraham Maslow asserts that safety holds priority over growth, which means that in the presence of threat defense is inevitable. One can hardly argue with him in the face of the evidence. But this is the reason that few humans experience much dialogue in the course of a lifetime.

Dialogue, then, above all else, is based (a) on faith in the self (b) entrusted to the other person in the exchange of communication. It does not necessitate full acceptance of the other person as he is. It does necessitate sufficient confirmation of the other as he is to entrust, to make oneself vulnerable to him.

Second, it means the one has a deep concern for the other person.[6] If dialogue exists between two people, each maintains an I-thou relationship with the other, that is, each holds the other as an inviolate entity, a person to be concerned about. Neither will use

the other for his own personal gain. The relationship is prized above any control or advantage. It is the break in such a relationship, when romantic, that is the source of all sad love songs, expressing the sickening emptiness when a deep faith in a relationship with another has withered. The relationship of dialogue is one where each assumes responsibility for the relationship, and indeed, for the other.

Third, in dialogue *we walk at the edge* of our knowledge and our security, for to trust an unstable relationship is to let a phrase flow freely, to invent, to question, to challenge, to explore—to test an idea in the saying.

Fourth, in dialogue one reveals himself as he is, and as he is affected by the other. If he does this he is open; to be open is to listen.

The purpose of our dialogue is to try our values in social practice, to nurture our value scheme, to put our ideals to the test, to translate between language level six (where we order our values) and language level one (where we feel the experience of living them.) In dialogue we make our life complete, give ourselves our sense of meaning. A common consequence of real dialogue is the response, "I didn't know you were like this. I never really knew how your felt." Then perhaps to the self, "He is changing, and so am I." Hasidic wisdom adds this:

Faith should not rest in the heart; it should also be expressed by word of mouth. The utterance of faith strengthens a man's faith.[7]

Dialogue strengthens faith and faith is the source of dialogue.

The Language of Dialogue

In this description of dialogue we have used scattered examples of

NOBODY
NEEDS
ME.

I
NEED
YOU.

Walk A Mile in My Shoes

Joe South

If I could be you and you could be me
  for just one hour,
If we could find a way to get inside each
  other's mind,
If you could see me through your eyes
  instead of your ego,
I believe you'd be surprised to see that
  you'd been blind.

Now your whole world you see around you
  is just a reflection,
And the law of karma says you reap
  just what you sow.
So unless you've lived a life of total per-
fection,
You'd better be careful of every stone that
  you throw.

And yet we spend the day throwing stones
  at one another,
Cause I don't think or wear my hair the
  same way you do.
Well I may be common people, but I'm
  your brother,
And when you strike out and try to hurt
  me, it's a hurtin' you.

There are people on reservations and out
  in the ghettos;
And, brother, there but for the grace of
  God, go you and I.
If I only had the wings of a little angel,
Don't you know I'd fly to the top of the
  mountain.
And then I'd cry.

Walk a mile in my shoes, walk a mile
  in my shoes.
And before you abuse, criticize and accuse,
Walk a mile in my shoes.

the language of dialogue. To fix the concepts and to initiate the attitudes of dialogue it may be helpful to speak further of the role and quality of the language. In so doing we should be careful to recognize that there are no gimmicks that work; the language that works is that guided by appropriate intent.

Yet the language that works is a guide to us in those moments when dialogue is threatened. We had a call from a man this morning whose first response to a proposed meeting was "Well, it is a little premature. You and I have not yet discussed———." In our urge to maintain the best of relations we responded. "Perhaps I have forgotten something that should be taken care of first. What do you think we ought to do before the meeting?" This response was guided by the need to preserve the dignity of our conversant. Thus the language was, we hope, appropriate. We have noted that the language of people who are able to talk to many people at deep levels is replete with phrases such as: "I may be wrong, but here is the way I see it . . . It could be . . . What would you think . . . I think what I am trying to say . . . Isn't there something missing here . . . What you say might just be so . . . I don't think I know if . . . " The statement is tentative, open to alteration. For some people these phrases seem unsure and in direct opposition to the description of the courage of dialogue. But the peculiar thing about the language of confidence is that on the surface it sounds weak. It is tentative in order to insure accommodation for the other person. Conversely, language that says "This is the way it is. There are no ands, ifs or buts . . ." on the surface sounds like it comes from the mouth of a strong man. Such

sure language allows if possible only one interpretation. But, again, it is the flexible man, seeing the possibility for several or many interpretations, who is strong, strong enough to accommodate, perhaps, his less flexible conversant.

Yet we hasten to add, strength is not wishy-washy accommodation to anything. It is not fearful confusion. And this should be added: the fearful conformist may use the language phrases of the strong man as a camouflage. "I really don't know what to think" may mean the speaker cannot tolerate the responsibility for taking a position—in which the nonverbal cues give us our best clues—but it is also the language of the man who truly has an open mind willing to listen and to find a position necessary to preserve a healthy relationship. When we are too sure of our words we are not listening to them or the words of others. We are listening to the fears which are demanding firm and legal definitions. Legal language is abstract, logical, and technically correct. But the language of dialogue is spontaneous, free, noncritical, tentative, reflective, searching—based on faith and tolerance. When people meet in dialogue, their language is not an analysis of the rights and privileges of each other, but a mutual participation of the lives involved.

1. Ludwig von Bertlanffy, "The Mind-Body Problem: A New View," in Floyd W. Matson and Ashley Montagu, eds., *The Human Dialogue* (New York: The Free Press, 1967), p. 233.

2. Erving Goffman, Interaction Ritual (New York: Doubleday & Company, Inc., 1967), pp. 5–45.

3. Martin Buber, *The Knowledge of Man* (New York: Harper & Row, 1965), p. 179.

4. Sidney M. Jourard, *Disclosing Man to Himself* (Princeton, N.J.: D. Van Nostrand Company, Inc., 1968), p. 123.

5. Martin Buber, "Distance and Relation," *Psychiatry*, 20 (1957), 97–104.

6. Milton Mayeroff, *On Caring* (New York: Harper & Row, Publishers, 1971).

7. Louis I. Newman, *Hasidic Anthology* (New York: Schocken Books, 1963), p. 104.

"Talk to me. I'm your mother."

Empathy Graphics, New York City

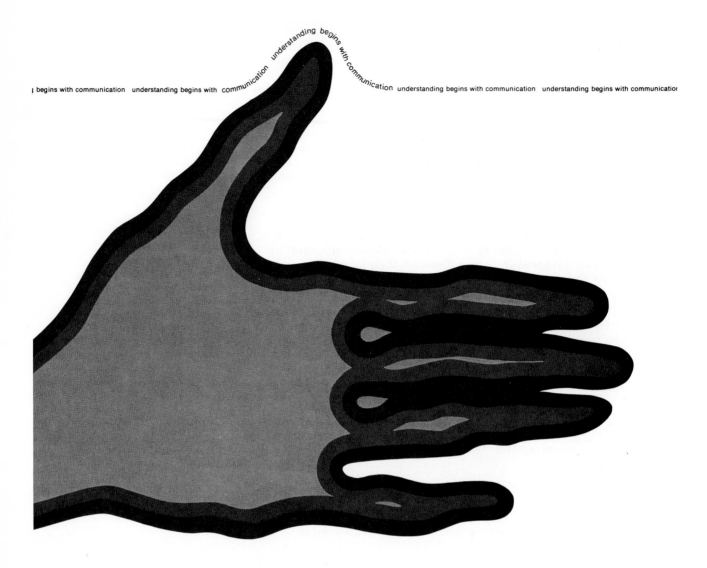

The old paper-between-the-hands-communication game

Number of players: It takes two.
Materials: Yourself, a stranger, hand cut-out.
How to play: Place your right hand on picture of hand. Have opposite
player place (his-her) right hand on opposite side. When both players
are in position, pull the paper out sharply with your left hand. Both
players then quickly close hands.
The *game* is over (or does it just begin?) when both players find they are
in the position to begin a friendship.
Who wins: Both players.

Courtesy of "Genesis," *Mountain Bell Magazine* (fall 1970).

The Interview

William D. Brooks

The interview is a form of dyadic communication involving two parties, at least one of whom has a preconceived and serious purpose, and both of whom speak and listen from time to time.[1] This definition indicates clearly that the interview is a *bipolar communication situation*. Although it is possible to have more than two persons in an interview, i.e., the group interview, team interview, or board interview, yet even these interviews are essentially bipolar: there are *two* parties. Thus, the interview is different from a small, problem-solving group in which three, four, five, or some limited number of persons present several points of view and then cooperate to find a satisfactory solution. The interview is also unlike debate, even though debate is dyadic and bipolar, in that no third party renders a decision or acts as an arbiter in the interview, as is the case in debate.

A second element in the definition of the interview is that at least one person, and perhaps both, has a *preconceived and serious purpose*. Two persons getting together and talking with neither having thought in advance about the purpose or objective to be accomplished does not constitute an interview. It might be social conversation, but it is not an interview. The word *serious* helps to differentiate the interview from social conversation for enjoyment.

The third element in the definition is: *both of whom speak and listen from time to time*. This places the interview clearly within the category of interpersonal communication. This element also emphasizes the constant two-way interaction that is a characteristic of any successful interview. The situation in which one person does almost all the talking is not an interview. It may be a private lecture, or an interrogation, but it fails to become an interview. When a "high-pressure" salesman delivers a memorized fifteen-minute presentation to a trapped customer, he is not engaged in a sales interview, but in a public speech since, like public speaking, it is a one-way form of communication with one initiator of messages. Goyer, et al. have stated: "Indeed, it is probably safe to suggest that if an expository interviewer finds himself talking uninterruptedly for as long as *two minutes*, he very likely is failing to 'get through' to his interviewee."[2] Interviewing demands that each party be a skillful participator in both sending and receiving messages. Not only do both participants send and receive messages, but they are also constantly engaged in moment-to-moment adaptations — in checking on the meanings of messages through soliciting and sending feedback. The effective participant in interviewing cannot depend absolutely on an advance outline or memorized

The interview is a form of dialogue in which at least one party has a preconceived and serious purpose and both parties speak and listen.

Abridged from SPEECH COMMUNICATION by William D. Brooks. © 1971, Wm. C. Brown Publishers. Used by permission.

speech. Unlike the debate situation, the interviewer or interviewee cannot plan his response while his colleague talks. Neither can the participant in an interview stop the communication process while he interprets what the other person has said and its meaning. Nor can he depend on words alone. He must be sensitive to nonverbal communication, to feedback, to feelings and attitudes, to the interpersonal relationships that exist and are developing, and to his own accuracy and efficiency in *intrapersonal* communication. The interview is one of the most demanding and sophisticated forms of communication, as well as one of the most potentially productive forms of communication, and as such, it calls into practice all those elements of intrapersonal and interpersonal communication discussed in this text.

Interview Purposes

Interviews are of several types and take place in many different contexts with a variety of purposes. Nevertheless, it is possible to classify interviews in terms of the *dominant* purpose the interviewer (the person who has the chief responsibility for achieving a successful outcome) has in mind. Interviews have been classified into ten types: (1) information-getting, (2) information-giving, (3) advocating, (4) problem-solving, (5) counseling, (6) application for employment or job, (7) receiving complaints, (8) reprimanding or correcting, (9) appraising, and (10) stress interviewing.[3]

In the information-getting interview, the objective is usually to obtain beliefs, attitudes, feelings, or other data from the interviewee. Public opinion poll and research surveys are typical well-known examples, but in fact, most people participate frequently in essentially the same kind of communication situation.

The purpose of the information-giving interview is to explain or instruct. Giving work instructions to a new employee or explaining the procedures and policies of the organization to a new member are examples of information-giving interviews.

Sometimes, a person wishes to modify the beliefs or attitudes of another person and attempts to do so through the persuasive interview. The sales interview is a typical example of the interviewer (the persuader or salesman) attempting to sway the interviewee (the respondent or customer) towards adopting his point of view. Another example of the advocating interview is the attempt of a subordinate to persuade his chairman, foreman, or boss to accept a proposal; or when you go to the bank to secure a loan you are a persuader engaged in a persuasive interview. Throughout life each of us engages in interviews in which we try to persuade another person to agree with us.

The problem-solving interview involves both information and persuasion just as does the problem-solving small group. In fact, the problem-solving interview could be classified as a two-person discussion or problem-solving group.

The counseling interview may be directly persuasive as one person tries to get the other to change his behavior in a prescribed manner, or it may be relatively non-persuasive (i.e., non-directive) in that its objective is to provide a situation in which the client can gain insight into his own problems. Counseling interviews focus on the *personal* problems of the person being advised. This type of interview requires a high degree of skill and psychological sophistication on the part of the counselor.

The employment interview, an interview in which virtually every member of society participates sooner or later, is a special type of interview that utilizes information-getting, information-giving, and persuasion as each party tries to get information from the other party and, perhaps, tries to persuade the other party.

Receiving complaints and reprimanding are specialized interviews which require the combination of several skills—persuading, problem-solving, counseling, information-giving, and information-getting. The purpose of the receiver of complaints is to do as much as possible to satisfy grievances. The purpose of the reprimand interview is to change the behavior of the interviewee favorably by helping him acquire new insight and motivation.

The appraising interview aims to inform the interviewee as to how well he is doing at his job and to give guidelines relative to his future performance. This interview of appraisal is related, in part, to the counseling interview.

Stress interviewing is often used as a testing procedure in which an opportunity is provided to observe how the interviewee reacts or behaves under pressure.

Participants in the Interview

The participants in interviews generally are most commonly referred to as *interviewer* and *interviewee*, although these terms are not the most appropriate for some interview situations. Terms such as counselor/counselee or persuader/persuadee are, for example, better terms for the

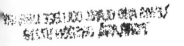

counseling situation and the persuasive interview. However, regardless of the term used—counselor, persuader, or interviewer—it refers to the party that carries the chief responsibility for achieving a successful outcome of the interview. It should be recognized, of course, that in many interviews both parties accept a responsibility for the successful outcome of the interview. This is especially true of the employment interview in which the employer wishes to "sell" his company and the applicant attempts to "sell" his qualifications.

The interviewee in most interview situations has the power of decision. In the information-getting interview the respondent (interviewee) decides whether to provide the information or not; in the reprimand and appraisal interviews the interviewee decides whether he will accept the correction or evaluation; and in the persuasive interview the respondent has the power of accepting or rejecting the persuasive attempt. In the employment interview, however, both parties share the decision-making power.

There are role-relationships in every interview as there are in other communication situations. Normally, it is the responsibility of the interviewer to take the initiative in the interview and to clarify role-relationships if such clarification is needed. It is not unusual in the employment interview for roles to change as the interview develops: e.g., at one time the applicant is the respondent and at another time the employer is the respondent. Since the functions of each interview participant vary widely among types of interviews as well as from specific interview to specific interview, it is unwise to think in terms of rigid, universal duties.

The heart of the interviewing process is the quality of the questioning.

The Question-Answer Process

There are many ways of classifying the various types of questions. Regardless of the classification system used, it appears to be a useful first step in developing skill in the question-answer process to be able to identify types of questions and their uses as well as types of answers. Our system calls for classifying interview questions into five basic types: open, closed, mirroring, probing, and leading.

Open Questions

Open questions call for a response of more than a few words. One type of open question, the open-ended question, is extremely vague in that it may do nothing more than specify a topic and ask the respondent to talk. An example is "What do you think about life?" or "Tell me a little about yourself."

A second kind of open question is more direct in that it identifies a more restricted topic area and asks for a reply on that restricted topic. In some classification systems this question is classified separately from open questions and is called the direct question. An example is "What did you do on your weekends last winter?"

Closed Questions

A second category of questions is the closed question. The closed question calls for a specific response of a few words. One type of closed question is the yes-no, or bipolar question. It calls for a "yes" or a "no" answer—or, perhaps, an "I don't know" reply. "Did you attend the last home basketball game last winter?" is a closed question. Similarly, "What two courses did you like most, and what two courses did you like least in high school?" is a closed question, though not a yes-no question.

One important principle related to the use of open or closed questions is that these types of questions tend to influence the length of the interviewee's responses. Open questions encourage the respondent to talk more, while closed questions discourage participation by the respondent.[4] Since one of the problems in most interviews is getting the interviewee to become freely involved and to participate in the interview, it is unwise for the interviewer to plan and use only closed questions. Neither should an interviewer in the informative, persuasive, or employment interview rely solely on open questions. Doing so, he may discover that, even though the interviewee does talk a lot he gives up very little specific information about himself. Further, the exclusive use of open questions often results in covering fewer topics than might have been possible with more direction and specificity. It is desirable to learn to use both types of questions. Generally speaking, open questions are more likely to be used in the early part of the interview or at the introduction of each new topic area, while closed questions are used as follow-ups for the responses to open questions.

Mirror Questions

Mirror questions are nondirective

techniques. The reason for using a mirror question is to encourage the interviewee to expand on a response that the interviewer believes was incomplete. Mirror questions are often restatements of what the interviewee has just said. If the interviewee has said: "I don't approve of legalizing abortion," a mirror question might be: "You say that abortion should not be legalized?" Closely related to the mirror question is the probe.

Probing Questions

Some questions are asked in order to probe more deeply into the reasons for an attitude or belief, or to elicit more specific information. Not all probes are questions of *why* or *how*, although those are common probing questions. There are a variety of other vocalizations that act effectively as probes and encouragements. Brief sounds or phrases such as "Uh-huh," "I see," "That's interesting," "Oh?" "Good," "I understand," and "Go on" have the effect of requesting further comment from the respondent. Probes and encouragements are introduced at any time—during pauses or while the interviewee is speaking. They indicate careful attention and interest, and they have the function of encouraging the respondent to "tell more" without specifying in a closed way the further response. It is important that an interviewer avoid the habit of relying on one reinforcing or probing word.

Equally as important as direct probing questions and sounds or phrases of encouragement is the use of silence. The inexperienced interviewer is often afraid of pauses and silences. He tends to fill every silence, and so doing, rushes through the interview.

Sometimes, if the respondent is slow in answering a question, the inexperienced interviewer may rush in to rephrase the question or to ask a new question. With experience, interviewers can learn when to use silence as a means of communication—as a probe, for example. Silences, if they are effective as probes, must be terminated by the respondent. Research findings indicate that silences of three to six seconds are most effective in getting the respondent to provide more information.[5] If the respondent does not terminate the silence within that time, the chances of his remaining silent increase. This means not only that the interviewer will have to speak, but that the use of silence will have been ineffective and that it will have had a damaging effect upon the interview situation. Hence, when one uses silence as a probe, he should be prepared to terminate the silence within six seconds or at such time as it seems destined to fail as a probing technique.

Leading Questions

Leading questions strongly imply or encourage a specific answer. They "lead" the respondent to an answer the interviewer expects. The leading question can be quite *detrimental* to the interview when used for the wrong reasons. If the interviewer wants straightforward, valid, and reliable information from the respondent, he will want to carefully avoid using leading questions. Cannell and Kahn state: "Questions should be phrased so that they contain no suggestion as to the most appropriate response,"[6] and Bingham, Moore, and Gustad state: "Avoid implying the answer to your own question."[7] If, however, the interviewer wishes to *test* the respond-

ent, to see if he *really* understands, or is *genuinely* committed, then the leading question may be quite useful. For example, when the speech therapist asks the mother of a stuttering child, "You are slapping his hands every time he starts to stutter, aren't you?" he is leading her to an incorrect answer unless she clearly understands that slapping the child for stuttering is inappropriate behavior. When this tactic is taken by the interviewer, he is sometimes referred to as the *devil's advocate*.

One type of leading question is the *yes-response* question, or the *no-response* question. "Naturally, you agreed with the decision, didn't you?" is an example of a yes-response question. One of the components of leading questions is *expectation*. If the interviewer asks, "Are you twenty-one years old?" the question is a direct, closed question, but it is not leading. If the interviewer, however, asks, "Of course, you are twenty-one years old, aren't you?" he indicates an expectation. Expectations can be identified by the syntax and logic of the question, but, intonation can communicate doubt, confidence, and *expectation*. Through intonation and emphasis one might make the question, "Did *you* agree with that decision?" a leading question. The intonation and emphasis could register surprise and incredulity at anything other than the expected answer.

Another form of the leading question is the loaded question, which uses loaded words and has high emotional connotations. It reaches "touchy spots" and strikes strong feelings. It may present a dilemma from which it is difficult for the respondent to escape. Questions that are not stated objectively are considered loaded. Various techniques are used to indicate the bias or expectation. Prestige may be used. "The President of the United States believes that the problem is serious. Do you agree?" is an example of using prestige to indicate the bias. The interviewer may also associate positive stereotypes with responses that are desired or negative stereotypes with responses that are not desired. It is apparent that loaded questions should be used with extreme caution, and probably not at all by the inexperienced interviewer. When used by an insightful and skilled interviewer, the loaded question may uncover important hidden information, attitudes, or feelings.

To gain an understanding of the question-answer process, one needs to become familiar with and be able to recognize the various types of questions that may be used. Through guided practice, he can develop skill in using questions. He must also develop skill in recognizing inadequate answers to his questions.

Inadequate Answers

One kind of inadequate response is the *ooververbalized response.* In one trial situation, the lawyer asked a witness how she came to be at a certain place at 1:30 A.M. She proceeded to tell in detail how she had spent the preceding twenty-four hours. After five minutes in relating what she had done between 7:00 A.M. and noon, the attorney was finally successful in interrupting her and requesting her to skip those details and tell why she was at that certain place at 1:30.

Another kind of inadequate response is the *irrelevant answer.* It simply has nothing to do with the question asked. It has no bearing on the subject or purpose of the interview.

A third unacceptable response is the *inaccurate response.* The information may be purposely or accidentally false, but it is inaccurate, detrimental, and unacceptable. Inaccurate responses are often difficult to detect, but when inaccuracy is suspected related questions and delayed, repeated questions may be asked to check consistency.

The *partial response* is a fourth kind of inadequate answer. Partial responses are easily detected if the interviewer is alert and thinking. If the interviewer is hastily taking the first small answer and rushing on to his next question, he may settle for partial responses when he should have probed and elicited more information.

Nonresponse is the fifth inadequate response. It is a rather serious response which may be ignored and the question dropped, or which may be probed if the interviewer thinks it would be profitable to do so. One of the most common weaknesses related to using questions in the interview is the tendency to take too much for granted, i.e., the interviewer too easily assumes that his interpretations of the interviewee's responses are accurate. He jumps to conclusions too quickly. He fails to check the meanings of the messages. The interviewer also assumes too quickly that the interviewee understands the question—that the respondent has the same frame of reference as does the interviewer. Such assumptions are not warranted, as has been stressed throughout this text. As interviewers and as interviewees we need to develop a critical attitude toward our questions and answers. We must curb the tendency to accept the first meaning that pops into our heads. The tendency to take things for grant-

ed, to presume, is not easy to correct. It is a common characteristic we all share. It is a subtle fault, and for this reason, we need to discipline ourselves—to stop and ask ourselves, "Now, what am I taking for granted here?" Successful interviewing requires effective interpersonal and intrapersonal communication.

We must remember that in the informational interview, information is forfeited when we omit data and meanings, when we distort statements (sometimes we mistake qualified statements for definite statements), and when we make additions to what the other person has said. We can prevent some of this forfeiting of information if we are systematic, if we employ verbal emphasis and attention factors, if we encourage and use feedback, if we summarize frequently, and if we are sensitive to the other person's viewpoint, frame of reference, experience, and intended meaning. We must remember that role differences, interpersonal attraction, thinking habits, attitudes, and poor listening habits can act as barriers to effective informational interviewing.

The Structure of the Interview

There are at least three parts to all interviews—the opening, the substantive part, and the closing. The initial stage, opening the interview, is quite important, for during this time the relationship between the interviewer and the respondent is established. The objectives of the opening are to establish confidence, trust, clarity of the purpose of the interview, and the identification of mutual goals. Rapport, an important element throughout the interview, is largely established in the opening stage of the interview. Some pre-interview acts also relate to the establishment of rapport. The request for an interview should *never* be made in terms that alarm or threaten the interviewee, for example; and the place selected for the interview should be private, comfortable, and conducive to a smooth and satisfactory interview operation. In addition to pre-interview planning, certain behavior during the opening of the interview can help to establish good rapport, confidence, and relaxation for the interview. The purpose of the interview should be clearly explained and the procedures indicated and mutually agreed to or adjusted.

The second phase of the interview is the substantive part of the interview that relies heavily upon the question-answer process previously discussed.

The final part of the interview is the closing. Some interviews come to natural closings as a result of the nature of the progress of the discussion or as a result of the inclination of the participants. Other interviews need to be continued, but circumstances dictate that they must be closed. Still other interviews could be continued profitably because things are going so well, but time dictates that they must be ended. Regardless of the reasons or conditions, the interview closing ought to contain a short summary by the interviewer, an opportunity for the interviewee to make additions and corrections, and an indication of the next steps, or where-to-go-from-here.

1. Robert S. Goyer, W. Charles Redding, and John T. Rickey, *Interviewing Principles and Techniques* (Dubuque, Iowa: Wm. C. Brown Book Company, 1968), p. 6.

2. Ibid., p. 14.

3. Ibid., pp. 7–8.

4. Stephen A. Richardson, Barbara S. Dohrenwend, and David Klein, *Interviewing: Its Forms and.Functions* (New York: Basic Books, Inc., 1965), p. 147.

5. See: R. L. Gordon, "An Interaction Analysis of the Depth-Interview" (Ph.D. diss., University of Chicago, 1954); and G. Saslow et al. "Test-Retest Stability of Interaction Patterns During Interviews Conducted One Week Apart," *Journal of Abnormal Social Psychology* 54 (1957): 295–302.

6. C. F. Cannell and R. L. Kahn, "The Collection of Data by Interviewing," in *Research Methods in the Behavioral Sciences*, ed L. Festinger and D. Katz (New York: Dryden Press, 1953), p. 346.

7. W. V. D. Bingham, B. V. Moore, and J. W. Gustad, "How to Interview" (New York: Harper & Brothers, 1959), p. 74.

The Language of Love: Communications Fights

George R. Bach and Peter Wyden

It is fashionable nowadays for intimates to complain about their "communications." The very word has acquired a certain cachet as if it were something ultra-modern. Husbands and wives accuse each other: "You never talk to me" or "You never listen to me." More honest couples take pride in confiding to each other, "We just can't communicate." Whatever the wording, these grievances are likely to be aired in a tone of acute frustration or resignation, much as if the partners were innocent victims of two electronic circuits that went haywire.

Executives know that communications are the life line of business; when the line becomes clogged or breaks down, two things occur: either (1) whatever shouldn't or (2) nothing. Intimates, on the other hand, usually just blame themselves or their mates for communications failures or wallow in lamentations of the "ain't-it-awful" variety. They rarely realize that intimate communication is an art that requires considerable imagination and creativity. They are almost never aware that only a conscious, resolute decision on the part of both partners to work at the problem—continually and for the rest of their lives—can produce good communications. And even if partners are ready to go to work to make their language of love serve them better, they don't know how to go about it.

The job is big because intimate communication involves a lot more than transmitting and receiving signals. Its purpose is to make explicit everything that partners expect of each other—what is most agreeable and least agreeable, what is relevant and irrelevant; to monitor continually what they experience as bonding or alienating; to synchronize interests, habits, and "hangups"; and to effect the fusion that achieves the *we* without demolishing the *you* or the *me*.

Intimates usually fail to understand that the language of love does not confine itself to matters of loving and other intimate concerns. It permeates *all* communications between lovers. For example, if one business acquaintance says to another, "I'm hungry," this message almost certainly needn't be weighed for emotional implications. It can be taken at face value and acted upon accordingly. However, if an intimate sends the same message to another intimate, he may be engaging in several activities:

1. expressing a private sentiment, perhaps "feeling out loud" just to gauge whether the partner's reaction is sympathetic or indifferent;

2. appealing emotionally to the partner in order to persuade

Intimate communication requires that the partners make explicit what they expect of each other.

"Grin and Bear It" by George Lichty
Courtesy of Publishers-Hall Syndicate

"Why do we have to have meaningful dialogues? . . .
I feel much better if we merely yell at each other!"

him to do or say something (perhaps, "Come on, let's go to the coffee shop");

3. transmitting meaningful information (perhaps, "I'm starved, but I can't stop to eat now").

Partner A, then, might well be putting his foot in his mouth if Partner B is saying, "You don't understand how busy I am" and "A" only shrugs and replies, "Why don't you go and have something to eat?" Maybe "B" wants "A" to bring him something to eat from the coffee shop so he can work and eat at the same time. Unfortunately, "A" can't divine this request—which "B" would never expect him to do if he were talking to a business colleague.

Many intimates stubbornly insist that there shouldn't be any communications problems between them. The folklore of romantic love leads lovers to believe that some sort of intuitive click or sensitivity links all intimates; that this should suffice to convey their deep mutual understanding; and that this miracle occurs simply because the partners love one another. So they demand to be divined. In effect, they say, "He ought to know how I feel" or, "You'll decode me correctly if you love me." This permits spouses to think they can afford to be sloppier in their intimate communications than they are in their nonintimate contacts.

Another reason why communications are such a problem is a psychological laziness that has many people in its grip. Encouraged by the romantic fallacy that the language of love falls into place as if by magic, they find it easy to shirk the task and shrug it off.

The third reason is that the popularity of game-playing and the role-taking in today's society

has encouraged the suspicion that transparency, even at home, may not be a good idea. This belief is usually grounded in the fear that candor would cause an intimate to reveal something about himself that might cool the partner. It creates still another temptation for partners to try to enjoy a free ride on the vague and often wrong presumption that they understand each other.

The easiest way to create communications problems is to withhold information from one's spouse. When partners don't confide in each other, they are likely to find themselves trying to tap their way through a vacuum, like blind people with white canes. The resulting fights can pop up at any time and place. For Herb and Lonnie Cartwright the place happened to be their kitchen. The time was the evening before they planned to give a big party:

LONNIE: I need another $30 for food for the party.

HERB: That's a lot of money for food.

LONNIE (*exasperated*): People have to eat!

HERB (*reasonable*): I know that.

LONNIE (*taking a deep breath before plunging into unaccustomed territory*): Ever since you bought that new insurance policy we're always strapped for cash.

HERB (*startled*): But it's in your name!

LONNIE (*vehemently*): I don't want you to die! Let's live a little now!

HERB (*shaken*): I resent that! After all, I was trying to do the right thing by you.

LONNIE (*with finality*): Then you shouldn't have bought the policy until after you get your next raise. I don't like to come to you like a beggar.

What happened here? These

Popeye by Bud Sagendorf

partners had kept each other in such ignorance over the years that they inevitably wound up poles apart on family financial policy. This wife, like so many others, thought of her husband as a money tree. One reason why she loved him was that he was such a good provider. She believed that, within reason, she could buy anything she wanted. But she carefully avoided a test of her notions by never expressing an interest in the family bank balance. To her, money was to spend, just like a child's pocket money. To her husband, on the other hand, money was the equivalent of security. He had told his wife that he had bought a big new insurance policy, but not how expensive it had been. The lesson of this case is that husbands would do well not to leave wives ignorant about personal finances or other basic realities of their life together.

When intimates refuse to impart strategic information that they possess, or when they refuse to react to information that is offered to them, they are asking for trouble. Sometimes a partner withholds information in the name of tact. This is especially true when it comes to sharing information about sexual preferences. There are times when the state of the union demands that transparency be tempered by tact. But much so-called tact is cowardice or deception—a cover-up to avoid confrontations and feedback from the opponent. The withholding of information only leads to worse explosions later.

Some husbands, for instance, don't tell their wives how broke they are. They "don't want her to worry." Suddenly a man from the loan company appears at home to repossess the wife's car. Not only is this crisis often unnecessary ("Honey, why didn't you tell me?

I could have borrowed the money from Dad!"). Often it leads to irreversible damage because it erodes the wife's trust in her spouse. In true intimacy stress is shared by partners.

There are partners, however, who, without knowing it, *cause* their spouses to withhold information. One such husband tended to get excited and be in the way when things went wrong at home. Then he lectured his wife that she should have managed better. When he went on business trips he called home daily and his wife always reassured him that things were fine. Usually they were, but one day the husband returned from a week's absence and was extremely upset to find that his wife had broken her ankle and hadn't said a word about it on the telephone. In her inner dialogue, the wife had said to herself, "He's no help in a crisis." The husband had brought this lack of trust upon himself.

When intimates are frustrated by their inability to communicate clearly and straightforwardly, they tend to confuse matters further by sending messages full of sarcasms, hyperboles, caricatures and exaggerations that befog or overdramatize. The list of these statics is almost endless, but here are some random examples:

"I'd just as soon talk to a blank wall." "You've got diarrhea of the mouth." "You did *not say that*; if you did, I didn't hear it!" "We have nothing to say to each other any more." "You always talk in riddles." "I've learned to keep my mouth shut." "You never say what you mean." "Why do you always interrupt me?" "You just like to hear the sound of your own voice." "You never stand up for yourself." "If I've told you once, I've told you a thousand times . . ."

When fight trainees are faced

with these statics as they try to communicate feelings and wishes to their partners, we sometimes tell them the ancient yarn about the Texas mule who was too stubborn to respond to commands. The owner decided to hire a famous mule trainer to cure the trouble. The trainer took one look at the mule and cracked him over the head with a two-by-four. The owner was appalled.

"That's dreadful," he said. "I thought you were going to train him!"

"Sure," said the trainer. "But first I have to get his attention."

Partners who must deal with statics need to review the techniques for getting a good fight started. The same goes for spouses who find themselves confronted with opponents who blanket out communications with jamming noises, the way the Communists used to jam Western radio broadcasts.

Some intimate jammers can be infuriatingly effective. Suppose a husband knows his wife wants to talk to him about his overspending. But the husband also knows his spouse loves to listen to gossip about his boss's sex life. The husband therefore rattles on interminably about fresh gossip he has just heard on the office grapevine and then dashes to the car to leave for work.

"Hey," shouts his wife. "We've got to talk about those bills!"

"Will do!" shouts the husband — and drives off.

Even partners who seem to appreciate the importance of open, unjammed communications rarely realize just how unambiguous their signals should be and how meticulously a message sender should solicit feedback from the recipient to check out whether his signal was understood as it was intended. Here is what often happens in the three stages of message sending: (1) the intention of the message, (2) the framing of the message, and (3) the interpretation of the message at the other end of the line.

Case No. 1: The wife tells the kids not to bother Dad. He is listening.

How Meant
"I'm protecting you"
How Sent
"Don't bother him."
How Received
"She's fencing me in."

Case No. 2: The husband doesn't bring any of his buddies home from his club. She asks him about it.

How Meant
"It's too much work for you."
How Received
"He's ashamed of me."
How Sent
"Oh, let's skip it."

Husbands and wives who wish to extricate themselves from a jungle of unclear signals find it helpful to fix within their minds the seemingly simple fundamentals of communication:

Obtain the attention of your receiver. Prepare him to receive your message. Send out your message clearly and with a minimum of extraneous static. Make sure your information is beamed toward the receiver's wave length. Stake out your own area of interest and stick to its limits. Keep your self and your receiver focused on the joint interest area. Stimulate your receiver to respond by acknowledging reception. Obtain feedback to check how your message was received.

These principles are known to anyone who ever placed an important long-distance phone call. Yet intimates, especially while under the emotional stress of conflict and aggression, tend to

ignore the basics even though they "know better." Their resistance against forging a clear connection is a sign that they find conflict stressful and don't like to accept the fact that they are involved in one.

This is why noncommunicators lead each other around the mulberry bush with such round-robin jabs as these:

SHE: You never talk to me.
HE: What's on your mind?
SHE: It's not what's on *my* mind; it's that I never know what's on *your* mind.
HE (*slightly panicky*): What do you want to know?
SHE (*jubilantly*): Everything!
HE (*thoroughly vexed*): That's crazy!
SHE: Here we go again.

This game of hide-and-seek may also go like this:

HE: You talk too much!
SHE: About what?
HE: About everything.
SHE: One of us has to talk!
HE: You talk, but you never say anything.
SHE: That's crazy.
HE: You're darned right!
SHE (*thoughtfully*): What do you mean?
HE (*wearily*): You make a lot of noise, but that makes it impossible for us to have a real talk.
SHE: Here we go again. . . .

Here's what happened after the latter fight, between two unmarried young people:

DR. BACH (*to the girl*): What was he really telling you?
GIRL: That he doesn't like me.
DR. B (*to the boy*): Is that what you wanted to convey?
BOY: No! I love her!
DR. B: You two are starving for real communication. You're

using words like fog to hide your true feelings.

Here are some exercises that help:

1. Diagnose how efficient or inefficient your present level of communication is. Is each partner candid and transparent? Does each get a chance to tell the other what's "eating him"? Does each partner really understand what the other is after? Once shortcomings are identified, the fight techniques outlined in previous chapters should be used to negotiate settlements.

2. Locate some of the causes of poor communication by owning up to yourself and to each other that you occasionally or habitually use one of the statics discussed in this and the next two chapters. Try to catch each other in the use of static and aggressively eliminate its use. Calls of "Static!" or "Foul!" may help.

3. Stop blocking communication by explicitly renouncing the use of static maneuvers.

4. Start making communication flow more freely by deliberately making yourselves accessible, open, and crystal-clear. From time to time, take new readings of the quality of your communications. Has improvement taken place?

5. Respond with full resonance. Be sure you are sharing your private view of yourself and the world with your partner. Expressive communication enhances intimacy; reflective communication is useful but secondary. The more intimate two people are, the more they take turns expressing their views freely.

I know you believe you understood what you think I said, but I am not sure you realize that what you heard is not what I meant.

An Overview of Transactional Analysis

Muriel James and Dorothy Jongeward

The crazy person says, "I am Abraham Lincoln," and the neurotic says, "I wish I were Abraham Lincoln," and the healthy person says, "I am I, and you are you." Frederick Perls[1]

Many people come to a time in their lives when they are provoked to define themselves. At such a time transactional analysis offers a frame of reference that most people can understand and put to use in their own lives.

Introduction to Structural Analysis

Structural analysis offers one way of answering the questions: Who am I? Why do I act the way I do? How did I get this way? It is a method of analyzing a person's thoughts, feelings, and behavior, based on the phenomena of ego states.[2]

Berne defines an ego state as "A consistent pattern of feeling and experience directly related to a corresponding consistent pattern of behavior."[3] The findings of Dr. Wilder Penfield, neurosurgeon, support this definition. He found that an electrode applied to different parts of the brain evoked memories and feelings long forgotten by the person.[4]

The implications are that what happens to a person is recorded in his brain and nervous tissue. This includes everything a person experienced in his childhood, all that he incorporated from his parent figures, his perceptions of events, his feelings associated with these events, and the distortions that he brings to his memories. These recordings are stored as though on video tape. They can be replayed, and the event recalled and even reexperienced.

Each person has three ego states which are separate and distinct sources of behavior: the Parent ego state, the Adult ego state, and the Child ego state. These are not abstract concepts but realities. "Parent, Adult, and Child represent real people who now exist or who once existed, who have legal names and civic identities."[5]

You can use transactional analysis to understand yourself better and improve your intimate communication.

The three ego states are defined as follows:

The *Parent ego state* contains the attitudes and behavior incorporated from external sources, primarily parents. Outwardly, it often is expressed toward others in prejudicial, critical, and nurturing behavior. Inwardly, it is experienced as old Parental messages which continue to influence the inner Child.

James-Jongeward, BORN TO WIN: Transactional Analysis with Gestalt Experiments, 1971, Addison-Wesley, Reading, Mass.

Andy Capp *by Reg Smythe*

The *Adult ego state* is not related to a person's age. It is oriented to current reality and the objective gathering of information. It is organized, adaptable, intelligent, and functions by testing reality, estimating probabilities, and computing dispassionately.

The *Child ego state* contains all the impulses that come naturally to an infant. It also contains the recordings of his early experiences, how he responded to them, and the "positions" he took about himself and others. It is expressed as "old" (archaic) behavior from childhood.

When you are acting, thinking, feeling, as you observed your parents to be doing, you are in your Parent ego state.

When you are dealing with current reality, gathering facts, and computing objectively, you are in your Adult ego state.

When you are feeling and acting as you did when you were a child, you are in your Child ego state.

According to structural analysis, each person may respond to a specific stimulus in quite distinct ways from each of his ego states; sometimes these ego states are in concert, sometimes in conflict. Let's look at the following examples.

To a stimulus of a piece of modern art

Parent: Good grief! What's it supposed to be!
Adult: That costs $350 according to the price tag.
Child: Ooo, what pretty color!

To a request for an office report

Parent: Mr. Brown is not cut out to be a supervisor.
Adult: I know Mr. Brown needs these by five o'clock.

Child: No matter what I do I can't please Mr. Brown.

Introduction to Analyzing Transactions

Anything that happens between people will involve a transaction between their ego states. When one person sends a message to another, he expects a response. All transactions can be classified as (1) complementary, (2) crossed, or (3) ulterior.[6]

Complementary Transactions

A complementary transaction occurs when a message, sent from a specific ego state, gets the predicted response from a specific ego state in the other person. Berne describes a complementary transaction as one which is "appropriate and expected and follows the natural order of healthy human relationship."[7] For example, if a wife who is grieving for her lost friend is comforted by a sympathetic husband, her momentary dependency need is answered appropriately.

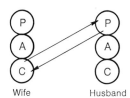

Wife   Husband

A complementary transaction can occur between any two ego states. For example, two people may transact Parent-Parent when lamenting their children's leaving home; Adult-Adult when solving a problem; Child-Child or Parent-Child when having fun together. A person from his Parent can transact with any of the ego states of another person. He can also do this with his Adult and

Knots

R. D. Laing

JILL   *I am frightened*
JACK *Don't be frightened*
JILL   *I am frightened to be frightened when you*
       tell me I ought not to feel frightened

       frightened
       frightened to be frightened
       not frightened to be frightened

       not frightened
       frightened not to be frightened
       not frightened to be not frightened

JILL   *I'm upset you are upset*
JACK *I'm not upset*
JILL   *I'm upset that you're not upset that I'm*
       upset you're upset
JACK *I'm upset that you're upset that I'm not*
       upset that you're upset that I'm upset,
       when I'm not.

JILL   *You put me in the wrong*
JACK *I am not putting you in the wrong*
JILL   *You put me in the wrong for thinking you*
        put me in the wrong.
JACK *Forgive me*
JILL   *No*
JACK *I'll never forgive you for not forgiving me*

Child. If the response is the expected one, the transaction is complementary. The lines of communication are *open* and the people can continue transacting with one another.

Gestures, facial expressions, body posture, tone of voice, and so forth, all contribute to the meaning in every transaction. If a verbal message is to be completely understood, the receiver must take into consideration the nonverbal aspects as well as the spoken words.

Crossed Transactions

When two people stand glaring at each other, turn their backs on each other, are unwilling to continue transacting, or are puzzled by what has just occurred between them, it is likely that they have just experienced a *crossed transaction*. A crossed transaction occurs when an unexpected response is made to the stimulus. An inappropriate ego state is activated and the lines of transacting between the people are crossed. At this point, people tend to withdraw, turn away from each other, or switch the conversation in another direction. If a husband responds unsympathetically to his grieving wife, "Well, how do you think I feel!" he is likely to cause her to turn away from him.

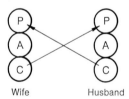

Wife   Husband

Crossed transactions are a frequent source of pain between people—parents and children, husband and wife, boss and employee, teacher and student, and so forth. The person who initiates a transaction, expecting a certain

response, does not get it. He is crossed and often left feeling discounted.

Ulterior Transactions

Ulterior transactions are the most complex. They differ from complementary and crossed in that they always involve more than two ego states. When an ulterior message is sent, it is disguised under a socially acceptable transaction. Such is the purpose of the old cliché: "Wouldn't you like to come up to see my etchings?" In this instance the Adult is verbalizing one thing while the Child, with the use of innuendo, is sending a different message.

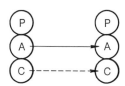

If a car salesman says to his customer with a leer, "This is our finest sports car, but it may be too racy for you," he is sending a message that can be heard either by the customer's Adult ego state or by his Child ego state. If the customer's Adult hears, he may respond, "Yes, you're right, considering the requirements of my job." If his Child responds, he may say "I'll take it. It's just what I want."

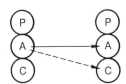

The Games People Play

People play psychological games with one another that are similar

JILL   *You think I am stupid*
JACK   *I don't think you're stupid*
JILL   *I must be stupid to think you think I'm*
       stupid if you don't: or you must be lying
       I am stupid every way:
       to think I'm stupid, if I am stupid
       to think I'm stupid, if I'm not stupid
       to think you think I'm stupid, if you don't.

JILL   *I'm ridiculous*
JACK   *No you are not*
JILL   *I'm ridiculous to feel ridiculous when I'm not.*
       You must
           be laughing at me
       for feeling you are laughing at me
           if you are not laughing at me.

How clever has one to be to be stupid?
The others told her she was stupid. So she made
herself stupid in order not to see how stupid
they were to think she was stupid,
because it was bad to think they were stupid.
She preferred to be stupid and good,
rather than bad and clever.

It is bad to be stupid: she needs to be clever
to be so good and stupid.
It is bad to be clever, because this shows
how stupid they were
to tell her how stupid she was.

WHAT'S THE MATTER WITH *HER*?

GAMES PEOPLE PLAY

Words and Music by
JOE SOUTH

Moderately

Verse:

Oh, the games peo-ple play now,
oth - er cry;
to you,
what you see,

ev -'ry night and ev-'ry
Break a heart then we
Sing-in' Glo-ry Hal -le-
What's hap-pen-in' to

day, now.
say good - bye;
lu - jah!
you and me.

Nev - er mean - in' what they
Cross our hearts and we
And they're try'n' to sock it
God grant me the se -

say, now.
hope to die.
to you.
ren - i - ty,

Nev - er say - in' what they mean.
That the oth - er was to blame.
In the name of the Lord.
To re - mem-ber who I am.

And they while a - way the ho - urs
Nei-ther one will ev - er give in.
They gon - na teach you how to me - di - tate;
'Cause you're giv-in' up your san - i - ty

In their i - vo - ry
So, we gaze at an
Read your hor-o-scope,
For your pride and your

(continued on page 113)

to games like monopoly, bridge, or checkers, that people play at social gatherings. The players must know the game in order to play— after all, if one person enters a card party ready to play bridge, and everyone else is playing pinochle, he can't very well play bridge.

All games have a beginning, a given set of rules, and a concluding payoff. Psychological games, however, have an ulterior purpose. They are not played for fun. Of course, neither are some poker games.

Berne defines a *psychological game* as "a recurring set of transactions, often repetitive, superficially rational, with a concealed motivation; or, more colloquially, as a series of transactions with a gimmick."[8] Three specific elements must be present to define transactions as games: (1) an ongoing series of complementary transactions which are plausible on the social level, (2) an ulterior transaction which is the underlying message of the game, and (3) a predictable payoff which concludes the game and is the real purpose for playing. Games prevent honest, intimate, and open relationships between the players. Yet people play them because they fill up time, provoke attention, reinforce early opinions about self and others, and fulfill a sense of destiny.

Psychological games are played to win, but a person who plays games as a way of life is not a winner. Sometimes a person acts like a loser to win his game. For example, in a game of *Kick Me* a player provokes someone else to put him down.

Student: I stayed up too late last night and don't have my assignment ready.
(ulterior: I'm a bad boy, kick me.)

The Born Loser by Art Sansom

Instructor: You're out of luck. This is the last day I can give credit for that assignment. (ulterior: Yes, you are a bad boy and here is your kick.)

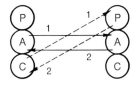

Though he may deny it, a person who is used to this game tends to attract others who can play the complementary hand and are willing to "kick" him.

Every game has a first move. Some first moves are nonverbal: turning a cold shoulder, batting a flirty eye, shaking an accusative finger, slamming a door, tracking mud in the house, reading someone's mail, looking woebegone, not speaking. Other first moves are verbal statements such as:

You look so lonesome over here by yourself . . .
How could you go to school wearing that get-up!
He criticized you. Are you going to take that?
I have this terrible problem . . .
Isn't it awful that . . .

Barbara and Tom's favorite game was *Uproar.* They both knew the first move in the game so either could start it. Once it was started, a predictable set of transactions occurred which climaxed with a loud fight. The outcome was always the same—hostile withdrawal to avoid closeness. This was their payoff for playing the game, the avoidance of intimacy.

To set up the game either Barbara or Tom provoked the other with nonverbal behavior such as sulking, chain-smoking, with-

(continued from page 112)

drawing, or acting irritated. When the partner was "hooked" into playing, the game was under way. As the game continued he/she got a put-off or a put-down. After exchanging many angry words, they finally withdraw from each other.

When Barbara starts the game, the transactions are:

Barbara: (Begins pouting and chain-smoking with exaggerated gestures)

Tom: "What's the matter? What's wrong?"

Barbara: "It's none of your business!"

Tom: (Goes out to the local bar)

Barbara: (Explodes in anger when he returns. A long battle ensues filled with accusations and counter-accusations. The payoff comes when Barbara breaks into tears, runs into the bedroom, and slams the door. Tom retreats to the kitchen for another drink. They make no further contact that evening.)

When Tom initiates the game, the transactions are:

Tom: (Fixes a drink for himself, goes off to the den, and closes the door.)

Barbara: "Why didn't you fix a drink for me? Is something wrong?"

Tom: "Can't I even have a few minutes alone!"

Barbara: "If you want to be alone, I'll leave!" (Barbara goes shopping, buys things they can't afford, and returns carrying several packages.)

Tom: (Explodes in anger about the way she spends money. The game comes full circle when she stamps away mad and he fixes his bed in the den.)

Games tend to be repetitious. People find themselves saying the same words in the same way, only the time and place may change. Perhaps the replay contributes to what is often described as "I feel as if I've done this before."

People play games with different degrees of intensity from the socially accepted, relaxed level to the criminal homicide/suicide level. Berne writes:

a) A First-Degree Game is one which is socially acceptable in the agent's circle.

b) A Second-Degree Game is one from which no permanent, irremediable damage arises, but which the players would rather conceal from the public.

c) A Third-Degree Game is one which is played for keeps, and which ends in surgery, the courtroom or the morgue.[9]

Games are individually programmed. They are played from the Parent ego state if the parent's games are imitated. They are played from the Adult ego state if they are consciously calculated. They are played from the Child ego state if they are based on early life experiences, decisions, and the "positions" that a child takes about himself and others.

Psychological Positions

When taking positions about themselves, people may conclude:

I'm smart.   I'm stupid.
I'm powerful.   I'm inadequate.

I'm nice.   I'm nasty.
I'm an angel.   I'm a devil.
I can't do anything right.   I can't do anything wrong.
I'm as good as anybody else.   I don't deserve to live.

When taking positions about others, people may conclude:

People will give me anything I want.   Nobody will give me anything.
People are wonderful.   People are no damn good.
Someone will help me.   People are out to get me.
Everybody likes me.   Nobody likes me.
People are nice.   Everybody's mean.

In general, the above positions are "I'm OK" or "I'm not-OK," and "You're OK" or "You're not-OK." The psychological positions taken about oneself and about others fit into four basic patterns.[10] The first is the winner's position, but even winners may occasionally have feelings that resemble the other three.

The First Position: I'm OK, You're OK

is potentially a mentally healthy position. If realistic, a person with this position about himself and others can solve his problems constructively. His expectations are likely to be valid. He accepts the significance of people.

The Second or Projective Position: I'm OK, You're not-OK

is the position of persons who feel victimized or persecuted. They blame others for their miseries. Delinquents and criminals often have this position and take on paranoid behavior which in extreme cases may lead to homicide.

The Third or Introjective Position: I'm not-OK, You're OK

is a common position of persons who feel powerless when they compare themselves to others. This position leads them to withdraw, to experience depression, and, in severe cases, to become suicidal.

The Fourth or Futility Position: I'm not-OK, You're not-OK

is the position of those who lose interest in living, who exhibit schizoid behavior, and, in extreme cases, commit suicide or homicide.

The person with the first position feels "Life is worth living." With the second he feels "Your life is not worth much." With the third he feels "My life is not worth much." With the fourth he feels "Life isn't worth anything at all."

1. Frederick S. Perls, *Gestalt Therapy Verbatim* (Lafayette, Calif.: Real People Press, 1969), p. 40.

2. Eric Berne, *Transactional Analysis in Psychotherapy* (New York: Grove Press, 1961), pp. 17–43.
    Cf. Paul McCormick and Leonard Campos, *Introduce Yourself to Transactional Analysis: A TA Handbook* (Stockton, Calif.: San Joaquin TA Study Group, Distributed by Transactional Pub., 3155 College Ave., Berkeley, Calif., 94705, 1969).
    Also see John M. Dusay, "Transactional Analysis," in *A Layman's Guide to Psychiatry and Psychoanalysis* by Eric Berne (New York: Simon & Schuster, 3rd ed., 1968), pp. 277–306.

3. Eric Berne, *Principles of Group Treatment* (New York: Oxford University Press, 1964), p. 364.

4. W. Penfield, "Memory Mechanisms," A.M.A. *Archives of Neurology and Psychiatry*, vol. 67 (1952), pp. 178–98.

5. Berne, *Transactional Analysis in Psychotherapy*, p. 32.

6. Eric Berne, *Games People Play* (New York: Grove Press, 1964), pp. 29–64.

7. Ibid., p. 29.

8. Eric Berne, "Transactional Analysis" in *Active Psychotherapy* by Harold Greenwald, ed. (New York: Atherton Press, 1967), p. 125.

9. Berne, *Games People Play*, p. 64.

10. Eric Berne, "Standard Nomenclature, Transactional Nomenclature," *Transactional Analysis Bulletin*, vol. 8, no. 32, October, 1969, p. 112.
    Cf. Zelig Selinger, "The Parental Second Position in Treatment," *Transactional Analysis Bulletin*, vol. 6, no. 21, January, 1967, p. 29.

To Talk to You

Jean Itzin

the words
I want to say
fall cringing
to the floor,
scurrying into corners
seeking shadows,
hiding from your gaze.

The Fine Art of Conversation

Jack Harrison Pollack

You can improve your communication skills by practicing several techniques and watching out for certain pitfalls.

Have you ever lost your voice at a gathering when you were trying hard to make a good impression by saying something bright? If so, you're not alone. Millions of men and women find social conversation their No. 1 problem. But if you learn how to talk interestingly, you'll no longer feel embarrassment at parties; you'll widen your circle of friends; and you'll lead a happier, more successful life.

Recently I attended a dinner party where our playful host recorded our conversation on a hidden tape recorder. Later he played it back to us. At first we were shocked, but soon we all began laughing at our silly chatter. One guest's observation was typical. "Gosh, I blabbed and blabbed without saying a thing!"

Today it is especially important to be a good conversationalist, for talk is the main entertainment at many parties. Our stay-at-home mothers and grandmothers had fewer challenges to hold their own in groups of talk-happy strangers. Today, party games are played much less often than they were a generation ago. Etiquette authority Amy Vanderbilt says, "Stimulating conversation is the best social entertainment today." Note the key word—"stimulating."

Unfortunately, many of us are tongue-tied after we've commented on the weather, our children, homes, and jobs. Women are of-

ten better conversationalists than men, but both sexes tend to be segregationalists in the field of talk. At countless gatherings men form a group to discuss dull business problems while the women form another circle to talk about illnesses, diets, children, relatives, and household problems. They are all deep in subjects they came to the party to escape.

What I am presenting are practical suggestions—10 of them—that will help make your conversation more sparkling.

1. Listen attentively

Conversation is more than mere talk. It entails listening, too. Most people need to learn how to listen effectively.

A bore has been defined as someone who talks when you want him to listen. An occasional interlude of silence may be what's needed to make your conversation delightful.

There are chatterboxes who seldom listen when you talk to them. Their restlessness and wandering eyes, in addition to their clucking tongues, give them away. The late humorist Robert Benchley once proved this by sauntering around a large gabby party making idiotic statements such as, "Tonight it may snow if the whistle stops." Few were aware that he was deliberately uttering nonsense.

B.C. *by Johnny Hart*

By permission of John Hart and Field Enterprises, Inc.

Many of us concentrate on what we plan to say, instead of giving attention to what the other person is saying. When we itch to speak, we can't listen with much care. And we don't fool the other fellow a bit.

A husband whose wife complained that he never *really* listened to her protested, "But dear, you've been talking for half an hour and I haven't said a word!" "Yes," she replied, "but you've been listening in a most annoying manner."

You don't have to lead the conversation to be a good conversationalist. At a recent party I watched a woman listen attentively to a man whose talk about old automobiles was enthusiastic. The woman knew nothing about this subject, but it was an exciting adventure for her to draw him out and learn something new. She showed curiosity and sincere enthusiasm. Although she hardly said a word, the appreciative man later told me, "She's a brilliant woman!"

2. Talk about what interests the other person

Probably the most effective conversational technique is steering the discussion around to a subject dear to the *other* person's heart. Whether it is his hobby, job, family, or travel, discover his conversational soft spot. You'll never have to worry about an awkward silence.

Talking about things other people are interested in will make you more popular. "Charm in conversation consists less in displaying one's own wit and intelligence than in opening the way for the *other* fellow to display his," reminds University of Minnesota psychologist Wendell White. You may not care much about skiing or gun manufacturing, but if your dinner partner does, encourage him to talk.

Dr. Arnold Gesell, the child-care authority, long had a reputation for being aloof and uncooperative with reporters. But he talked to me freely after I discovered his great interest in photography.

Several years ago Dr. Benjamin Spock refused to be interviewed by any writer. At a medical conference I showed him a page of a manuscript I was preparing about his childhood. "Where did you get this material about me?" he demanded. "Isn't it true?" I parried. "Yes, but I'd rather you didn't print it!" he exclaimed.

What I did print was much more—told me by Dr. Spock after his protests. Why did he talk? Because I had focused the conversation on a subject that enormously interested *him*, even though he was on the defensive.

It helps to know a person's background. At the beginning of an interview with New York Judge Justine Wise Polier about a juvenile delinquency article, I mentioned that I had known her late father, the great Rabbi Stephen S. Wise. My interview was much more productive after I revealed this fact.

Talking to a person sincerely about *his* deep interests has another advantage. You'll be so engrossed that you won't have time to be self-conscious about yourself.

3. Avoid dull details

Your conversation is livelier and more pertinent when you omit unnecessary facts. "The secret of being tiresome is in telling everything," warned Voltaire. If you edit yourself as you talk, you won't be like the man Churchill described as "having the gift of compressing the largest amount of words into the smallest amount of thought."

All of us know the person who, when telling a story, digresses: "Let's see, was it Friday or Saturday? Well, it must have been about 10 o'clock, because I had just left my sister's house, and I . . ."

Other windbags overwhelm you with detailed chronological reports. If you ask such a person where he spent his vacation, he can't answer simply, "Cape Cod." Instead, he'll filibuster with a dreary step-by-step log of the journey.

4. Avoid trite expressions

Many people beat cliches to death in their conversations. Don't let yourself be described as "a person of few words who uses them over and over again."

"Slang," says Amy Vanderbilt, "can lend a little color to your conversation. But it can easily become second nature, so you seem to suffer from a poverty of language." Your conversation will be much brighter if you use meaningful words.

And don't quote yourself. Few of us are so witty as Bernard Shaw, who could say, "I often quote myself. It adds spice to my conversation!"

5. Make yourself clear

You may have a good mind, but unless you express yourself logically you may be thought stupid. Don't jump from topic to topic. Conversation is more interesting when you stick to one subject long enough for give-and-take enjoyment of it. "The best conversationalists keep the talk concrete so that the emotions get engaged

as well as the mind," says University of Iowa English professor John C. Gerber.

When being introduced, beware of unclear expressions such as "I've heard so much about you!" The person hearing it may wonder. "Just *what* has he heard?" It's unwise to remark, "My, how you've changed!" The other person often wonders, "Have I changed for the better or worse?"

You can add to clarity of speech by looking a person in the face when talking with (not *at*) him. Don't talk so softly that others have to lean forward to hear you.

And don't make your conversation difficult to understand by slurring words together.

6. *Ask questions sincerely*

Most people are complimented when you ask their opinion or advice, for you are giving them a sense of superiority. If you learn how to ask questions sincerely, your conversation will improve tremendously.

At a party, the best way to get people to talk is to put them at ease, so ask questions that establish a rapport by showing sincere interest. People talk most easily when they are relaxed.

I once met a shy chap named Leo Godowsky at a Connecticut party. I knew nothing about him, but within 10 minutes I had learned that he was married to George Gershwin's sister Frances; his father had been a famous composer-pianist; and because his father outranked him as a musician, he had turned to color photography—a field in which he made many important inventions.

If you find yourself next to a shy person, don't tease him as a Washington society woman once did when she was seated near President Calvin Coolidge at a

dinner party. "Oh, Mr. President," she said, "I made a bet today that I could get you to say more than two words." "You lose," deadpanned taciturn Calvin.

7. *Use tact when you disagree*

One secret of successful conversation is learning to disagree without being disagreeable. It isn't what but *how* you speak that often makes all the difference. Ben Franklin used to remark diplomatically, "On this point, I agree. But on the other, if you don't mind, may I take exception?"

Arguments about politics, religion, or divorce used to be taboo. But nowadays a friendly argument on controversial topics often enriches a conversation. "Today almost any topic is discussible, if there is a reason to discuss it and if the discussion is conducted with taste and discretion," Amy Vanderbilt believes.

But don't start an argument with a sweeping statement such as, "I loathe Tennessee Williams' plays. His characters are degenerate." Such an opinionated remark will cause all sides to line up too violently for polite conversation.

And don't argue about facts. Be more interested in where the conversation is leading than in winning an argument over some trivial fact.

Most important, don't flatly contradict anybody—even when you're sure he is wrong. Use subtlety.

8. *Think before you interrupt*

To interrupt is often discourteous, but sometimes you feel obliged to break into a conversation. Your interruption will appear less offensive if you use a graceful

phrase such as, "John, may I add something to what you just said?" or "Your story, Alice, reminds me of . . ."

Never interrupt anyone just to tell a story. You don't have to tell stories to be a good conversationalist. People who tell joke after joke aren't so popular as is generally believed. Your story should be told spontaneously and fit the occasion. Some of the biggest bores I know will interrupt a serious discussion to tell the latest parlor joke.

9. Develop a tolerant attitude

It's difficult to enjoy the conversation of someone who annoys you. But try to distinguish between what is said and the person who is saying it. Facts, after all, are impersonal. Concentrate on the subject under discussion. If you try to develop a tolerant attitude — even toward tactless individuals — you'll be a much better conversationalist.

The best way to handle tactless remarks is to parry them. Occasionally at a party someone used to say to me, "You look like———————[an actor who's no matinee idol]." I'd smile and say, "Gee, I'm lucky to have a double. I wish I had his bank account."

Think before you speak! Everything that pops into your head isn't necessarily wise to say. You can make enemies for life through a thoughtless remark or a story that is embarrassing or hurtful to someone in your group.

10. Be generous in giving praise

Everybody enjoys being admired for something. Your conversation will be richer if you learn how to

---

Conversational Avoiding

Roger Price

No subject affords greater opportunities for study and promises richer rewards than conversational avoiding.

Because of the volume of talk that constantly floods civilization, the beginning avoidist will sometimes be trapped into listening to what is being said to him. There is a great danger here (of becoming involved in something, usually more listening), and the following rule should be obeyed at all times:

THE ONLY THING AN AVOIDIST EVER LISTENS TO IS NOTHING.

Frequently, though, you will find it necessary to take certain steps to make sure that there is nothing for you not to listen to (this sentence must be read twice before it makes any sense). Hence, avoidist conversation.

Avoidist conversation should be employed immediately when anyone inclines his torso toward you at an angle of more than ninety degrees.

Whenever this sort of danger threatens (or any other time you feel like it), you may avoid by employing eight tested remarks of such extreme dullness that the avoidee will experience a partial paralysis lasting approximately four minutes, while trying to think up an answer. These remarks are:

1. A girl I used to go with when I was in high school just got a job with the Telephone Company.

2. I got this suit three years ago in Pittsburgh for fifty dollars.

3. I went to bed early last night, but I didn't get to sleep until after midnight.

4. I ate hardly anything for lunch today, just a salad and some pie and coffee.

5. I read in the papers that Alf Landon is going back into politics.

6. My little boy will be eight years old next month. You oughta hear him talk.

7. I sure wish I'd kept up with my piano lessons when I was a kid.

8. I can take better pictures with a little Brownie box camera than I can with those real expensive ones.

(Note: When traveling, the following may be substituted for No. 5: "I used to live down that street.")

Memorize these eight tested remarks and use them at every opportunity. Properly spaced, they should keep the avoidee off balance and silent for a period of thirty minutes. At the end of that time, if danger still exists, start all over again, repeating the same speeches, word for word.

Use only these tested remarks at first. Later, once you have mastered the timing and proper descending inflection, you will be able to improvise your own remarks indefinitely.

If you cannot remember the eight tested remarks, just mutter. Try reciting the names of all the state capitals without moving the lips.

...THE ART OF COMMUNICATION SUFFERS SOMEWHAT AT THE CONVERSATIONAL LEVEL.

compliment people sincerely and naturally.

Several years ago I called on Bernard Baruch to get a story. He politely declined to talk, and started to usher me out. I commented on a large oil painting of him over his living-room fireplace. "That's a very good picture of you," I observed. "Oh, that's not *really* a good picture of me," he said. "I was too stern then. I was thinking about the atom bomb." And the Elder Statesman then talked frankly with me for an hour. I didn't get the story that I'd come for, but I left with a much better one.

Sometimes it's suitable to use flattery in a kidding way. When I visited artist Norman Rockwell in Vermont I told him right off, "My editors want me to profile you because they consider you a 'Great Living American.' " "Me?" he laughed modestly. "That's a joke." But he enjoyed the remark, and I was off to a good start.

You can also flatter people by suggesting that they have hidden talents. Many big businessmen beam when I ask them, "With your gift for expression, did you ever consider becoming a writer?"

Used skillfully, flattery can cover social mistakes. At a party, I overheard a man introduce a lovely young woman by the wrong name. "My name is Sylvia, not Elizabeth," she corrected stiffly. "I'm sorry. I was thinking of Elizabeth Taylor, because you look so much like her," the man nonchalantly explained.

You can use flattery in voicing appreciation. Don't just tell your P.T.A. speaker, "I enjoyed your talk." Comment specifically on something he said, or ask him to amplify one of his remarks.

It's flattering to people when you remember their names. James Farley makes a point of remembering unusual names, such as "Hepzibah." The people he greets often say gratefully, "Why, you're the only person who ever remembered my name."

Try practicing the suggestions among these 10 that apply most to you. If you correct your conversational faults you'll get more—much more—out of life. You'll be able to talk to anybody, about anything.

Prods

1. How does a conversation with a friend differ from a public speech? Be as specific as you can; consider type of language, kinds of nonverbal behavior, and amount of risk involved.
2. Talk with the personnel director of a large organization about his or her interviewing style—the purpose of an interview, the criteria for judging its success, and the kinds of questions used.
3. Think of a conversation you recently had with a close friend. How might you have helped improve the conversation? What might the other person have done to improve it?
4. List five parent messages you received today. How have they influenced your behavior? Think of the way in which you use your Adult and Child. Describe two situations where both were used.
5. What TA games do you like to play? How do you know when you're playing them? What can you do to stop them?
6. With whom do you have intimate communication? Describe the relationships and explain how they differ from other relationships.

Differences in sender-receiver backgrounds, personalities, and expectations are likely to distort any message — especially one that is transmitted serially.

Alterations, omissions, and additions can occur in serially reproduced messages because of the motives and assumptions of communicators.

In organizations the grapevine distributes information to members through serial reproduction.

Rumors are transmitted when people use serial communication to reproduce messages during social conversation.

Relationship

2
Serial

Distortion in Communication

John R. Freund and Arnold Nelson

Differences in sender-receiver backgrounds, personalities, and expectations are likely to distort any message—especially one that is transmitted serially.

There is a children's game called "Telephone," in which a word or phrase is whispered from one child to another through a long series until, at the "end of the line," words emerge which generally bear little resemblance to the original message. Anyone who has played the game tends to attribute the distortion of the message either to the means of communication (whispering) or to the impulses of the children participating, which might lead them to distort the message deliberately in order that the game may be successful.

Few people realize that similar distortion occurs when adults participate, speak in normal tones and seek wholeheartedly to get the message through the series intact. . . . The distortion is not confined to superficial changes in wording, but works as much havoc upon the ideas contained in the original message as could be expected if they were to be subjected to deliberate misrepresentation. . . . The changes made by any one speaker are small in comparison to the cumulative effect of these changes. . . .

In ordinary communication between one sender and one receiver no message is transmitted without some change, however small. Frequently, though, the changes are so small as to go undetected, and their very existence rests upon deductions about what must be true rather than what can be seen to be true. If someone insists, for instance, that he knows exactly what I mean when I say, "I had a flat tire yesterday," I cannot dissuade him by pointing to a tangible change in the uttered message, or signal, as he repeats it. If, however, the communication process can be "stretched out" through serial reproduction of the message, the otherwise invisible changes in meaning can be detected in visible alterations in the reproduced signals. The process is somewhat like that by which plants and flowers can be "seen" growing in fast-motion movies.

A closer analogy exists in the occurrence of noise in high fidelity recording equipment. An expensive high fidelity set reduces noise to levels that cannot be detected by the ear. But that it still exists can be demonstrated by recording from one such set to another and back again several times. Each successive recording acquires all of the preceding noise and adds its own. The original signal, however, remains unreinforced; and if this process is carried on long enough, the signal will be lost in the accumulated noise.

But distortion in communication between human beings is more than just the effects of the accumulation of noise, as a brief analysis of the process will show. When one person talks to another, the message (which is transmit-

From "Distortion in Communication" by John R. Freund and Arnold Nelson in READINGS FOR COMMUNICATION, ed. Ralph N. Miller. © Communication Staff, Western Michigan University.

B.C. *by Johnny Hart*

By permission of John Hart and Field Enterprises, Inc.

ted as a signal only once) occurs in at least four different forms:

1. The message at its source (in the mind of the speaker before it is uttered)

2. The message as it is uttered (altered from its first form to fit the speaker's preconception of his listener's ability to understand him)

3. The message as it is perceived and retained by the listener (altered from its second form by the listener's individual background of experience)

4. The message as it is remembered by the listener (altered from its third form by the activity of selection and rejection)[1]

It can be seen, consequently, that the distortion that occurs in any particular message may be the result of a number of causes which are locked in the minds of the sender and the receiver and have nothing whatsoever to do with external "noise." Furthermore, we can see that by examining a serially reproduced message we will be able to see the results of an accumulation of these invisible changes, which frequently take the form of a definite change in the signal at the end of the series.

In order to understand the way in which a serially reproduced message is related to the normal communication process, the reader may wish to examine the following diagram. Here, the four forms of the message are represented by their numbers, as above.

Speaker	Speaker	Speaker	Speaker
A	B	C	D
3−4	1−2 --> 3−4		1−2
1−2 --> 3−4		1−2 --> 3−4	

Three things should be observed: first, only one form of the message (number 2) exists as an observable signal; second, each speaker is involved in all four forms of the message; and third, two forms of the message (numbers 1 and 4) are merged. This third point means that Speaker B in the diagram makes use of the fourth form of the message as the raw material out of which he frames his signal to Speaker C. Some interesting things happen in this merger but exactly how they happen is a complicated affair, more complicated than the terms "remembering" and "forgetting" suggest. Three causes of distortion that have impressed us are these:

1. The influence of the speaker's and listener's background of experience.

2. The influence of the personality of the speaker or listener.

3. The influence of faulty prediction on the part of speaker or listener.

The last item may need some clarification. Any kind of communication involves prediction on the part of both the speaker and listener. A speaker may have a faulty "image" of his listener and alter the signal on the basis of that image. This alteration could easily yield a confused impression for the listener. Or the listener may have a very fixed notion of what the speaker is going to say, and this predictive "set" will cause him to fail to perceive or recall the actual signal.

One further cause of distortion ought to be mentioned inasmuch as it is very nearly confined to serially reproduced messages: this is the sweeping, structural change that occasionally alters a message so drastically that we are at a loss to explain the

Original Message

Speaker A

Speaker B

Speaker C

Speaker D

Speaker E

change in terms of what was contained in the message immediately preceding it. Our first guess is likely to be that we have come upon a very weak link in a chain of listeners. The explanation becomes clear, however, when we examine the whole series. If we do so, we can see that in every retelling of the message more details of varying importance are lost or altered slightly. As a result of the steady, somewhat random loss of details, the structure of the whole message tends to become imbalanced and finally unstable. This is accompanied by a corresponding strain upon the mind of the listener. The results of the strain are finally manifested in a reordering of all the details into a new form which "makes sense" and is structurally satisfying, even though it is an extreme distortion of the original message. The diagram at left attemps to illustrate this kind of structural change. Imagine that the geometric figures represent the "meaning" of the whole message and that each dot stands for a detail.

It can be seen that the original triangle slowly loses one of its supporting corners. To us, it still vaguely resembles the original triangle, but we must remember that Speaker E receives only what is sent by Speaker D. To him, apparently, it resembles nothing, and therefore he feels obliged to alter it into the neat little symmetrical figure that becomes his message.

This brings us to a final question. What can be learned from observing the process of serial reproduction besides the somewhat dismal generalization that all communication tends toward distortion? Can anything be done to halt—or at least to retard—distortion? A few general principles may be offered, which, however, are not easily observed in practice.

First, if there is an opportunity for feedback to be employed, it helps to diminish distortion. A better term, perhaps, is "reverberation," for feedback from the listener must be coupled with "feed forward" on the part of the speaker, an attitude which anticipates verbally difficulties which the listener may not realize he is encountering. Successful reverberation—immensely difficult to achieve—is probably the greatest single deterrent to distortion in any kind of communication.

The two final principles are somewhat related to reverberation. The first applies to the sender of the message. He must endeavor to exercise forward responsibility. Speaker B has a powerful urge to feel responsible to Speaker A—to deliver A's message intact. This urge frequently overwhelms the much more important responsibility that B has to Speaker C. The result of a failure to exercise forward responsibility is loss of contact with the listener—and, of course, distortion.

Finally, the listener has the responsibility of maintaining the faculties of prediction and recall in a state of equilibrium. While he is listening he must constantly predict what he thinks the message is going to be, and just as constantly check his predictions and alter them on the basis of what he can recall of what has actually been said.

In spite of everything, something of the original message will be lost if the signal is not short enough to be memorized. Paradoxically, an awareness of this fact is often of aid in bringing about the attitude that is most conducive to the preservation of the message.

1. Ian M. L. Hunter, in *Memory: Facts and Fallacies* (Baltimore, Penguin Books Inc., 1957), pp. 14–16, distinguishes "retention" from "remembering" in the following way: Retention is an unobservable brain process which is "a necessary condition for remembering for, without it, there would be nothing to remember." Remembering is a process "by means of which the effects of past learning manifest themselves in the present," and is able to be observed, at least somewhat.

Serial Communication of Information in Organizations

William V. Haney

An appreciable amount of the communication which occurs in business, industry, hospitals, military units, government agencies— in short, in chain-of-command organizations—consists of serial transmissions. *A* communicates a message to *B*; *B* then communicates *A*'s message (or rather his *interpretation* of *A*'s message) to *C*; *C* then communicates his interpretation of *B*'s interpretation of *A*'s message to *D*; and so on. The originator and the ultimate recipient of the message[1] are separated by "middle men."

"The message" may often be passed down (but not necessarily all the way down) the organization chain, as when in business the chairman acting on behalf of the board of directors may express a desire to the president. "The message" begins to fan out as the president, in turn, relays "it" to his vice presidents; they convey "it" to their respective subordinates; and so forth. Frequently "a message" goes up (but seldom all the way up) the chain. Sometimes "it" travels laterally. Sometimes, as with rumors, "it" disregards the formal organization and flows more closely along informal organizational lines.

Regardless of its direction, the number of "conveyors" involved, and the degree of its conformance with the formal structure, serial transmission is clearly an essential, inevitable form of communication in organizations. It is equally apparent that serial transmission is especially susceptible to distortion and disruption. Not only is it subject to the shortcomings and maladies of "simple" person-to-person communication but, since it consists of a series of such communications, the anomalies are often *compounded*.

This is not to say, however, that serial transmissions in organizations should be abolished or even decreased. We wish to show that such communications *can be improved* if communicators are able (1) to recognize some of the patterns of miscommunication which occur in serial transmissions; (2) to understand some of the factors contributing to these patterns; (3) to take measures and practice techniques for preventing the recurrence of these patterns and for ameliorating their consequences.

I shall begin by cataloguing some of the factors which seem-

Alterations, omissions, and additions can occur in serially reproduced messages because of the motives and assumptions of communicators.

William V. Haney, "Serial Communication of Information in Organizations" in CONCEPTS AND ISSUES IN ADMINISTRATIVE BEHAVIOR, Sidney Mailick and Edward H. Van Ness, Eds., © 1962. Reprinted by permission of Prentice-Hall, Inc., Englewood Cliffs, New Jersey.

WHY YOU Ⓧⓔ☆!!, Ⓧⓔ☆!!.

A TRUE POET ALWAYS RHYMES HIS CUSS WORDS.

12·15

ingly influence a serial transmission.

Motives of the Communicators

When *B* conveys *A*'s message to *C* he may be influenced by at least three motives of which he may be largely unaware.

The Desire to Simplify the Message

We evidently dislike conveying detailed messages. The responsibility of passing along complex information is burdensome and taxing. Often, therefore, we unconsciously simplify the message before passing it along to the next person. It is very probable that among the details most susceptible to omission are those we already knew or in some way presume our recipients will know without our telling them.

The Desire to Convey a "Sensible" Message

Apparently we are reluctant to relay a message that is somehow incoherent, illogical, or incomplete. It may be embarrassing to admit that one does not fully understand the message he is conveying. When he receives a message that does not quite make sense to him he is prone to "make sense out of it" before passing it along to the next person.

The Desire to Make the Conveyance of the Message as Pleasant and/or Painless as Possible for the Conveyor

We evidently do not like to have to tell the boss unpleasant things. Even when not directly responsible, one does not relish the reaction of his superior to a disagreeable message. This motive probably accounts for a considerable

share of the tendency for a "message" to lose its harshness as it moves up the organizational ladder. The first line supervisor may tell his foreman, "I'm telling you, Mike, the men say that if this pay cut goes through they'll strike—and they mean it!" By the time "this message" has been relayed through six or eight or more echelons (if indeed it goes that far) the executive vice president might express it to the president as, "Well, sir, the men seem a little concerned over the projected wage reduction but I am confident that they will take it in stride."

One of the dangers plaguing some upper managements is that they are effectively shielded from incipient problems until they become serious and costly ones.

Assumptions of the Communicators

In addition to the serial transmitter's motives we must consider his assumptions—particularly those he makes about his communications. If some of these assumptions are fallacious and if one is unaware that he holds them, his communication can be adversely affected. The following are, in this writer's judgment, two of the most pervasive and dangerous of the current myths about communication.

The Assumption That Words Are Used in Only One Way

A study indicates that for the 500 most commonly used words in our language there are 14,070 different dictionary definitions— over 28 usages per word, on the average.[2] Take the word *run*, for example:

> Babe Ruth scored a *run*.
> Did you ever see Jesse Owens *run*?

I have a *run* in my stocking.
There is a fine *run* of salmon this
year.
Are you going to *run* this company
or am I?
You have the *run* of the place.
Don't give me the *run* around.
What headline do you want to *run*?
There was a *run* on the bank today.
Did he *run* the ship aground?
I have to *run* (drive the car) down-
town.
Who will *run* for President this
year?
Joe flies the New York-Chicago *run*
twice a week.
You know the kind of people they
run around with.
The apples *run* large this year.
Please *run* my bath water.

We could go on at some length
—my small abridged dictionary
gives eighty-seven distinct usages
for *run*. I have chosen an extreme example, of course, but
there must be relatively few
words (excepting some technical
terms) used in one and in only
one sense.

Yet communicators often have
a curious notion about words
when they are using them, i.e.,
when they are speaking, writing,
listening, or reading. It is immensely easy for a "sender" of a
communication to assume that
words are used in only one way—
the way he intends them. It is
just as enticing for the "receiver"
to assume that the sender intended his words as he, the receiver,
happens to interpret them at the
moment. When communicators
are unconsciously burdened by
the assumption of the mono-usage
of words they are prone to become
involved in the pattern of miscommunication known as *bypassing*.

*Bypassing: Denotative and Con-
notative.* Since we use words to
express at least two kinds of
meanings there can be two kinds
of bypassings. Suppose you say to

**As Teachers
Requested It**   **As Coordinators
Ordered It**   **As Curriculum Staff
Wrote It**

**As the Art Department
Designed It**   **As Teachers
Implemented It**   **What the
Student Wanted**

From a mimeographed school publication in a Utah school district.

me, "Your neighbor's grass is certainly green and healthy looking, isn't it?" You could be intending your words merely to *denote*, i.e., to point to or to call my attention, to the appearance of my neighbor's lawn. On the other hand, you could have intended your words to *connote*, i.e., to imply something beyond or something other than what you were ostensibly denoting. You might have meant any number of things: that my own lawn needed more care; that my neighbor was inordinately meticulous about his lawn; that my neighbor's lawn is tended by a professional, a service you do not have and for which you envy or despise my neighbor; or even that his grass was not green at all but, on the contrary, parched and diseased; and so forth.

Taking these two kinds of meanings into account it is clear that bypassing occurs or can occur under any of four conditions:

1. *When the sender intends one denotation while the receiver interprets another.*

2. *When the sender intends one connotation while the receiver interprets another.*

A friend once told me of an experience she had had years ago when as a teenager she was spending the week with a maiden aunt. Joan had gone to the movies with a young man who brought her home at a respectable hour. However, the couple lingered on the front porch somewhat longer than Aunt Mildred thought necessary. The little old lady was rather proud of her ability to deal with younger people so she slipped out of bed, raised her bedroom window, and called down sweetly, "If you two knew how pleasant it is in bed, you wouldn't be standing out there in the cold."

3. *When the sender intends only a denotation while the receiver interprets a connotation.*

For a brief period the following memorandum appeared on the bulletin boards of a government agency in Washington: *Those department and sections heads who do not have secretaries assigned to them may take advantage of the stenographers in the secretarial pool.*

4. *When the sender intends a connotation while the receiver interprets a denotation only.*

The Assumption That Inferences Are Always Distinguishable from Observations

It is incredibly difficult, at times, for a communicator (or anyone) to discriminate between what he "knows" (i.e., what he has actually observed—seen, heard, read, etc.) and what he is only inferring or guessing. One of the key reasons for this lies in the character of the language used to express observations and inferences.

Suppose you look at a man and observe that he is wearing a white shirt and then say, "That man is wearing a white shirt." Assuming your vision and the illumination were "normal" you would have made a statement of *observation*—a statement which directly corresponded to and was corroborated by your observation. But suppose you now say, "That man bought the white shirt he is wearing." Assuming you were not present when and if the man bought the shirt that statement would be *for you a statement of inference*. Your statement went *beyond* what you observed. You inferred that the man bought the shirt; you did not observe it. Of course, your inference may be correct (but it could be false: perhaps he was given the shirt as a gift; perhaps he stole it or borrowed it; etc.).

Nothing in the nature of our

Blondie by Chic Young

© King Features Syndicate, Inc., 1972.

language (the grammar, spelling, pronunciation, accentuation, syntax, inflection, etc.) prevents you from speaking or writing (or thinking) a statement of inference *as if* you were making a statement of observation. Our language permits you to say "Of course, he bought the shirt" with certainty and finality, i.e., with as much confidence as you would make a statement of observation. The effect is that it becomes exceedingly easy to confuse the two kinds of statements and also to confuse inference and observation on nonverbal levels. The destructive consequences of acting upon inference as if acting upon observation can range from mild embarrassment to tragedy. . . .

Trends in Serial Transmission

These assumptions,[3] the mono-usage of words, and the inference-observation confusion, as well as the aforementioned motives of the communicators, undoubtedly contribute a significant share of the difficulties and dangers which beset a serial transmission. Their effect tends to be manifested by three trends: omission, alteration, and addition.

Details Become Omitted

It requires less effort to convey a simpler, less complex message. With fewer details to transmit the fear of forgetting or of garbling the message is decreased. . . . The essential question, perhaps, is which details *will be retained*?

1. Those details the transmitter wanted or expected to hear.

2. Those details which "made sense" to the transmitter.

3. Those details which seemed important *to the transmitter*.

4. Those details which for various and inexplicable reasons seemed to stick with the transmitter—those aspects which seemed particularly unusual or bizarre; those which had special significance to him; etc.

Details Become Altered

Among the details most susceptible to change were the qualifications, the indefinite. Inferential statements are prone to become definite and certain. What may start out as "The boss seemed angry this morning" may quickly progress to "The boss was angry."

A well-known psychologist once "planted" a rumor in an enlisted men's mess hall on a certain Air Force base. His statement was: "Is it true that they are building a tunnel big enough to trundle B-52's to—(the town two miles away)?" Twelve hours later the rumor came back to him as: "They are building a tunnel to trundle B-52's to—." The "Is-it-true" uncertainty had been dropped. So had the indefinite purpose ("big enough to").

Details Become Added

Not infrequently details are added to the message to "fill in the gaps," "to make better sense," and "because I thought the fellow who told it to me left something out."

The psychologist was eventually told that not only were they building a tunnel for B-52's but that a mile-long underground runway was being constructed at the end of it! The runway was to have a ceiling slanting upward so that a plane could take off, fly up along the ceiling and emerge from an inconspicuous slit at the end of the cavern! This, he admitted, was a much more "sensible"

Permutation Personified

Despite telemetering advances, improvements in mechanical transmission of data and collating total knowledge, there are occasional breakdowns in communication. We're indebted to a traveler recently returned from Miami for this example.

Operation: Halley's Comet

A COLONEL issued the following directive to his executive officer:

"Tomorrow evening at approximately 2000 hours Halley's Comet will be visible in this area, an event which occurs only once every 75 years. Have the men fall out in the battalion area in fatigues, and I will explain this rare phenomenon to them. In case of rain, we will not be able to see anything, so assemble the men in the theater and I will show them films of it."

EXECUTIVE OFFICER to company commander:

"By order of the colonel, tomorrow at 2000 hours, Halley's Comet will appear above the battalion area. If it rains, fall the men out in fatigues. Then march to the theater where the rare phenomenon will take place something which occurs only once every 75 years."

COMPANY COMMANDER to lieutenant:

"By order of the colonel in fatigues at 2000 hours tomorrow evening. the phenomenal Halley's Comet will appear in the theater. In case of rain in the battalion area, the colonel will give another order, something which occurs once every 75 years."

LIEUTENANT to sergeant:

"Tomorrow at 2000 hours, the colonel will appear in the theater with Halley's Comet, something which happens every 75 years. If it rains, the colonel will order the comet into the battalion area."

SERGEANT to squad:

"When it rains tomorrow at 2000 hours, the phenomenal 75-year-old General Halley, accompanied by the Colonel, will drive his Comet through the battalion area theater in fatigues."

rumor than the one he had started, for the town had no facilities for take-offs and thus there was nothing which could have been done with the B-52's once they reached the end of the tunnel!

Distortion in serial communication can be reduced by being aware of sources of change and by systematically using ways to maintain accurate reproduction of messages.

Correctives[4]

Even serial transmissions, as intricate and as relatively uncontrolled communications as they are, can be improved. The suggestions below are not sensational panaceas. In fact, they are quite commonplace, common sense, but uncommonly used techniques.

1. *Take notes.*

2. *Give details in order.*
   Organized information is easier to understand and to remember. Choose a sequence (chronological, spatial, deductive, inductive, etc.) appropriate to the content and be consistent with it. For example, it may suit your purpose best to begin with a proposal followed by supporting reasons or to start with the reasons and work toward the proposal. In either case take care to keep proposals and reasons clearly distinguished rather than mixing them together indiscriminately.

3. *Be wary of bypassing.*
   If you are the receiver, query (ask the sender what he meant) and paraphrase (put

what you think he said or wrote into your own words and get the sender to check you). These simple techniques are effective yet infrequently practiced, perhaps because we are so positive we *know* what the other fellow means; perhaps because we hesitate to ask or rephrase for fear the other fellow (especially if he is the boss) will think less of us for not understanding the first time. Querying and para- phrasing are *two-way* respon- sibilities and the sender must be truly approchable by his receivers if the techniques are to be successful.

This checklist may be help- ful in avoiding bypassing:

Could he be denoting something other than what I am?
Could he be connoting something other than what I am?
Could he be connoting whereas I am merely denoting?
Could he be merely denoting whereas I am connoting?

4. *Distinguish between infer- ence and observation.*
Ask yourself sharply: Did I *really* see, hear, or read this— or am I guessing part of it? The essential characteristics of a statement of observation are these:

   1. It can be made only by the observer.
      (What someone tells you as observational is still inferential for you if you did not observe it.)
   2. It can be made only *after* observation.
   3. It stays with what has been observed; does not go beyond it.

This is not to say that infer- ential statements are not to be made—we could hardly avoid doing so. But it is important

A Communications Problem

A U.S. Navy court of inquiry has reported its finding on the Israeli attack June 8 on the *USS Liberty,* and it is an amazing document, not so much for what it says as for what is left unsaid.

It should not be surprising that the court of inquiry did not make a judgment, for it could not, on the reasons for the attack, which killed 34 Americans and wounded 75. Israel has apologized and said the attack was made in error, and a final judgment must await the evidence from her side which was outside the naval court of inquiry's jurisdiction.

But surely it is most surprising to learn from the Navy's finding that hours before the *Liberty* was hit the Joint Chiefs of Staff had ordered her to move far- ther from the Sinai coast, and that "the messages were misrouted, delayed and not received until after the attack." The *Liberty* at the time was in international waters, but no closer than 13.6 nautical miles from land.

Our government has said that the *Liberty* was there to provide radio commu- nications in case an American evacuation from the Middle East became neces- sary. That seems fair enough—but is it all?

The *Liberty* was not just another communications ship. She contained all the latest, sophisticated electronic gear, and may well have had the capacity to eavesdrop on land communications near by. The Pentagon has declined com- ment on reports that her mission was to monitor Israeli and Egyptian radio transmissions from the battlefield.

Readers will recall that after the war began, Israel was able to quote por- tions of a phone conversation between Egypt's Nasser and Jordan's King Hus- sein in which they discussed plans, later carried out, to try to blame the United States for the destruction of their planes. Here was another example of the fruits of electronic monitoring.

But the shocking thing in the court of inquiry's finding was the failure, some- where between the Joint Chiefs of Staff in Washington and the eastern Mediter- ranean, to communicate quickly with the most modern communications ship in the world.

The warning implicit in this applies not merely to the Navy's communications system, but to the communications network whose use or misuse can control all of our many terrible weapons of destruction.

Congress ought to find out more about it, and sooner than it took the Penta- gon to get a message to the *Liberty.*

Courtesy of the Boston Globe: Editorial "A Communications Problem" June 30, 1967.

or even vital at times to know *when* we are making them.

5. *Slow down your oral transmissions.*
   By doing so, you give your listener a better opportunity to assimilate complex and detailed information. However, it is possible to speak too slowly so as to lose his attention. Since either extreme defeats your purpose, it is generally wise to watch the listener for clues as to the most suitable rate of speech.

6. *Simplify the message.*
   This suggestion is for the *originator* of the message. The "middle-men" often simplify without half trying! Most salesmen realize the inadvisability of attempting to sell too many features at a time. The customer is only confused and is unable to distinguish the key features from those less important. With particular respect to oral transmission, there is impressive evidence to indicate that beyond a point the addition of details leads to disproportionate omission.

7. *Use dual media when feasible.*
   A message often stands a better chance of getting through if it is reinforced by restatement in another communication medium. Detailed, complex, and unfamiliar information is often transmitted by such combinations as a memo follow-up on a telephone call; a sensory aid (slide, diagram, mockup, picture, etc.) accompanying a written or oral message, etc.

8. *Highlight the important.*
   Presumably the originator of a message knows which are its important aspects. But this does not automatically insure that his serial transmitters will similarly recognize them. There are numerous devices for making salient points stand out as such; e.g., using underscoring, capitals, etc., in writing; using vocal emphasis, attention-drawing phrases ("this is the main point . . . ." "here's the crux . . .," "be sure to note this . . ."), etc., in speaking.

9. *Reduce the number of links in the chain.*
   This suggestion has to be followed with discretion. Jumping the chain of command either upward or downward can sometimes have undesirable consequences. However, whenever it is possible to reduce or eliminate the "middlemen," "the message" generally becomes progressively less susceptible to aberrations. Of course, there are methods of skipping links which are commonly accepted and widely practiced. Communication downward can be reduced to person-to-person communication, in a sense, with general memos, letters, bulletins, group meetings, etc. Communication upward can accomplish the same purpose via suggestion boxes, opinion questionnaires, "talk-backs," etc.

10. *Preview and review.*
    A wise speech professor of mine used to say: "Giving a speech is basically very simple if you do it in three steps: First, you tell them what you're going to tell them; then you tell; then, finally, you tell them what you've told them." This three step sequence is often applicable whether the message is transmitted by letter, memo, writ-

ten or oral report, public address, telephone call, etc.

Summary

After the last suggestion I feel obliged to review this article briefly. We have been concerned with serial transmission—a widespread, essential, and yet susceptible form of communication. Among the factors which vitiate a serial transmission are certain of the communicator's motives and fallacious assumptions. When these and other factors are in play the three processes—omission, alteration, and addition—tend to occur. The suggestions offered for strengthening serial transmission will be more or less applicable, of course, depending upon the communication situation.

An important question remains: What can be done to encourage communicators to practice the techniques? They will probably use them largely to the extent that they think the techniques are needed. But do they think them necessary? Apparently many do not. When asked to explain how the final version came to differ so markedly from the original, many of the the serial transmitters in my studies were genuinely puzzled. A frequent comment was "I really can't understand it. All I know is that I passed the message along the same as it came to me." If messages were passed along "the same as they came," of course, serial transmission would no longer be a problem. And so long as the illusion of fidelity is with the communicator it is unlikely that he will be prompted to apply some of these simple, prosaic, yet effective techniques to his communicating. Perhaps a first step would be to induce him to question his unwarranted assurance about his communication. The controlled serial transmission experience appears to accomplish this.

---

1. "The message," as already suggested, is a misnomer in that what is being conveyed is not static, unchanging, and fixed. I shall retain the term for convenience, however, and use quotation marks to signify that its dynamic nature is subject to cumulative change.

2. Lydia Strong, "Do You Know How to Listen?" *Effective Communication on the Job*, Dooher and Marquis, eds. (New York: American Management Association, 1956), p. 28.

3. For a more detailed analysis of these assumptions and for additional methods for preventing and correcting their consequences, see Willian V. Haney, *Communication: Patterns and Incidents* (Homewood, Ill.: Irwin, 1960), chs. III, IV, V.

4. Most of these suggestions are offered by Irving J. and Laura L. Lee, *Handling Barriers in Communication* (New York: Harper & Bros., 1956), pp. 71–74.

Management Communication and the Grapevine

Keith Davis

Professor of Management, Arizona State University, Tempe, Arizona

A particularly neglected aspect of management communication concerns that informal channel, the grapevine. There is no dodging the fact that, as a carrier of news and gossip among executives and supervisors, the grapevine often affects the affairs of management. The proof of this is the strong feelings that different executives have about it. Some regard the grapevine as an evil— a thorn in the side which regularly spreads rumor, destroys morale and reputations, leads to irresponsible actions, and challenges authority. Some regard it as a good thing because it acts as a safety valve and carries news fast. Others regard it as a very mixed blessing.

Whether the grapevine is considered an asset or a liability, it is important for executives to try to understand it. For one thing is sure: although no executive can absolutely control the grapevine, he can *influence* it. And since it is here to stay, he should learn to live with it.

As for the research basis of the analysis, the major points are these:

1. *Company studied*—The company upon which the research is based is a real one. I shall refer to it as the "Jason Company." A manufacturer of leather goods, it has 67 people in the management group (that is, all people who supervise the work of others, from top executives to foremen) and about 600 employees. It is located in a rural town of 10,000 persons, and its products are distributed nationally.

In organizations the grapevine distributes information to members through serial reproduction.

2. *Methodology*—The methods used to study management communication in the Jason Company are new ones. Briefly, the basic approach was to learn from each communication recipient how he first received a given piece of information and then to trace it back to its source.

Significant Characteristics

In the Jason Company many of the usual grapevine characteristics were found along with others less well known. For purposes of this discussion, the four most

Abridged from "Management Communication and the Grapevine" by Keith Davis in *Harvard Business Review*, Jan.-Feb., 1953, 31: 43–49. © 1953 by the President and Fellows of Harvard College; all rights reserved.

Blondie by Chic Young

significant characteristics are these:

1. *Speed of transmission* — Traditionally the grapevine is fast, and this showed up in the Jason Company.

2. *Degree of selectivity* — It is often said that the grapevine acts without conscious direction or thought — that it will carry anything, any time, anywhere. This viewpoint has been epitomized in the statement that "the grapevine is without conscience or consciousness." But flagrant grapevine irresponsibility was not evident in the Jason Company. In fact, the grapevine here showed that it could be highly selective and discriminating. Whether it may be *counted on* in that respect, however, is another question. The answer would of course differ with each case and would depend on many variables, including other factors in the communication picture having to do with attitudes, executive relationships, and so forth.

3. *Locale of operation* — The grapevine of company news operates mostly at the place of work. Since management has some control over the work environment, it has an opportunity to influence the grapevine. By exerting such influence the manager can more closely integrate grapevine interests with those of the formal communication system, and he can use it for effectively spreading more significant items of information than those commonly carried.

4. *Relation to formal communication* — Formal and informal communication systems tend to be jointly active, or jointly inactive. Where formal communication was inactive at the Jason Company, the grapevine did not rush in to fill the void; instead, there simply was lack of communication. Similarly, where there was effective formal communication, there was an active grapevine.

Informal and formal communication may supplement each other. Often formal communication is simply used to confirm or to expand what has already been communicated by grapevine. This necessary process of confirmation results partly because of the speed of the grapevine, which formal systems fail to match, partly because of its unofficial function, and partly because of its transient nature. Formal communication needs to come along to stamp "Official" on the news and to put it "on the record," which the grapevine cannot suitably do.

Spreading Information

Human communication requires at least two persons, but each person acts independently. Person A may talk or write, but he has not *communicated* until person B receives. The individual is, therefore, a basic communication unit. That is, he is one "link" in the communication "chain" for any bit of information.

The formal communication chain is largely determined by the chain of command or by formal procedures, but the grapevine chain is more flexible. There are four different ways of visualizing it, as Exhibit I indicates:

1. *The single-strand chain* — A tells B, who tells C, who tells D, and so on; this makes for a

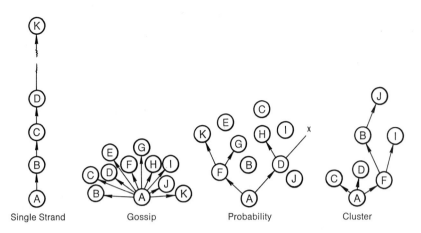

Exhibit I. *Types of communication chains*

Single Strand   Gossip   Probability   Cluster

tenuous chain to a distant receiver. Such a chain is usually in mind when one speaks of how the grapevine distorts and filters information until the original item is not recognizable.

2. *The gossip chain* — A seeks and tells everyone else.

3. *The probability chain* — A communicates randomly, say, to F and D, in accordance with the laws of probability; then F and D tell others in the same manner.

4. *The cluster chain* — A tells three selected others; perhaps one of them tells two others; and then one of these two tells one other. This was virtually the only kind of chain found in the Jason Company, and may well be the normal one in industry generally.

Active Minority

The predominance of the cluster chain at the Jason Company means that only a few of the persons who knew a unit of information ever transmitted it — what Jacobson and Seashore call the "liaison" individuals.[1] All others who received the information did not transmit it; they acted merely as passive receivers.

For example, when a quality-control problem occurred, 68% of the executives received the information, but only 20% transmitted it. Again, when an executive planned to resign to enter the insurance business, 81% of the executives knew about it, but only 11% passed the news on to others. Those liaison individuals who told the news to more than one other person amounted to less than 10% of the 67 executives in each case.

These active groups varied in membership. There was no evidence that any one group consistently acted as liaison persons; instead, different types of information passed through different liaison persons. However, as will be shown later, some individuals were invariably communication "isolates"; they received and transmitted information poorly or not at all.

The above findings indicate that if management wants more communication, it should increase the number and/or effectiveness of its liaison individuals.

Liaison individuals tend to act in a predictable way. If an individual's unit of information concerns a job function in which he is interested, he is likely to tell others. If his information is about a person with whom he is associated socially, he also is likely to tell others. Furthermore, the sooner he knows of an event after it happened, the more likely he is to tell others.

In other words, three well-known communication principles which are so often mentioned in relation to attitudes also have a major influence on the spread of information by liaison individuals:

1. Tell people about what will affect them (job interest).

2. Tell people what they want to know, rather than simply what you want them to know (job and social interest).

3. Tell people soon (timing).

Conclusion

If management wants to do a first-class communication job, at this stage it needs fewer medicines and more diagnoses. Communication analysis has now passed beyond "pure research" to a point where it is immediately useful to top management in the individual firm. The patterns of communication that show up should serve to indicate both the areas where communication is most deficient and the channels through which information can be made to flow most effectively.

In particular, no administrator in his right mind would try to abolish the management grapevine. It is as permanent as humanity is. Nevertheless, many administrators have abolished the grapevine from *their own minds.* They think and act without giving adequate weight to it or, worse, try to ignore it. This is a mistake. The grapevine is a factor to be reckoned with in the affairs of management. The administrator should analyze it and should consciously try to influence it.

1. Eugene Jacobson and Stanley E. Seashore, "Communication Practices in Complex Organizations," *The Journal of Social Issues*, vol. VII, no. 3, 1951, p. 37.

The Basic Law of Rumor

A large part of ordinary social conversation consists of rumor mongering. In our daily chitchat we both take in and give out lungfuls of gossip or rumor.

The two basic conditions for rumor are that (1) the theme of the rumored story must have some importance to the speaker and listener and (2) the true facts of the story being rumored must be ambiguous in some way. The amount of rumor in circulation varies with the importance of the subject to the individuals concerned and the ambiguity of the evidence pertaining to the topics at issue. The relation between importance and ambiguity is multiplicative, for if either aspect is zero, there is no rumor.

For instance, a U.S. citizen is not likely to spread rumors concerning the market price for camels in Afghanistan; the subject has no importance for him, ambiguous though it is. Ambiguity alone does not launch or sustain rumor. Nor does importance. If I receive a legacy and know the amount involved, I am resistant to rumors that exaggerate its amount. Knowledge through education is a main factor in eliminating ambiguity and rumor.

Purposes or Motives in Rumor Transmission

Any human need may provide the motive power to rumor. Sex interest accounts for much gossip and scandal; anxiety is the power behind the macabre and threatening tales we often hear; hope and desire underlie pipe-dream rumors; and hate sustains accusatory tales and slander. Rumor relieves primary emotional urges. It justifies a person's feelings about a situation and explains why he feels that way. Thus rumor serves the major end of rationalization, which is one way we order a disorganized situation.

To find a plausible reason for a confused situation is itself a motive, and this pursuit of closure helps to account for the vitality of many rumors that are born out of curiosity. For example, a stranger whose business is unknown to the small town where he takes up residence will breed many rumors about why he has come to town.

Rumors are transmitted when people use serial communication to reproduce messages during social conversation.

A rumor spreader is usually unaware of the extent to which he reflects himself in the stories he spreads. If the story we hear gives an interpretation of reality that conforms to our secret lives, we tend to believe and transmit it. We project ourselves and our desires into our interpretation and continuation of rumor.

Characteristics of Rumor

Rumor is ordinarily specific or topical; it deals with clearly ident-

---

Adapted from a student paper for an undergraduate course in organizational communication. Student's name unknown.

ified events or personalities—e.g., Mrs. X, a movie actor, the Russians. Hearsay reports of happenings, gossip, slander, and hopeful or dire predictions of coming events are among the concrete forms that rumor takes.

A rumor implies that a truth is being communicated. This implication holds even when the teller prefaces his tidbit with the warning, "It is only a rumor, but I heard. . . ."

Rumor thrives in the absence of secure standards of evidence. This criterion is akin to ambiguity. Also closely related is the principle of distortion, which we find in most forms of human communication, including legends, courtroom testimony, recounting of past experiences, witticisms, proverbs, biography, and even the writing of history. Since we cannot always know when secure standards of evidence are present, we often cannot tell whether we are listening to fact or fantasy. In rumor the source of evidence often recedes to nothing more than "They say . . ." or "I have it on good authority. . . ."

When the standards of evidence are within the informant himself, we must judge whether our informant really knows what he is talking about. We can be fairly sure that a scientist telling us about his specialty is not passing on a rumor. Our physician is less prone than our friends to believe or tell rumors of magical cures or improbable epidemics. All individuals have within themselves secure, standards of evidence concerning matters in which they are expert. It is often difficult for an outsider, however, to judge the degree of their expertness and impartiality.

On most matters, we are all inexpert, and to that extent are rumor prone. We have neither time nor patience to check what we hear against outside standards of evidence, even when such standards are available. In general, a healthy scepticism is far more advisable than gullibility.

Prods

1. What can happen in a conversation with a friend when either or both of you assume that you know what the other is talking about? What can you do to check your assumptions? Try one of them.

2. Ask a friend who works in a large organization to describe to you the number and order of steps in which a message travels from a high-ranking manager to a low-ranking employee. What are the potential sources of distortion in that network?

3. Identify an instance where distortion in the serial reproduction of a message was caused by differences in the backgrounds or personalities (or both) of the people involved.

4. Look up *fast* in the dictionary. How many meanings are listed? Write five sentences using a different sense of *fast* in each one. What implications for serial communication can be drawn from this exercise?

5. You and a friend see a man wearing a dark blue suit and carrying a briefcase get into a shiny limousine. You say to your friend, "He's probably a wealthy businessman." What two elements of communication are you confusing in this statement? What might you have said differently?

6. Talk to the director of communication, personnel director, or some other manager in a large organization about the operation of the grapevine in his or her company. How fast is it? How accurate is it? What does the manager do to improve its accuracy? Do certain individuals in the company tend to contribute to the flow of the grapevine more than others?

7. Select three friends who are likely to spread a rumor fast and far, and tell them that the university is about to adopt a new policy on grading. After three days ask some other friends whether they heard about the new policy and, if so, who told them, when and where, and whether they believe it's true.

Blondie by *Chic Young*

A small group is a collection of individuals who communicate face-to-face and depend on each other to a significant degree.

Leadership in a group involves the interaction between a person and the members of the group, all of whom assume various roles at various times.

Problem solving in your group will be more efficient if you follow a pattern or sequence.

Relationship

3

Small Group

Introduction

Lawrence B. Rosenfeld

Without talking, form groups with no more than four members. Once your group is formed, discuss the following questions:

1. What is a group?
2. What effect does the classroom environment have on the group?
3. What cues did the members give each other to indicate that they were part of the group that was formed?
4. What effect does the lack of oral verbal communication have on interaction?
5. Have you attained a group identity?
6. Can you describe the personalities of each of the members?
7. Can you differentiate among the roles that are being enacted? Who is the leader?
8. What problems are encountered, and how are they handled? . . .

Human existence is dependent upon society; without social life no human life would be possible. Society is sustained by communication; communication makes human life possible. Social life and communication are two words which imply sharing and participating, but the 1970s is witnessing the rise of existential loneliness, the increased use of the word *alienation*. As interaction decreases, as we find ourselves farther and farther apart, we become less than social, and human life becomes less than what it could be.

One reason for decreased human contact may be the increased technological sophistication of our generation. Why take the time to walk to a friend's house when it is so much easier to call on the telephone? But the telephone is not real human contact. Human contact is replaced by the telephone voice. Similarly, radio, television, and the movies have separated us from each other, formed barriers between us, eliminated the necessity for human contact. Without human contact communication is curtailed, aborted. We sit and listen, or sit and watch, and realize that we cannot affect the course of action in what we observe. In a sense, communication has not taken place, if, indeed, communication is a form of exchange through which people can come into contact with each other's minds (Newcomb, Turner, and Converse 1965).

Our age, though, may be coming to realize the necessity for human contact. The rise of sensitivity groups, training groups, group marathons, human relations workshops, and the increased use of groups in academic and business settings, all provide evidence that the most efficient means for insuring "survival" is in human contact, face-

A small group is a collection of individuals who communicate face-to-face and depend on each other to a significant degree.

to-face interaction: interpersonal communication.

Generally, groups provide a variety of experiences. Whether the specific purpose is to provide companionship, share information, solve a particular problem, or provide the group members with therapy, all groups are valuable because they serve the following purposes:

1. Encourage meaningful interaction. Meaningful interaction can best take place when there is face-to-face contact, when individuals acknowledge and adjust to each other's presence. What constitutes meaningful interaction varies from group to group. For example, *casual groups* are not established to solve a particular problem, but rather to provide members with friendship, interesting conversation, and companionship. To the extent that these things are provided, the interaction is meaningful.

2. Facilitate the learning of problem-solving procedures. Working in groups provides individuals with the opportunity to better understand a variety of views as members present and defend opposing views. During idea development members learn to critically evaluate the ideas of others. Problem solving also entails learning how to deal with conflicts, and how to affect a compromise. Individuals in *problem-solving groups* discover alternatives which are not possible under circumstances where directives and orders are the usual methods for solving problems. Although all groups are problem-solving groups to some extent, the main characteris-

tic of the problem-solving group is that a group goal is established which centers on a problem, goal, or task, and interaction results in a group-generated solution.

3. Facilitate the development of commitments. Individuals in a group normally develop commitments to both the group and its decisions. Group members feel a sense of responsibility and loyalty to one another; as a consequence, group-generated decisions have a higher probability of being enacted than decisions derived from authority figures. *Consciousness-raising groups*, which concentrate on creating an intense group identity, develop strong commitments in group members for each other, as well as for the group's decision to end oppression. Women's Liberation is an example of a consciousness-raising group (Chesebro, Cragan, and McCullough 1971).

4. Provide a background for understanding the impact of communication, and developing awareness of other people. We affect one another by communicating, and in the small group setting we have the opportunity to learn what our impact as communicators is on others. The small group can provide a means whereby we observe our own behavior, and where we can see how different forms of behavior elicit different responses.

The information flow in the small group setting is intense: not only is factual information presented, but each participant also is bombarded with his own and others' feelings, wishes, commands, desires, and needs. This information may be imparted verbally, nonverbally, intentionally, or unintentionally. The more directly individuals work with others, the better opportunity they will have to become aware of and sensitive to the feelings and emotions of others. *Therapy groups*, such as sensitivity training groups, function with the expressed intent of helping individuals by increasing their awareness. This awareness helps group members to build an individual identity which will facilitate social interaction (Rogers 1970). . . .

Groups may be defined according to certain attributes. Homan's (1950) definition focuses exclusively on *interaction*: "A group is defined by the interaction of its members. [Each member of the group] interacts more often with [the other members] than he does with outsiders" (p. 84). A group may be defined in terms of the *patterns* of its interaction. The definition offered by Merton (1957) specifies that there is patterned interaction which can be identified, and that members have expectations of each other in terms of adherence to the patterns of interaction. These patterns of interaction are usually the result of established norms. Other definitions focus upon *perceptions*: a group is a group if individuals outside the group perceive it to be a group, and if group members themselves perceive the group. Smith (1945) offers such a definition when he writes that a group consists of individuals "who have a collective perception of their unity and who have the ability or tendency to act and/or are acting in a unitary manner toward the environment" (p. 227).

Cartwright and Zander's (1968) definition of "group," the one used to guide this study of small

group behavior, is broad enough to encompass the many diverse definitions already presented, yet specific enough to help focus our attention. They define a group as "a collection of individuals who have relations to one another that make them interdependent to some significant degree" (p. 46). This definition provides parameters for group size (as the size increases the opportunity to influence other members decreases), group interaction (it is the result of the interdependency among members), and perceptions (members perceive themselves as part of a group because of the mutual interdependency and influence). The point Cartwright and Zander make about interdependency is worth repeating — individuals in a group influence and are influenced by the other members.

Even with this definition, there is still disagreement about groups. One question related to this problem is, "How real are groups?" From a psychological perspective, the only objective reality is the individual. The social psychological perspective also focuses on the individual, but emphasizes the individual in society. The sociological perspective views the group as a conceptual reality, i.e., it may be described without reference to the individual members. The group must be analyzed at the group, not the individual, level. Anthropologists view groups in terms of cultural forces, and developmental stages common to all primates. The writings of Levi-Strauss (1964) and Ardrey (1970) are examples of this approach to the group.

There is difficulty in working from extreme positions. Viewing the group as *only* the sum of its individuals, or as meaningful *only* when studied as a conceptual entity, or as *only* the result

of cultural forces, greatly reduces our understanding of the group as an individual and social phenomenon. Campbell (1958) has taken a middle-of-the-road position by admitting that groups vary in the degree to which they have a real existence. One of his most important considerations is the degree to which all the components (individuals) of the entity (group) share a *common fate*, that is, the extent to which they experience similar outcomes. If individuals are perceived as constituting a group, and they appear to be bound together in a relationship where each person shares a position relative to each other person, then the group is seen as a viable entity, something capable of independent existence. A second factor Campbell notes is *similarity*. Perceived member similarity affects whether they will be perceived as a group. Motorcycle gangs may be perceived as a group because members possess the same type of motorcycles and they dress similarly (leather jackets, emblems, or hats). The last consideration, less important than the other two, is *proximity*. The degree to which the members of a unity occupy a common space, or are in close proximity, affects the degree to which they are perceived as a viable entity. It is easier to attribute "groupness" to individuals who share physical environments than to individuals who are physically separated. Whether or not a group is perceived as an entity varies with the strength of these three perceptions. When common fate, similarity, and proximity are perceived, the individuals will be perceived as a group. When none of these are perceived, a group will not be perceived. Between these two points lies a range of responses.

A group is a highly complex

structure. It consists of individuals, with all their personal characteristics, interacting with one another in a given environment on a particular task. McGrath and Altman (1966), synthesizing and critiquing small group research, found that the research is concerned with three levels of reference: the *individual*, the *group*, and the *environment*. On the level of the individual, the concern has been with the personality characteristics, abilities, attitudes, and group position of each of the group members. On the group level, group abilities, training, experience, interpersonal relations, and structure have been studied. On the environmental level, the concern focuses upon conditions imposed upon the group, such as the task, operating conditions, and, possibly, the social conditions.

Information provided on the level of the individual is insufficient to predict the level of group performance; information provided on the level of the group alone also is insufficient to predict the level of group performance. Group capabilities may serve to set an upper limit on a group's performance potential. Likewise, information about the environment is insufficient to predict group performance, although it obviously affects it. Therefore, it is necessary to see the combined perspectives of all three approaches to help us better understand small group phenomena.

The component parts of small group interaction are interdependent; they share a relationship in which change in one part produces changes in the others. Studying the *parts*, such as members' personality characteristics and interpersonal relations, without some picture of how these parts fit into a *whole*, is a sure way to develop a false picture

West Side Story

Jet's Song

When you're a Jet,
You're a Jet all the way
From your first cigarette
To your last dyin' day.
When you're a Jet,
If the spit hits the fan,
You got brothers around,
You're a family man!
You're never alone,
You're never disconnected!
You're home with your own —
When company's expected,
You're well protected!
Then you are set
With a capital J,
Which you'll never forget
Till they cart you away.
When you're a Jet,
You stay
A jet!

When you're a Jet,
You're the top cat in town,
You're the gold-medal kid
With the heavyweight crown!

When you're a Jet,
You're the swingin'est thing.
Little boy, you're a man;
Little boy, you're a king!

The Jets are in gear,
Our cylinders are clickin'!
The Sharks'll steer clear
'Cause every Puerto Rican
'S a lousy chicken!

Here come the Jets
Like a bat out of hell —
Someone gets in our way,
Someone don't feel so well!
Here come the Jets:
Little world, step aside!
Better go underground,
Better run, better hide!
We're drawin' the line,
So keep your noses hidden!
We're hangin' a sign
Says "Visitors forbidden" —
And we ain't kiddin'!
Here come the Jets,
Yeah! And we're gonna beat
Every last buggin' gang
On the whole buggin' street!

On the whole!

Ever — !
Mother — !
Lovin' — !
Street!

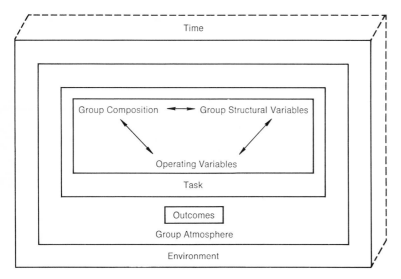

Fig. 1.1. *A graphic model of small group interaction*

of group interaction. Figure 1-1 depicts the relationships among the component parts of small group interaction. Group process takes place over *time*, and with the passage of time change occurs. Group interaction, then, is dynamic—the relationships among component parts are in constant flux.

Group composition includes a host of variables pertaining both to individual group members and how they interact with each other. Individual characteristics include each member's personality, attitudes, beliefs, self-concept, and perceptions of the other members. Interactive variables include group size, combined problem-solving skills, and how well different members can work together. Although it seems that group composition is a "given," such is not necessarily the case. For instance, group procedures which maximize individual usefulness may serve to increase friendly attitudes.

Two group *structural variables* are of concern: the communication network and the attraction

network. Communication networks can differ according to type of structure, tightness (how flexible that structure is), and effectiveness (the relationship between the structure and task requirements). The attraction network includes not only who likes whom, but also the formation of cliques and subgroups, and their effects on social-emotional and task development.

Operating variables include the kinds of procedures the group uses in its deliberations, the roles enacted, and the norms and standards set under which the group functions. Deliberation procedures are highly varied. A group may decide to research a problem before discussing it, to divide the problem into small parts which individuals may attack separately, or any one of an infinite number of other procedures. The roles enacted in a group also affect its operation. The number of roles and the willingness and abilities of members to assume necessary roles constitute only three aspects of role enactment which affect the group's

behavior. Because norms prescribe the limits of acceptable behavior, they too must be considered in an analysis of group interaction. Group standards are another aspect of interaction. The extent to which members agree on norms and other evaluative criteria (of task solutions, for instance) will affect the degree to which value conflicts are avoidable.

The *task* provides the general framework within which the group operates. It is the prime reason, the rationale, for the group's existence. Aspects of the task which affect the other components of group interaction are critical task demands, that is, those aspects of the task which make certain abilities and procedures crucial to task solution; the complexity of the task; its difficulty; and the goals.

The *outcomes* of group interaction may be analyzed in terms of the quality, quantity, appropriateness, and efficiency of the solution or decision, and member satisfaction with the outcomes. It is important to note that a group's outcomes affect its subsequent interaction; outcomes are not simply the result of group interaction. A solution, for example, does not develop during the last minutes of discussion. The last minutes of discussion result from a decision to accept a certain solution. Last minute interaction is aimed at reinforcing the decision, and insuring that the members are in agreement. According to Collins and Guetzkow (1964), member satisfaction is a function of task success, success in solving interpersonal problems, and member position in the group. Both high power and a position of centrality produce member satisfaction.

The *group atmosphere* is the emotional framework within

which the group operates. The group atmosphere or climate may be hostile, it may be conducive to work, and it may be affected by the task, the environment (which can create pressures under which the group must operate), and group composition.

Group interaction, structural and operating variables, atmosphere, task, and outcomes take place within a given *environment*. The environment places limitations on the group, and may serve as a facilitative or debilitative agent for task accomplishment. The environment includes such things as the physical area in which the group meets, the materials it either does or does not have, and other groups with which the group may or may not be in competition. Time limits are also an environmental restriction.

Proficiency in small group interaction is enhanced by experience and knowledge. The aim of this book is to provide you with both. Knowledge of the various dimensions and perspectives of small group phenomena, combined with both supervised and unsupervised experiences, should increase your effectiveness and satisfaction as a group member. If this were the only rationale for studying small group behavior, it would be sufficient, given the increasing use of groups in our society. But another, possibly more important, rationale is that the small group can, and usually does, function as a microcosm of the larger society. Consequently, the study of small group dynamics will help group members view and, hopefully, understand their social behavior better. . . .

Groups Versus Individuals

Although it may sound like heresy in this age of "group think," it should be quite obvious that under many conditions groups are *not* useful. Before considering the conditions which affect the decision of whether to employ a group or an individual to solve the particular problem at hand, take time to do the following. Divide your class into small groups with four to six members each. Select several individuals to work alone.

Ask each group and each individual to generate test items for an examination on small group dynamics. Groups should follow a brain-storming procedure, that is, each idea generated should not be subject to discussion until all ideas have been exhausted. The object, for both the groups and individuals, is to generate as many items for the examination as possible.

Ask each group member, as well as each individual, to estimate the temperature of the room. Group members should add their estimates together, then divide by the total number of members to obtain a group average. Now obtain a class average for all the groups.

Solve the following problem: A farmer must cross a river but he has a problem. He has a bale of grass, a wolf, and a lamb with him, and the boat can hold only the farmer and *one of the three at a time.* If he leaves the lamb alone with the grass, the grass will be eaten. If he leaves the wolf with the lamb, the lamb will be eaten. How can he transport the wolf, the lamb, and the grass safely to the other side?

Develop a short crossword puzzle on any topic. Each puzzle must have at least ten words.

Complete a crossword puzzle. Do not use any of the puzzles generated during the fourth problem; use one from your daily newspaper or a magazine. . . .

The following are important aspects to consider in deciding whether to use an individual or a group to solve a particular problem. Depending upon the particular circumstances, some will be more important than others. Which are most important can only be determined by the task and socio-emotional functions your group must perform. A yes response indicates that a group should be used to solve a problem; a no response indicates that an individual should be used.

1. Are many steps required to solve the problem?

2. Are there many parts to the problem?

3. Will the solution be difficult to verify?

4. Are the individuals involved likely to perceive the problem as an impersonal one?

5. Will the problem be of moderate difficulty for the individuals who constitute the group?

6. Is a great deal of information required to solve the problem? Would a single individual be unlikely to possess it?

7. Does the problem demand a division of labor?

8. Are many solutions desired?

9. Are many man-hours required for the problem's solution?

10. Will individuals have to assume a great deal of responsibility for the solution?

11. Are the proposed solutions likely to be diverse?

12. Are the attitudes concerning the problem likely to be diverse?

13. Is it unlikely that group members will engage in nontask-oriented behavior?

The Relationships among People in a Communication Situation

Dyadic

Serial

Small Group

Speaker-Audience

Charles Harbutt/Magnum
Ron Partridge/BBM Associates

Robert Lightfoot/VAN CLEVE Photography
Jeffrey Blankfort/BBM Associates

Will Blanche/Design Photographers International, Inc.
Mickey Palmer/Design Photographers International, Inc.

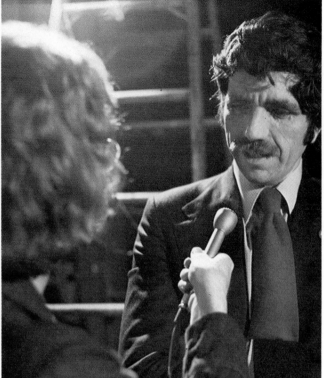

left: G. Jacobsen/Design Photographers International, Inc.
upper right: Marion Bernstein
lower right: Burt Glinn/Magnum

Group Climate

Jack Gibb

The Supportive Atmosphere

When the new observer comes into a group for the first time, he is able to sense a feeling about the group which we might call an atmosphere or a climate. Even a highly sensitive observer may have difficulty in describing these feelings. It may be helpful to select one of the many *schema* that have been offered for describing climates and use that example to show the distinction between a supportive climate and a defensive climate.

There is some evidence that a supportive climate maximizes the learning in the classroom. Certain kinds of behavior on the part of the teacher and of the students in a classroom tend to produce supportiveness. Because the teacher is such a critical member of the group, her behavior will be most important in the climate setting, particularly in the early stages of the development of the group. As indicated in Figure 1, the behav-iors that produce what has been called a "supportive climate" are a shared problem-solving attitude, feelings of acceptance, empathy toward other group members, and listening to the remarks of others. Creative, active listening is a difficult process. People can sit quietly and take a bodily attitude of attending but can, in reality, be formulating their next speech or devising a strategy for some later movement in the group. Perhaps a more active and difficult process is one of attempting to empathize or "feel into" the behavior of other members of the group. Many writers have talked about the significance of acceptance of the person and his attitudes. Here again, the teacher's behavior is critical in determining norms of acceptance of a wide range of student attitudes.

Perhaps the key determiner of the supportive climate is the attitude of willingness to share in a problem that the group holds in common. Here the group member communicates the willingness to enter with the other persons into a relationship in which they jointly explore the problem that confronts them. This willingness may occur at fairly deep levels of the personality. In occasional classes, one finds the teacher and the students engaged in a kind of joint inquiry in which all members of the group are trying to find answers to their problems. Learning is seen as a common quest in which many members of the classroom group can serve as resource persons. Learning to learn from others is one of the necessary skills for implementing such a climate.

On the right-hand side of Figure 1 are listed some of the effects of such a climate in the classroom. When such a climate exists, students and teachers feel less need to defend themselves from others, to protect their own attitudes and ideas from attack. Self-initiated activity occurs more readily under supportive climates. Members grow and develop as autonomous persons. When people listen to others, the individuals who are speaking get a chance to achieve a kind of catharsis or purging of their own emotions and feelings. This release is probably a necessary step in the reduction of the normal tensions that occur in all interpersonal relationships. When people feel supported and comfortable, they are able to perceive better. People who sense that they are accepted and understood tend to be released from their own defensiveness and tend to reach out in counteracceptance and counterempathy toward the other members of the group. A supportive climate exists only in degree. The observer of the classroom will wish to be sensitive to diagnostic

shared-problem-solving attitude	→	Supportive Climate	→ − defensiveness
acceptance	→		→ + initiating behavior
empathy	→		→ + growth
listening	→		→ + catharsis
			→ + perceptiveness
			→ + acceptance and empathy

Fig. 1. *The supportive climate*

SOURCE: J. R. Gibb, *Factors Producing Defensive Behavior within Groups*, IV, Annual Technical Report, Office of Naval Research, Contract Nonr-2285 (01), November 15, 1957.

Abridged from "Group Climate" by Jack Gibb in *The Dynamics of Instructional Groups*, ed. Nelson B. Henry, © 1960 National Society for the Study of Education. Used by permission of the National Society for the Study of Education.

The climate of a group can develop defensively or supportively, depending upon the verbal and nonverbal behaviors of its members.

advice giving	→		→ +	defensiveness
censoring	→		→ +	responding
defense	→	Defensive		behavior
persuasion	→	Climate	→ −	growth
controlling	→		→ −	perceptiveness
punishing	→		→ −	empathy

Fig. 2. *The defensive climate*

Source: As for figure 1.

signs in the development of such a climate.

The Defensive Atmosphere

A contrasting climate is described in Figure 2.

As indicated in Figure 2, certain behaviors tend to produce and heighten the defensive level of the group. Because of the nature of our classroom activities, most teachers tend to engage in a considerable amount of persuasional activity. They give advice, control the activities of the students in many ways, try by subtle influence to persuade and "guide" the behaviors of the students that come under their tutelage. Less subtly, the teacher may use punishment, evaluation, and censoring as mechanisms for keeping the group in line. These behaviors tend to produce similar behaviors in the class, the total end product of which is a defensive climate. This persuasional and selling climate is characteristic of our culture and tends to be carried over into the schoolroom. The dynamics of competition for extrinsic rewards are such as to produce defensiveness. Most of the strains of the schoolroom tend to promote defensive climates. The teacher is usually under strong pressure from within himself and from those administratively above him to cover a certain amount of ground, to mold the students in certain prescribed patterns, to reward what is accepted as good behavior, to guide and counsel students who deviate from accepted patterns of behaving. By administering extrinsic rewards for conforming behavior and by attempting to control the behavior of members, the teacher inevitably builds resistance and defense in the schoolroom.

As is indicated on the right-hand side of the figure, certain kinds of behavior inevitably result when defensive climates are produced.

Oftentimes behavior tends to reproduce itself in kind. Thus, defensiveness tends to produce more defensiveness. As classroom members become threatened by extrinsic reward systems, competition, and discipline, there is an increased feeling of necessity to defend one's own image. As people defend themselves, they engage in the kinds of behavior which produce counter self-preserving feelings in others. Accompanying this feeling of increased defensiveness is an increase in responding behavior. Students and teachers are responding to and, in a sense, controlled by the behavior of others. It is less possible for people to grow in defensive climates than in climates where they feel less need to protect their own images. People see the world less clearly. There is less tendency to feel one's self into the position of the other per-

Andy Capp by Reg Smythe

son. When there is less empathy, there is less understanding and countersupport. When climates become largely defensive, they tend to reproduce themselves.

Thus, it requires a major educative act on the part of the teacher to counteract the defensiveness of the group.

A Way of Thinking about Leadership and Groups

Thomas Gordon

First of all, leadership can be conceptualized as an interaction between a person and a group, or, more accurately, between a person and the members of a group. Each participant in this interaction may be said to play a role, and these roles in some way must be differentiated from each other. The basis for this differentiation seems to be a matter of influence—that is, one person, the leader, influences, while the other persons respond.

The determination of the kind of stimuli that will facilitate group action is a function of the nature of the group's goals and the reaction of the group to the contribution (stimuli) of the individual. Stated more simply, a potential "leader" of a group somehow must perceive what it is the group wants, he must contribute something that will move the group closer to that goal, and finally his contribution must be "accepted" before he can be said to have patterned the group's behavior. Thus a leader also must be led, in that he is influenced by the behavior of the group members to the extent that the group's norms, problems, and goals actually determine the kind of contribution that will pattern the

group's behavior. In this sense, leadership is truly a process of interaction.

Thus, leadership is also relative to the situation. What will pattern group behavior in one situation may not in another. For a member of an athletic team to try to inspire in his teammates a fighting spirit may be an act of leadership when the team is losing but may invoke ridicule when the team is assured of winning by a large margin. Because a group itself is a moving, changing social system, its requirements for leadership will usually be different from time to time. This is not to deny, though, that a *particular* group may always require certain functions to be performed, so that a certain few members in a group may continuously emerge as leaders more often than others, even over a long period of time in the life of the group. The principle that "leadership is relative to the situation" also need not exclude the possibility that there may be certain "universal functions" that always facilitate change or movement in many or all kinds of groups. Perhaps it is more accurate, then, to say that the *pattern of leadership* is relative to the situation. Some specific functions

"A Way of Thinking About Leadership and Groups," from *Group-Centered Leadership*, by Thomas Gordon. Houghton Mifflin Company, 1955. Reprinted by permission of the publishers.

Leadership in a group involves the interaction between a person and the members of the group, all of whom assume various roles at various times.

Am I a Good Group Participant?

Leland P. Bradford

All during our lives we find ourselves sharing in group activity. We belong to our family, the Scouts, the softball team, the Spanish club, or the church choir. Sometimes we belong to groups just for short periods of time. We go to camp, or we attend a special discussion meeting, or we are on the Valentine's Day party committee.

By the time we get to high school we feel that we know a lot about groups. But now and then we come away from our group activity feeling dissatisfied with the way things are going. There is apparent lack of interest, or there is bickering among the members; the group seems to be growing away from its common relationship and goal.

This sometimes happens because we are not functioning well as units in our group. Since it is we who make up the group, we must always be conscious of our contribution to it. To get at the root of our common group problems, we must first ask ourselves, "Am I a good group participant?"

Below are indicated some of the roles of a good group member. You may play several or all of these roles in your group at some time; in fact, the more roles you play, the better. You should not feel that your place in the group is determined by one role only. If you find that you have not been participating enough, resolve now to be a better group member, and watch how your group will come alive, both for you and for everyone else in it.

1. *Do I propose new ideas, activities, and procedures?* Or do I just sit and listen?

2. *Do I ask questions?* Or am I shy about admitting that I do not understand?

(continued on page 157)

may be required at all times in a single group or at various times in all groups, but the total pattern of leadership functions will be unique for each group and perhaps even for each situation confronting a group.

Probably the principal significance of such a conception of leadership is that it shifts the focus of attention from a *single* leader to a role that potentially may be occupied by *any group member* who is able to emit appropriate stimuli which facilitate group action toward a goal. True, in some groups one member during a short period may occupy that role more frequently than other members, as when a group is engaged in reaching a particular goal and the functions required to attain this end can be carried out best by one member. Yet our definition allows for the emergence of a new leader when the group selects a new goal.

A complicating factor, yet one that does not detract from the usefulness of our definition, is the common phenomenon of a group situation in which one person acquires a relatively permanent and often formal or institutionalized role of group leader. This may occur more or less informally when the group learns to depend upon one member as a reliable source of stimuli, as with a group that becomes committed to relatively unchanging and limited goals. Or it may occur formally, as in so many of our larger organizations, when a person is given a formal and designated role (and usually a title). Even when leadership roles become institutionalized in this way, a leader to be "followed" (or to continue having his actions pattern group behavior) must be perceived by the members as facilitating the group's efforts at reaching some goal.

One further element needs to be added to this conception of leadership. Often overlooked, yet of great significance, is the possibility that once a person is perceived as a leader in one situation, the members may in future situations tend to respond more readily to *his* behavior than to others'. This is to say that stimuli from one who has been perceived *already* as a leader may have a higher probability of directing the group's behavior, perhaps because of the attitude that somehow he is a more "legitimate" source of influence. . . . The potential for leadership behavior may not be equally distributed throughout a group, even though our conception of leadership fosters the notion that any member through his own behavior *can* pattern the behavior of the group.

The Nature of the Group

Leadership cannot be examined without considering some of the characteristics of the group in which leadership operates. By conceptualizing leadership as an interaction between an initiator (or facilitator) and those who respond to or accept the facilitation, we become obligated to examine the situation in which this interaction occurs—namely, the group itself.

Why People Join Groups

Let us first assume that people join groups because they perceive that membership in a group somehow will provide satisfaction of some basic need. Membership in a group is not merely a matter of chance, for people actively search for relationships with others in a group situation because of the promise or expectation that they will be rewarded

(continued from page 156)

3. *Do I share my knowledge when it will prove helpful to the problem at hand?* Or do I keep it to myself?

4. *Do I speak up if I feel strongly about something?* Or am I shy about giving an opinion?

5. *Do I try to bring together our ideas and activities?* Or do I concentrate only on details under immediate discussion?

6. *Do I understand the goals of the group and try to direct the discussion toward them?* Or do I get off the track easily?

7. *Do I ever question the practicality or the "logic" of a project, and do I evaluate afterwards?* Or do I always accept unquestioningly the things we do?

8. *Do I help to arrange chairs, serve refreshments, and even clean up when the session is over?* Or do I prefer to be waited on?

9. *Do I encourage my fellow group members to do well?* Or am I indifferent to their efforts and achievements?

10. *Do I prod the group to undertake worthy projects?* Or am I happy with mediocre projects?

11. *Am I a mediator and a peacemaker?* Or do I allow ill feeling to develop?

12. *Am I willing to compromise (except where basic issues such as truth and justice are involved)?* Or do I remain inflexible?

13. *Do I encourage others to participate and to give everyone else a fair chance to speak?* Or do I sit by while some people hog the floor, and do I sometimes dominate it myself?

through the satisfaction of certain needs. Furthermore, people will continue in a group only if they continue to have an expectation of need satisfaction.

In order that this explanation may not convey the notion that human behavior is controlled through some kind of "pleasure principle," a restatement of the above is required. The problem here is to avoid giving the impression that human behavior can be explained simply by invoking a principle that people seek what gives them immediate reward or pleasure and avoid what does not. To explain human behavior, and in this case the behavior of individuals leading to membership in groups, a more appropriate concept is *self-actualization*. By this is meant the basic tendency for individuals to actualize their potential.

Such a theory of the basic tendency of man allows us to modify our earlier proposition about why people join groups. Thus, people join groups because they perceive them as a possible means for self-actualization—a way of actualizing their own capacities. A group, therefore, promises the individual an opportunity to grow, develop,

fulfill, enhance, create—or simply to *become* that for which he has the potential.

The Task of the Group

Assuming that a group consists of individuals seeking self-actualization, the essential task of the group becomes the selection of goals, and of means for reaching those goals, which will provide the maximum self-actualization of its members. Put in another way, the task of the group is to adjust to the changing needs of its members—to find the best solutions to its continuous problem of meeting their needs. But because the needs of one individual may often conflict with the needs of another, a group must find ways of fulfilling the needs of each person at the least expense to all other members. It must find some formula for distributing its available, and usually limited, means for satisfying the needs of its members. Consequently, a group is in a continuous state of adjusting to the tension, conflicts, and problems arising from the ever-changing needs of its members.

Improving Conference Leadership

Stanley G. Dulsky
Chicago Psychological Institute

The conference technique has been widely adopted by industry as a basic method of training. Much has been written on how to conduct a conference, how to set up the physical facilities, scheduling the meetings, etc. However, strange as it may seem, not enough attention has been devoted to the leadership role of the conference leader.

The writer has conducted conference meetings for the past seven years, and has also participated, for the past three years, in the training of conference leaders. As a result of this experience, it has become apparent that there are certain basic psychological principles which should be known to a conference leader, and which, if practiced, will enable him to become more effective as a trainer.

I. Encourage "Sounding Off"

The conference leader must always have a permissive, accepting attitude in order to encourage the expression of negative feelings. The technical term for this principle is *catharsis*. In popular parlance it is called "getting it off your chest." It is one of the oldest psychological principles known. It is a common element in all forms of psychotherapy.

The conference leader shows his permissive, accepting attitude by never evaluating an opinion.

Evaluation of response must be left to the conference members who, sensing this permissive atmosphere, will evaluate freely, and quickly agree or disagree with another member's statement. An example of the accepting attitude and evaluation by other members is as follows.

During a training conference one member said, with a great deal of feeling, "I believe that these meetings are a waste of time." By this statement he meant, of course, to attack management policy in regard to training by the conference technique, as well as, perhaps, the abilities of the conference leader himself. No sooner had the leader reflected (see point No. 5), "You feel you're not getting anything from these conferences," than several members immediately "jumped" on the dissenting member by vigorously disagreeing with him, and proceeded to indicate specifically how they had been helped by past discussions of various topics.

2. Promote Discussion and Active Cooperation

Most conference leaders need to become more aggressive in promoting discussion and drawing in all members of the conference.

One of the reasons why the conference type of learning situation is so effective is that conference members participate actively. Psychologists call this *active learning*. It is the opposite of passive learning, where material

You can improve your work with small groups by applying certain principles of leadership.

is given, usually in lecture form, to an audience. In a training conference there is no lecturing by a leader. The opinions and conclusions come from the conference members, and come only as a result of their active cooperation and thinking.

Use of Open-End Questions

Too many conference leaders fail to promote discussion to the extent that they might. They do not "throw" enough questions. Or they ask questions that are easily answered by yes or no. The following are some examples of questions that the conference leaders should ask to promote discussion.

(After one member has given an opinion): "And what do you think about that?"

(After a remedy or plan of action has been presented): "What advantages do you see in that plan?" or "How would that affect the X Department?" or "How would that promote safety?"

One of the most difficult problems for the conference leader is how to get every conference member to participate. Again, we present some suggestions.

(If a certain group is silent): "We don't know how the inspectors (modify for group) feel about this."

(If women in a mixed group are silent): "We haven't heard from the ladies on this."

Summarize Frequently

Another technique to promote discussion is the frequent use of the *summary*. Many leaders fail to use this device with the result that after five or ten minutes the members "don't know where we are." Attention lags, members lose interest, the conference bogs down.

The leader should always summarize after one member has spoken at length, after a conflict of opinion between two or more members, after definite conclusions or opinions have been reached. This stimulates the members who have not been in the discussion and shows them "where we are," keeps them on the beam. It also affords the leader the opportunity to pull back the discussion from those who have monopolized it and to throw an overhead question to the others.

Two conference members argue in favor of a point, two are opposed. These four have been talking about five minutes. The leader enters the situation in this way: "We've certainly had a lively discussion on this question. Some of us believe that (summarizes pro arguments) and others believe that (summarizes con arguments). What do the rest of you think about it?"

3. Inflate Egos

Most conference leaders need to become more alert to opportunities to inflate the ego of a conference member. This is particularly important for reticent members.

A basic need of all people is the need for status, for being looked up to, for feeling important. Some of this feeling comes naturally to a conference member because of the intrinsic nature of the conference. For example, if a conference member makes a statement or ventures an opinion or draws a conclusion that is agreed with by the other conference members, it is obvious to him that he has said something which is important and which has the approval of his colleagues. Although the leader may not directly comment on this remark, the fact that the others have accepted it is important to the member. This is "natural" ego-inflation.

The leader can help this process and should in certain cases, particularly with reticent members. Examples of the ego-inflation technique by the leader follow.

(After a member has made a remark): "Isn't that a point we ought to consider?" (Note: There is no evaluation here.)

—or "In the light of Mr. Jones' comment, do we want to modify our conclusion?"

—or "Let's consider the effects of John's suggestion."

—or "Jones brought up a disadvantage from *his* point of view. How would it affect the rest of you?"

4. Promote Competition

The conference leader should be on the alert to promote competitiveness among members for the purpose of bringing out the two sides of a problem.

A sense of competition is present in a conference group, although not usually to a very pronounced degree. However, when leadership is effective, each member is motivated to express himself to greatest advantage. Each member wants to be regarded by the others as having sound judgment, and each member wants the others to know that, on the basis of his long experience in his position, he has found certain principles to be true. This competitive aspect arises most frequently when there is a difference of opinion, and each member of the opposing side feels strongly urged to defend his position by mustering the strongest arguments he can.

As an example of the competitive aspect and of how far the leader may safely let it go, consider the following excerpt from a conference. This took place in a supervisory discussion about waste of time on the job.

One conference member said, "I don't think our people waste a lot of time around here." Before the leader could say anything, a second conference member quickly commented, "I disagree with you, Joe. I think they do." Here we have a situation where one man's judgment is pitted against another's. In a sense, both have challenged each other, and are ready to square off in the ring. The leader picked up these two remarks, and said: "We have a disagreement here. One of us believes that employees do waste time; the other believes that they do not. Joe, since you were first, would you like to tell us why you believe as you do?" After Joe had given his arguments and after his opponent had been asked to give his, the leader pulled the discussion back, and threw it out to the rest of the group with the remark, "And what do the rest of you think about this now?"

In the above example the competitive spirit broke out spontaneously without any help from the leader. However, in some groups the leader may have to foster it. Below are some suggestions.

"I wonder if all of us would agree with what Joe just said."

"Mr. Smith feels that . . . Is there anyone who thinks differently?"

"John's experience leads him to believe that . . . Has anyone's experience here been otherwise?"

5. Reflect

The conference leader can make excellent use of a technique that has been used very effectively in a form of psychological therapy known as non-directive counseling. The technique is called *reflection*. There are two levels of reflection: (a) reflections of content (rewording what a person says) and (b) reflection of feeling (clarifying and drawing out the feeling tone behind the state-

ment). This technique is advantageous in providing emotional release for conference members, and also in keeping the discussion moving.

As an example of *reflection of content*, we cite the following excerpt from a conference.

In a discussion of the company practice of inducting new employees, a supervisor said, "I think we do a terrible job around here on new employees." The leader responded, "You feel that our present practice leaves much to be desired." The conference member agreed with the leader's statement, and then went on to explain why he thought the present method was terrible. Although the leader could have merely asked the conference member to amplify his remark, the leader achieved the same end with greater benefit to the conference member by reflecting.

An example of *reflection of feeling* is seen in another excerpt from a conference.

One member said, "I don't believe suggestions are really welcomed here because they don't listen to us." The leader reflected as follows: "*You* feel that management doesn't value your opinions, and doesn't have much confidence in your judgment."

Conference leaders without psychological training might find this suggestion the most difficult of all to grasp and to use. However, if the principle is understood, the leader can begin to apply it in his conferences. Here is an additional example.

Supervisor Smith complains bitterly and at length that the new employees are difficult to manage, that they lack motivation to do a good job, that they waste time, and asks what the younger generation is coming to, etc. Leader reflects: "You feel that you don't understand the new employees and therefore aren't quite sure how to handle them."

You Can Be a Better Leader

Louis Cassels

The average executive spends about 60 percent of his time in meetings and conferences. This recent survey finding points up the fact that ability to work in and through small groups is one of the most useful skills a manager can have.

Like most management skills, this one has to be developed. Managers who are adept at human relations on a man-to-man basis may be clumsy at working with groups.

Here are six suggestions for improving your performance as leader or member of a business work group. They come from Dr. Gordon L. Lippitt, a professional psychologist who is program director of the National Training Laboratories.

Dr. Lippitt's organization has done pioneering research in group processes for twelve years. Founded in 1947, NTL concentrated initially on training leaders of educational, religious, and civic groups. But in recent years managers have constituted a large proportion of its clientele.

To work more effectively in group situations a businessman needs to develop:

1. Awareness of his own impact on a group.

2. Insight into the needs, abilities, and reactions of others.

3. Sincere belief in the group approach to problem solving.

4. Understanding of what makes a group tick.

5. Ability to diagnose the ailments of a sick group.

6. Flexibility as a leader or member.

The first two qualities are closely related. Both require what Dr. Lippitt calls sensitivity.

Awareness

Many people who are alert to human responses in their ordinary business and social contacts become quite insensitive when they are functioning in a group. They plow ahead, intent on their own role or contribution, and never pause to observe the effect of their behavior on the others. People tend to act this way for at least two different reasons.

Some feel vaguely insecure in a group situation. Their nervousness causes them to develop calluses on their mental antennae which would normally pick up the nuances of response from others. Some are born actors who are so exhilarated by the opportunity to impress several people at once that they can be brought down to earth only by the most blatantly negative reaction from the captive audience.

You probably know already which of these types you are. If not, a little self-analysis should enable you to find out. In either case, the antidote is to make a conscious effort at future meetings to observe how you are acting, how much or how little you are talking, how attentively you are listening when others talk, and how your behavior is affecting the rest of the group.

Unless you are a remarkable fellow, you will probably be surprised at what you learn about yourself when you become a participant-observer rather than merely a participant. You may find, for example, that the sense of humor which you always considered to be a welcome relief from tension is actually an irritant and a distraction to others. Or you may learn that some of your colleagues regard your habit of doodling as a sign of boredom rather than concentration.

Sensitivity is doubly important if you are leader of the group. Your status means that your impact on the proceedings, for better or worse, is likely to be greater than anyone else's. It also means that you are less likely to be told, by any overt word or gesture, when you are rubbing the group the wrong way. You will have to rely on much subtler forms of feedback—the expression on a man's face, the tone of his voice, the tense or relaxed atmosphere of the meeting itself, the apathy or enthusiasm which the group exhibits when you call for ideas.

As a group leader, and to only slightly less extent as a member, you need also to recognize the effects of other people's behavior on you. You don't have to like a man in order to work effectively with him in a group, but it is important that you realize that you don't like him—and to differentiate between his personality, which irritates you, and his ideas, which may be extremely valuable.

For example, you may have a violent prejudice against people who chew gum. It is not necessary that you abandon this prejudice if you find yourself in a group that includes an incurable gum chewer. But it is necessary that you recognize the existence of your prejudice and make allowances for it in appraising or responding to a statement which your gum-chewer has made between chomps.

Insight

Insight into the needs and abilities of others is another form of sensitivity that pays big dividends in group leadership. All human beings share certain basic needs—for affection, acceptance, recognition, a sense of belonging, a sense of achievement.

If an individual finds that some or all of these needs are being satisfied through his participation in a group, he will be an enthusiastic and constructive member. On the other hand, if the group consistently ignores or frustrates his needs, he is likely to become hostile or apathetic. He may have no idea that these subconscious psychological drives are affecting his group performance. But a sensitive leader can learn to spot the symptoms and take corrective action.

One highly effective way to satisfy an individual member's psychological needs—and at the same time improve the effectiveness of the entire group—is to probe constantly for unexpected abilities. You call a man into a meeting to serve as an expert on some particular phase of the business that is assigned to him. But if you give him a chance to participate broadly, you may find he has a lot of wisdom to contribute on some entirely different matter.

That helps his ego—and adds a valuable human resource to the potential of the group.

The Group Approach

Many executives appoint committees, call meetings and go through the motions of consulting others because that is the way they are expected to act. But they never really delegate decision-making powers to any group. They walk into a meeting with their minds made up, and manipulate the group until it arrives at—and rubber stamps—the decision already reached. To such executives, group procedures are a sham—a device for persuading people they are participating when in reality they are not. To use a group in this way is worse than a waste of time. People know when they are being manipulated, and they always resent it.

There may be times when an executive will want to call a group together simply to announce a decision. That is perfectly legitimate provided it is made clear that the meeting was called purely to communicate a decision for which higher management accepts full responsibility. But you should never pretend that the group itself is taking part in the decision.

There are also occasions when it is far wiser for a manager to turn a problem over to a group for solution, with no strings attached. Many of the problems that arise in modern business are so complex that no one man, however brilliant, can possibly have all of the expert knowledge required to solve them correctly. The group approach enables you to bring a wide variety of experiences, backgrounds, viewpoints and technical competences to bear on a problem.

Group procedures also tend to lead to more creative solutions. It is remarkable how many people have their best thoughts when they are stimulated by the thoughts of others.

Another important reason for letting a group solve a problem is that people feel committed to a decision which they have helped to reach. If you must rely on others to implement a decision, you will do well to let them participate genuinely in the decision-making process. Even if you feel compelled to dictate the basic policy, you can usually delegate to an appropriate group the task of working out details of its implementation.

Understanding

An understanding of what makes a group tick will enable you to follow several basic rules for releasing the group potential.

The first step is to define clearly the problem about which a decision is to be made. Try to get a single, sharply focused question before the group. More time is wasted in meetings because of failure to pinpoint the problem than for any other reason.

The next step is to clarify the jurisdiction of the group. How much latitude does it have for reaching a decision? Is it serving merely in an advisory capacity, or is it fully responsible for a binding decision? Uncertainty on these points will cause members to be wary about giving their opinions.

Try to create a relaxed, permissive atmosphere. Let it be known that you want contributions—and candor—from all participants, that no one is there just to listen and nod.

Withhold your own ideas about a solution, if you have any, until late in the session. If you put them on the table too early, you may give the group the false impression that you have already made up your mind and are merely looking for yes men.

Elicit as many ideas as possible before beginning to evaluate or criticize any particular solution. If you let the evaluation process begin too soon, it will choke off the production of alternative solutions and rivet attention on the first few ideas advanced.

Dissociate ideas from the men who put them forward. Never refer to "Jack's plan" or "Jones' proposal." Keep personalities and personal rivalries out of the picture as far as possible by giving each proposal a neutral designation—"plan A" or "suggestion No. 1."

Don't ask the group to guess when it's possible to get facts. If it is difficult to weigh the relative merits of one or more solutions without further investigation or testing, postpone a decision until a later meeting.

Aim for a consensus of the group, rather than take a vote. A consensus is usually not too hard to obtain if you allow skeptics to record their misgivings, and if you make it clear that the decision will be subject to revaluation later if necessary.

Diagnose the Ailments

Sometimes you can impanel a group of highly competent men, follow all of the right procedures, and still the group won't come alive and produce. That's when you need diagnostic ability.

If you have developed self-insight and sensitivity toward others, you may be able to figure out what's wrong. You don't have

to psychoanalyze the members. Just look a little below the surface of their conduct. Try to detect the unexpressed feelings and motivations that are causing them to fight among themselves or to run from the problem.

Watch for "hidden agendas"— the real interests that a group member is trying to further while professing to talk about the problem at hand. It may be necessary to bring some of these hidden agendas into the open—to lay aside the official problem until you have dealt with the distracting troubles.

Generally, it is best not to rely entirely on your own diagnostic powers, but to enlist the help of the group itself in analyzing its difficulties. A good technique for doing this is to distribute simple mimeographed forms—usually called "post-meeting reports"—to be filled out anonymously by all participants immediately after adjournment. How did you think today's meeting went? What did you like best about it? What did you dislike most? What should we do differently next time?

After you have used this blind questionnaire technique a few times, you may find that the members of the group are prepared to do the evaluating out loud at the close of the meeting. When you thus succeed in making a group conscious of its own procedures, and of its own responsibility to criticize and correct its inadequacies, you are on your way to mature and fruitful group activity.

Flexibility

The final piece of advice to those who have to participate in a large number of group meetings is: Try being flexible.

Many different roles must be

played in a group other than leader and member. For example, a group needs idea givers and idea evaluators, question askers and information providers, critics and supporters, challengers and summarizers, stirrer uppers and peacemakers.

Most people tend unconsciously to cast themselves in the same role or roles at every meeting they attend. But it is much better for the group—and for your relations with the group—if you vary your role from time to time.

Try out a new role and see how you feel about it, and how the others react to it. If you've always been an idea giver, see how well you can function as a supporter, or vice versa. You'll be amazed at how much more you can accomplish in a group through a little versatility.

Group Problem Solving

John K. Brilhart

Focus on the Problem before Solutions

What would you think if you drove into a garage with a car that was running poorly and the mechanic almost immediately said, "What you need to fix this buggy is a new carburetor and a set of spark plugs." If your reaction is like mine, you would get out of there as fast as your ailing auto would let you. A competent mechanic, after he asked questions about how the car was acting and observed how it ran, would put it on an electronic engine analyzer. After gathering information by these means he would make a tentative diagnosis, which he would check by direct examination of the suspected parts. Only then would he say something like, "The problem is that two of your valves are burned, and the carburetor is so badly worn that it won't stay adjusted properly."

Our two hypothetical mechanics illustrate one of the most common failings in group (and individual) problem solving: solution centeredness. Irving Lee, after observing many problem-solving conferences and discussions, found that in most of the groups he studied there was "a deeply held assumption that because the problem was announced it was understood. People seemed too often to consider a complaint equivalent to a description, a charge the same as a specification.[1] Maier, after many years of studying problem-solving discussions in business and industry, stated that "participants as well as discussion leaders focus on the objective of arriving at a solution and fail to give due consideration to an exploration of the problem."[2] Groups tend to act like a surgeon who scheduled an operation when a patient complained of a pain in his abdomen, like a judge who handed down a deci-

Problem solving in your group will be more efficient if you follow a pattern or sequence.

Abridged from *Effective Group Discussion* by John K. Brilhart. © 1967 Wm. C. Brown Company Publishers. Used by permission of the publisher.

Brainstorming Triggers Ideas

An agent recently came to us seeking help. She wanted an idea. We didn't have the idea she wanted, but we suggested a technique we hope will help her come up with the idea. The technique is called brainstorming. Maybe you can use it sometime. Here's how it works.

Start with a problem. (In the example above it was a title for a newsletter.) Appoint a small committee—three to five persons—and let it meet in a place where there are no distractions. State the problem as a question. Ask each member to answer with the *first* thought that comes to his mind. Appoint a recorder and begin.

There are probably only two hard and fast rules for a brainstorming session.

1. If you have a thought, get it out of your head and on paper. Speak out without hesitation. If you leave the thought loitering around in your mind, it will just clutter up the path of other ideas. Write down every brainstorm—no matter how silly or trite or foolish it may sound at the moment.

2. Don't rush it. Give the session time to work. We think a half hour would be a bare minimum and it may run a half day. Brainstorming is not likely to be effective if the committee members have to leave for another meeting in five minutes.

When all the committee members feel satisfied that they have exhausted their ideas, put the list away and let it simmer for a few days. *This is important!* When you look at it again, one of the brainstorms may seem just right—the idea you have been seeking. On the other hand, one of the "silly" ideas may trigger a brand new thought which is just what you wanted.

(continued on page 167)

Reprinted from "Brainstorming Triggers Ideas" in *Inside Information*, November, 1966. © 1966 *Inside Information*. Used by permission of the Information and Publications Department, University of Maryland.

sion as soon as he had read the indictment, or like the hunter who shot at a noise in the bushes and killed his son. Solution-centeredness has harmful effects:

1. *Partisanship is encouraged.* Participants spend a lot of time arguing the merits of their pet proposals. The group often becomes hopelessly split, or negative feeling is aroused which will affect future discussions.

2. *Ineffectual solutions tend to be adopted.* There is a tendency to spend much time debating the first and most obvious solutions, which are usually taken bodily from other situations and are not based on the facts of the present case. New, innovative ideas are not considered.

3. *Time is wasted.* Solution-at-once methods often result in a sort of pinwheel pattern. The problem is mentioned; someone proposes a solution which is argued at length; someone points out that an important aspect of the problem has been neglected; someone then goes back to the problem to see if this is so. This problem-solution cycle may be repeated indefinitely, wasting time on solutions which do not fit the facts of the case. At first, focus on what has gone wrong rather than what shall be done about it.

Begin with a Problem Question Rather Than a Solution Question

Consider the following situation: A student leader asks his group, "How can we get rid of a club president who is not doing his job, without further disrupting the club?" Such a statement of the problem appears insoluble, like how to eat a cake and have it too. The apparent dilemma is the result of incorporating a solution (get rid of the president) into the statement of the problem. The better procedure is to separate the solution from the problem, then focus on understanding the details of the problem. Once this has been done, appropriate solutions will usually emerge. Our student leader might ask, "How might we get good leadership for our club?" Then the group can dig into what is expected of the president, how the incumbent is acting, what members are complaining about, what is wrong, and why. Answers to these questions about the problem may lead to tentative solutions: "Send him to a leadership training laboratory," "Have the sponsor instruct him in his duties," "Ask him to resign," "Temporarily assign part of his duties to the executive committee members" and the like. See if you can distinguish between the following problems which include solutions (solution questions) and those which focus on what is wrong:

How can I transfer a man who is popular in the work group but slows down the work of others?

What can be done to alleviate complaints about inadequate parking space at our college?

How might we reduce theft and mutilation in the college library?

How can we get more students to enroll in physics?

What action shall we take in the case of Joe Blevins who is accused of cheating on Professor Lamdeau's exam?

Map the Problem Situation

To help develop problem mindedness, think of the problem as a large uncharted map with only

(continued from page 166)

Take the naming of *Inside Information* as an example of how the technique works. We (the Information and Publications staff) wanted to develop a "tip sheet," "communication guide," "house organ," or some kind of newsletter. The organizing committee met and made some decisions about format, content, publication dates, etc., and then went into a brainstorming session to find a name. We came up with the following in the first session:

Sign Posts	Flashback
For Public Information	Inside Information
Information Quotient	Show and Tell
Focal Points	Oriole Oracle
Pencil Points	Key Notes
Pertinent Points	The Bulletin
Salient Points	Illuminator
The Transmission Line	Quizling
Fishing Cord	Unclassified
Extension Cord	Unclassified Information

As you can see, most of them connote some phase of communication—but not all. After the ideas had simmered for a week, the committee met again and suggested a few more titles. Finally, we selected *Inside Information* because of the double, or even triple, meaning it might convey. This was to be our internal organ for carrying our communcations ideas to you. The title suggested that the newsletter might carry more than run-of-the-mill announcements, and it could be our way of bringing you into our confidence and into our departmental work—our way of introducing ourselves to you.

Next time you are searching for an idea, why not try brainstorming?

Spitballing with Flair

Spitballing, or brainstorming, is something like a group-therapy session in which the patient is the product and the doctors are the admen. Recently, Time Correspondent Edgar Shook sat in on a brainstorming meeting at Chicago's North Advertising Inc. The patient: Flair, a new Paper Mate pen with a nylon tip. Among the doctors: North President Don Nathanson, Creative Director Alice Westbrook, Copy Chief Bob Natkin and Copywriters Steve Lehner and Ken Hutchison. The dialogue, somewhat condensed:

Natkin: We have what I think must be the first graffiti advertising campaign, which we've been running in teen-age magazines. The reason I bring this up is that it could be translated into TV and could be very arresting.

Westbrook: I love graffiti.

Natkin (reading from graffiti ads): "Keep America beautiful. Bury a cheap, ugly pen today. Buy a Paper Mate." Some research has been done on this and it looks like it's working. "Draw a flower on your knee with a Paper Mate Flair."

Westbrook: Why not "navel"?

Natkin: They wouldn't let us say it. We are going to compromise. It was going to be "Draw a flower around your genitals with a Paper Mate Flair." Then they'd say "knee" and we'd say "navel," and we'd meet in the middle.

Westbrook: Body paint is going to get hotter and hotter.

Nathanson: Did you read that memo I sent out about the bosoms? God, I think bosom makeup is going to be big.

Westbrook: I do too. I know just the color for it too.

Nathanson: You know, you can do a fantastic industrial campaign on the idea of a silent pen. Because just think of the noise level. I mean, nothing is noisier than these competitor's pens. Everybody quiet. Just listen. (*He scratches first with the competitor's pen, then with a Flair.*)

Westbook: Boy, that really moves me.

Lehner: Picture the kind of thing you would get if you were awarded the Legion of Honor. Real parchmenty, with a great big heraldry and wax and stamps. And on the certificate it says, "The American Anti-Noise League." And you hear the announcer say with great . . .

Hutchison: Flair.

Lehner: . . . "From the American Anti-Noise League, for exceptionally smooth writing without scratching or squeaking." You hear a trumpet. Tah-Tah! We dissolve to another document. "To Flair from the United Cap Forgetters Council: for having a new kind of ink that won't dry out if you leave the cap off overnight." And a couple of trumpets. Bum-Bum! And on to a third document. "To Flair from the National Pen Pounders Association: for having a smooth, tough,

(continued on page 169)

vague boundaries. The first task facing the problem-solving group is to make the map as complete as possible (in other words, to fully diagnose the situation). The leader of the group should urge the members to tell all they know about the situation: facts, complaints, conditions, circumstances, factors, details, happenings, relationships, disturbances, effects. In short, what have you observed? What have others observed? What have you heard?

At best the "map" of the problem will be incomplete, with full detail in some parts, but gaps or faint outlines in others. Members will disagree on some details. Some observations may be spotty and fleeting. Sometimes the members will admit they do not know enough about the problem to deal with it intelligently. The author remembers a group of students concerned with recommending solutions to a severe shortage of parking space at a large university. The discussants soon decided they did not have enough information to make wise recommendations. They tried to list the types of information they would need before proceeding to talk about solutions. Soon investigating teams were out interviewing, getting maps, collecting records and reading. The subsequent discussions led to a clear description of the many problems involved, and ultimately to a set of recommendations with which the entire group was pleased. These recommendations were presented to proper authorities, and most of them put into effect within three years. When a group gets into a discussion of what must be done to get needed information, the spirit of teamwork is something to behold! And the solutions usually work.

Perhaps the greatest obstacle to problem-centered thinking is the leader or other member who comes to the group with the problem solved in his own mind. Needed is the spirit of humility, which does not know too much and realizes all of us know only a part.

Agree Upon Criteria

Many times there is a lack of "reality testing" before a decision is made final. Other times, a group cannot agree on which of two or more possible solutions to adopt. If the problem has been fully explored, the most likely source of difficulty is a lack of clear-cut standards, criteria, or objectives. In many discussions there is a need for two considerations of criteria: first, when formulating the specific objectives of the group; second, when stating specific standards to be used in judging among solutions. Until agreement (explicit or intuitive) is reached on criteria, agreement on a solution is unlikely.

From the beginning of the discussion, the group needs to be clearly aware of the limitations placed upon it. This is sometimes called the group's area of freedom. The group which tries to make decisions affecting matters over which it has no authority will be both confused and frustrated. For example, the area of freedom for a group of university students includes recommending changes in teaching methods, but students have no authority to make or enforce policy governing such changes. A committee may be given power to recommend plans for a new building, but not to make the final decision and contract for the building. Any policy decision or plan of action must be judged by whether or not it fits into the group's area of

(continued from page 168)

nylon point that won't push down." And you've got three trumpets going, and an announcer comes back in and says, "Flair even looks like a better way to write." We would play it very straight. Very pompous. Like Robert Morley's voice when he says these words. You get a kind of electricity between the silliness.

Westbrook: Let's face it. People just don't get emotionally involved with their pens. I think there's the danger of taking yourself too seriously when you're talking about a thing like that.

Lehner: We have other ideas that we think would be stronger at this point in time. For instance, one thing that we're playing with now is a guy sitting at his desk . . .

Westbrook: A big, snappy executive.

Lehner: And his secretary is with him and this guy is making notations like a guy would. Writing. "Yeah." "No." "See me . . ."

Westbrook: "You're fired." Stuff like that.

Lehner: And when the girl goes out of the room, he takes a leather portfolio, looks around, opens it up and starts doodling some very silly, funny little things. And the announcer says: "Introducing a new executive status symbol — Flair. To the casual observer, Flair is a dignified, serious, executive pen. But when you're alone, Flair reveals its true identity as the executive play pen. The greatest doodler in the world. This Christmas give him the executive play pen, Flair."

Westbrook: That's a great line! I think we ought to pretend like we got some new colors and see what we can do with it.

Nathanson: What a television color commercial it could be, with fuchsias and, oh, I don't know, you name them. You know, orchid colors. You'll get women to write letters wih orchid . . .

Westbrook: You could have a black pen with white ink or a white pen with black ink. Sort of an integrated pen, you know. (*Laughter*.) It could be called "the soul pen."

Nathanson: Black paper!

Westbrook: With white ink! That's groovy!

Nathanson: With blue paper!

Westbrook: Purple paper with pink ink! Pink paper with purple ink!

Nathanson: Brown ink! We present them with a whole slew of marvelous ideas. Sealskin and alligator pens!

Westbrook: Phony fur pens! Wouldn't you love a fur pen? A mink pen? How about a tiger pen? Or a leopard pen? Would you believe an alligator pen?

Natkin: How about a grey flannel pen?

Westbrook: Grey flannel is out. How about a turtleneck pen?

(*To learn what, if anything, resulted from this meeting, watch your TV set.*)

freedom. Thus, if a committee is authorized to spend up to $500, it must evaluate all possible ideas by that absolute criterion.

It is important to rank criteria, giving priority to those which must be met. Ideas proposed can be rated yes or no on whether they meet all the absolute criteria, and from excellent to poor on how well they measure up to the less important criteria.

Single words, such as *efficient*, are not criteria, but categories of criteria. Such words are so vague that they are meaningless when applied to possible solutions. They can be used to find specific criteria. Criteria should be worded as questions or absolute statements. For example, the following criteria might be applied to plans for a club's annual banquet:

Absolute — Must not cost over $400 for entertainment.
Must be enjoyable to both members and their families.

Questions — How convenient is the location for members?
How comfortable is the room?

Defer Judgment When Finding Solutions

Instead of evaluating each possible solution when it is first proposed, defer judgment until a complete list of possible solutions has been produced. Much of the research already quoted indicates that the process of *idea getting* should be separated from *idea evaluation*. Judgment stifles unusual and novel ideas. New ideas come from a minority, and do not have the support of experience or common sense. It is a good idea to list the proposed solutions on a chart or chalkboard. Encouragement should be given to combine, modify, or build upon previous suggestions. Get as many ideas as you can, and permit no criticism of them until after the list is complete.

Plan How to Implement and Follow up

Many times a group will arrive to no avail at a policy decision, a solution to a problem, a resolution or some advice. No plans are made for putting it into effect or to see if the ideas are received by the proper authorities. Every problem-solving discussion should terminate in some plan for action; no such group should consider its work finished until agreement is reached on who is to do exactly what, by what time, and how. If a committee is to make recommendations to a parent body, the committee should decide who will make the report, when he will make it, and in what form. If this report is to be made at a membership meeting, the committee members may then decide to prepare seconding or supporting speeches, may decide how to prepare the general membership to accept their recommendations and so forth. A neighborhood group that has decided to turn a vacant lot into a playground would have to plan how to get legal clearances, who to get to do the work, where to get the materials (or at least from whom), and how to check on the use children get from the playground. No good chairman or leader of a problem-solving group would fail to see that the group worked out details of how to put their decisions into effect.

━━━━━━━━━━━━━━━━━━━━━━━━

Creativity will improve your problem-solving ability.

━━━━━━━━━━━━━━━━━━━━━━━━

Brainstorming

Occasionally a problem-solving group may want to engage in a full-fledged brainstorming discussion. Brainstorming depends on the deferment of judgment; many auxiliary skills and techniques can be used to advantage. Brainstorming can be applied to any problem if there is a wide range of possible solutions, none of which can in advance be said to be just right. The process of brainstorming can be applied to any phase of the discussion: finding information (What information do we need? How might we get this information?), finding criteria (What criteria might we use to test ideas?), finding ideas (What might we do?), or implementation (How might we put our decision into effect?). In addition to what has been said about creative problem solving, the following rules of brainstorming should be presented to the group:

1. *All criticism is ruled out while brainstorming.*
2. *The wilder the ideas, the better.* Even offbeat, impractical suggestions may suggest practical ideas to other members.
3. *Quantity is wanted.* The more ideas, the more likelihood of good ones.
4. *Combination and improvement are wanted.* If you see a way to improve on a previous idea, snap your fingers to get attention so it can be recorded at once.

It is often advantageous to have in the discussion group both people with experience and people quite new to the specific problem (for a fresh point of view). A full-time recorder is needed to write down ideas as fast as they are suggested. Sometimes this can be done with a tape recorder, but a visual record that all can see is best. Be sure the recorder gets all ideas in accurate form.

The flow of possible solutions can sometimes be increased by asking idea-spurring questions. One can ask: "How can we adapt (modify, rearrange, reverse, combine, minimize, maximize) *any general solution*?" A concrete suggestion can be used to open up creative thinking in a whole area. For example, someone might suggest: "Place a guard at each door." The leader could then ask, "What else might be done to increase security?" When the group seems to have run out of ideas, try reviewing the list rapidly; then ask for a definite number of additional suggestions to see if you can get more ideas. Usually you will get many more, including some very good ones.

1. Irving J. Lee, *How to Talk with People* (New York: Harper and Brothers, 1952), p. 62.

2. Norman R. F. Maier, *Problem-Solving Discussions and Conferences* (New York: McGraw-Hill Book Company, 1963), p. 123.

Prods

1. How many small groups do you belong to? Which one is most effective? Why? What specific factors influenced your choice?
2. Chat with a manager of a local company about the number of small groups in his or her unit. In the manager's opinion, which are more effective and which are less effective. Determine why.
3. Could answers to questions 1 and 2 be secured better by a group or by an individual? Why?
4. Think of a group to which you belong. Is the climate primarily defensive or supportive? Cite specific examples to support your answer.
5. Ask the convention manager of a local hotel to evaluate a recent conference held there. What type of conference was it? How large? What kinds of leadership problems occurred during the conference? What did the conference leader(s) do to improve the efficiency of the conference?
6. List twenty possible ways to improve national elections, and note how long this task took you. Ask three to five other people to work together on such a list, and note the time they spent. Did the group produce a larger number of better ideas? Explain the results.

A public message deals with matters of concern to a large group or to several small groups.

Organizing messages around a body of information of interest to listeners will enhance your effectiveness as a speaker.

A public speaker is someone who seeks to inform or influence an audience.

Relationship

4

Speaker-Audience

The Public-Communication Perspective

George A. Borden, Richard B. Gregg, and Theodore G. Grove

The word *public* moves the messages we are going to be dealing with beyond the sphere of individual privacy. Of course, persons may respond to a public message either individually or in private. But the messages we are talking about either are intended to reach many people or, in the case of private messages which receive public exposure, have the potential of reaching many people.

To say that a message is intended for widespread public consumption or even for the consumption of a few score persons implies certain things about the nature of the message. Generally a public message concerns matters that have relevance to a group or groups of people; it contains meaning that is in the public domain. The concept of *public*, as we have just used it, is necessarily a complicated one which we shall explore further at various points in our discussion. We cannot easily maintain a distinction here between public and private; certainly the usual superficial distinctions will not do. While it may usually be held that such topics as sexual behavior are of a private nature, the legitimate theater, movies, television, magazines, novels, published scientific reports which have been popularized, and the growing public discussion of population control have all focused widespread attention on various aspects of sex. One can turn to almost any area of behavior which may be considered private and find that public conversation has been conducted on it.

Perhaps an example or two will help us understand the nature of public interest. A teacher who decides to lecture a student on the vices of inadequate classroom behavior or improper study habits probably chooses to do so in the privacy of an office. The subject to be discussed, at this time, concerns only the student involved. To be sure, some of what is said may be generally applicable to the whole student body, but, for the moment, very specific and individual behaviors are the salient points of the discussion, and others need not discuss, evaluate, or vote on the matter. Similarly, when a group of corporation executives gather to discuss the proper marketing techniques for a new product, they refrain from airing their views in public. Once again, there is a public relevance because decisions reached in the discussion will affect the consumer. But, for the moment, the interests of the discussants do not include the production of mes-

> *A public message deals with matters of concern to a large group or to several small groups.*

George A. Borden, Richard B. Gregg, and Theodore G. Grove, SPEECH BEHAVIOR AND HUMAN INTERACTION, © 1969. Reprinted by permission of Prentice-Hall, Inc., Englewood Cliffs, New Jersey.

Beetle Bailey *by Mort Walker*

sages for public consumption or for influencing public behavior.

Public messages are statements which are of interest to many people; the number may be 200 or several million. But the message must have a certain significance to a particular segment of the public before we can conclude that it is a public message.

In another sense, the language of a public message is more general than specific and more pluralistic than individualistic. Generally, public messages do not contain queries about personal health, murmurs of individual endearment, or the individual abbreviations one hears in a conversational setting. In private the language code tends to be very flexible and elaborate, filled with personal phrasing and connotation; but in public it is restricted so that the recipients' understandings of the message overlap. Of course the public language code may be technical and specialized and therefore somewhat mystifying to the average person. The terminology of psychologists or philosophers assembled in convention is highly technical. But, for the immediate public attending the convention, the code is understandable and a part of its lexicon.

Another dimension of the public-communication situation which differentiates it from interpersonal or small-group activity has to do with interaction between speaker and listener. In a public situation, the receiver of a message has less opportunity for interaction with the communicator than he does in a face-to-face or small-group situation. Consequently, the pressures to conform with the ideas expressed by the communicator are probably not so great, and the opportunities for influencing the communicator, at least the immediate opportuni-

ties, are not so prevalent. As we shall see later, communicator-listener interaction plays a significant role in determining the final effect of a public message.

No doubt you will be able to find various exceptions to the general distinctions we have just noted. One of the problems confronting any student of communication is that of knowing where to draw realistic boundaries—realistic in the sense that they do not distort the nature of the communication process too severely. We trust that our distinctions place the communication we shall be examining into a workable context; we make no claim that these boundaries are hard and fast.

The Communicator

Common sense tells us that the perceived character of the speaker is one of the factors which shape an auditor's response to a verbal message. All of us know certain individuals who command our respect for one reason or another and other individuals whom we hold in comparatively low esteem. We tend to grant a certain amount of credibility to the statements of people we respect, but we are likely to discount the opinions of those individuals we hold in low esteem. As a result of this understandable human behavior, the respected person has an easier time convincing us that his point of view is correct than does someone we do not like.

Aristotle listed ethos, the character of the speaker, as one of the three means of artistic persuasion in speaking.[1] . . . The concept of ethos has occupied a central place in the study of oral communication ever since Aristotle proclaimed its potent, persuasive force. In recent years studies on

the influence of a speaker's personality, character, or authoritativeness have provided empirical confirmation of the early Greek observation. Various studies in psychology, sociology, speech, education, and communication deal with differing aspects of ethos. Andersen and Clevenger, in their excellent summary of experimental research in ethos, state that the findings are neither sufficiently numerous nor sufficiently sophisticated to enable one to draw definite conclusions about the operation of ethos.[2]

Clearly Aristotle did not think it desirable to judge the character of the speaker on the basis of any prior impression. Rather, he felt the speech itself must contain the elements by which an auditor decides that the speaker is good or evil, credible or fraudulent. Nonetheless, it is equally clear that auditors do allow prior impressions to influence their reaction to a message, so we must include more in a realistic concept of ethos than Aristotle was willing to include. We need first to draw a distinction between genuine ethos and perceived ethos.

Obviously, the more we know about an individual through personal contact, the better able we are to make judgments of his honesty, sincerity, geniality, humanitarianism, and so on. When people with whom we are familiar express their opinions, we have some idea of whether they are objective or biased, realistic or visionary, probing or superficial. In other words, we have some insight into their real character.

Auditors of public communication are seldom in a position to render judgments based on intimate knowledge. Consequently many different factors, some genuine signs of character and some spurious and misleading,

influence the image, or perceived ethos, of a speaker. Andersen and Clevenger[3] suggest the term *image* because it refers to the ideas an auditor has about the character of a speaker, whether those ideas are correct, partially correct, or totally erroneous. An auditor may accept what a communicator says because he has heard the communicator described as an expert on his subject. Or the communicator may be a member of the same political party as the auditor or share the same religious viewpoint or express the same biases during the course of his statement or just be good looking. For any of these and similar reasons an auditor may tend to accept the statements of the communicator without serious question. On the other hand, if a communicator belongs to an opposing political party or interest group, possesses a differing ethnic background, expresses "unacceptable" biases or values, or is slovenly in personal appearance, these facts may provide justification for dismissing his statements summarily. As human beings we may deplore an auditor's reasons for liking or disliking a speaker, but as students of communication we must realize that the image of the speaker held by the auditor, for whatever reason, in some measure affects the auditor's response to the speaker's message.

The Message

The message, that is, what the communicator says or writes, purports to be the central element in the transaction that takes place between communicator and auditor. We use the word *purports* deliberately because at times a message has less importance than does some other element of the communicative situation. We have just talked about occasions when our image of the communicator can determine whether we accurately perceive and evaluate a message. Past experience and knowledge stored in our memory system may cause us to misinterpret and misjudge the intent of a message. Personal predispositions, biases, and needs all influence the reception and processing of a message.

Nevertheless, when human minds come into contact with one another during the course of communication, the message is one of the primary means of accomplishing that contact, and therefore it must always be considered an important variable.

Three basic elements of messages can be separated for analysis: the ideational, or content, element, i.e., the meaning; the organizational characteristics, or the form of the message; the linguistic element, or the language used to express the meaning. We need to remember that these elements are not perceived as discrete units by an auditor, even though we talk about them as if they were. Messages, particularly spoken ones, are perceived holistically, and we cannot realistically assess the impact of one element apart from the impact of the others.

When we ask "What does the message mean?" or "What is the point of the message?" we are referring to the content element of communication. The communicator has certain ideas he wants to explain or express, a certain point of view about a subject he wants to project, or particular argumentative claims he wishes to have accepted. This is what the message is all about; it is the residual meaning the communicator hopes the receiver will remember when the communication act is over and all else is forgotten. In a well constructed message, the major ideas constituting the residual message stand out and are easily ascertained.

If the message is anything other than assertion, the communicator must include supporting ideas, illustrations, explanations, and other data to uphold the major ideas. In addition, nearly all messages, particularly those that are argumentative or persuasive in intent, either explicitly or implicitly express attitudinal stances, value judgments, ethical presuppositions, and other bits of emotional data. Obviously, the longer a message, the more secondary illustrative and supporting material it is likely to contain.

No matter how we describe message content, the important point is that meaning does not ultimately reside in the message but rather in the minds of receivers. The various ideas that make up the message—the examples, the statistics, the authoritative references, and the appeals—all act as stimulators which trigger meaning in the minds of receivers. To the extent that the understanding and experience of the receivers overlap with those of the communicator, there will be identity of meaning. But to a significant degree meanings remain essentially individualized and private, human experiences do not precisely overlap, and the particular needs and values of one individual lead him to perceive a problem differently from the way his neighbor does. We often see what we want to see and hear what we want to hear in a message. Therefore it is difficult to generalize about auditor reactions to a message from an examination of the components of the message alone.

For analytical purposes, we may separate the form of a message—

that is, the way in which it is organized for presentation, the order in which ideas are presented, and the placement of supporting data or evidence in relation to major ideas—and discuss it apart from the content. Various studies have been undertaken to determine whether one organizational pattern is more effective than another, either in terms of persuading or bringing understanding. The results of such studies are too varied or the attitude changes measured are too insignificant to allow the formulation of any meaningful generalizations. At times stronger arguments ought to be stated first, and at other times they are better left until last; sometimes both sides of an issue should be presented, and on other occasions only the favored side should be discussed, etc. We would be hasty to conclude, however, that the form in which a message is cast is meaningless. We may more wisely conclude that it does not make sense to measure the influence of form apart from content, situation, audience, and other variables. The human auditor tends to respond holistically, not compartmentally, and his reactions simply do not stand still for neat slicing. But it is precisely because the mind reacts holistically, abhorring the formless and imposing closure and pattern wherever possible, that the form of a message is an important ingredient in the total analysis. Thus we may gain insight into the workings of a message by examining the formal skeleton shaping the content.

Without language there would be no message as we are talking about it here, so it goes without saying that the linguistic element deserves our attention. There is general agreement that man's development of language, the symbol system he uses to convey meanings to his fellows, is one of the things which most clearly separates him from other animals. The very existence of language illustrates man's unique capacity to internalize his environment and to reproduce it in a symbolic form. Language not only represents external reality but also encompasses emotional responses to that reality; thus, when we examine the meanings contained in language, we are dealing with human reality or reality as man sees it. The reality represented in linguistic meaning may not, and in fact often does not, accurately portray what is in the external world. But language does convey symbolically what man believes is there, and that is what we must be concerned with.

We often think of language as the primary means of conveying meaning in communication, but this is not an accurate understanding of what linguistic symbols do. Rather than carrying meaning from one mind to another, language symbols evoke meaning in the minds of auditors. For communication to be successful in terms of achieving understanding, there must be some correspondence of meaning between the speaker who uses a symbol and the auditor who hears it. We assume a certain generality of meaning on the part of individuals who speak the same language, and correctly so because without this generality there could be no linguistic communication. But we must grant the general assumption with care because no two individuals have precisely the same experiences and they are not likely to have precisely the same meanings for words. Obviously the more abstract the term, the less we can assume similarity of meaning between communicator and auditor. The symbol *dog* probably evokes similar meanings more often and more easily than does the symbol *justice*. To compound the difficulty, language, as we have already seen, is attitudinal to a large extent. Linguistic symbols evoke emotional feelings which are as much a part of the meaning as any physical object to which the symbol may refer. Politicians, advertising agents, propagandists, and the like capitalize daily on the rhetorical aspects of language, that is, on the ability of language to evoke attitudes of value and judgment which can ultimately lead to action. Therefore it behooves those of us who are interested in understanding communication to be aware of the linguistic element of a message both for the meaning (or lack of it) evoked and for the attitudes engendered.

We have discussed message characteristics only briefly, but the reader should recognize by now that what humans bring to a message is probably more important than what the message contains. Thus everything discussed in this book is ultimately related to human reaction to messages.

The Audience

Traditionally, textbooks on speech and oral communication deal with communication from the standpoint of the speaker. In so doing they sustain the point of view of the Greeks and Romans, who were primarily interested in providing useful techniques for effective speaking. They did not overlook audiences, to be sure, because a communicator had to know something about the kind of audience he was speaking to, its interests and values, its sociological makeup, and other pertinent personal characteristics in order to compose an appropriate

and successful message. The basis of the traditional point of view was the assumption that the principal initiator in a communicative act is the speaker. If he adjusts successfully to his audience, he can achieve his purpose. A corollary assumption was that a speaker who fails to evoke the intended response from his listeners has not successfully utilized or manipulated all the materials at his disposal in light of what he knows about his audience.

The traditional focus has some validity of course, but it is not the whole picture. In the past few years, researchers in communication have given increased emphasis to audiences, realizing that they are as influential in determining the nature and effect of a message as is any other element in the communicative process.

Anyone interested in understanding how man behaves during the process of communication must devote considerable time and effort to determining the nature of audiences for here he may discover his most useful leads. Here he must realize that an audience is not passive but makes demands of a communicator at the same time the communicator is placing demands on his audience. We may realistically describe a communicative act as a symbolic transaction involving a bargain between communicator and auditor; the interaction between the parties involved is never unidimensional but always reciprocal.

We describe audiences in various ways depending upon what characteristics we choose as being definitive. We may start with size. At one end of a continuum we place small audiences, such as local P.T.A. groups, civic clubs, or church groups. On the other end of the continuum we place the international audience be- cause our rapidly developing systems of international communication make it possible for a multitude of persons from different countries to hear a public message or to see a public message or both. At various points along the continuum we place audiences of other sizes — local radio and T.V. audiences, large numbers of people gathered in one hall as at our national political conventions, and, of course, the national television audience, which changes in size depending upon the nature of the communicative event. Or we may devise a continuum based on similarity characteristics, grouping very homogeneous audiences at one end and extremely heterogeneous audiences at the other.

A second dimension is that of homogeneity or heterogeneity in terms of audience beliefs, attitudes, goals. etc. Obviously, a communicator directs his messages more easily to those audiences with similar beliefs than to those with widely differing and divergent points of view. On one end of our continuum we may place audiences made up of small, local groups of people drawn together by a common interest, while at the other end we may again place the international audience, made up of groups of people in various countries who are interested in the subject matter of a message for one reason or another but who react differently depending upon their particular attitudes and goals. In between we may place audiences united by a general goal but still having sufficient differences over how to achieve the goal to account for differing reactions to the same message. The audience at one of our national political nominating conventions is a case in point; usually all delegates are united by a desire to advance the welfare of their party, but divergent local and regional problems may cause divisions on specific party policy. Obviously the more heterogeneous an audience is in terms of attitudes and beliefs, the wider the appeal of a message has to be to achieve its purpose; hence the more general and abstract its terminology is likely to be.

One conclusion from our brief attention to the nature of audiences is clear: The audience is an extremely important element in the communication process not only because it is the recipient of the message and will react to it but also because it can exert considerable controlling influence over the entire nature of the communicative act.

Climate of Opinion

So far we have been focusing on the inherent elements of the act of public communication — the communicator, the message that is communicated, and the audience to whom the communication is directed. Now we must broaden our perspective to include those situational and social phenomena which exert their influence on any act of public communication. In so doing, we shall be dealing with a very nebulous and immeasurable constellation of physical acts and events, social attitudes and values, and public moods and feelings which we call the *climate of opinion*. A climate of opinion inevitably surrounds every act of public communication, so it is necessary to understand the way in which this social milieu can substantially affect the impact of such communication.

It is difficult to delineate any pattern of climate-of-opinion elements which can be expected to hold from one communicative situation to another. Generally we

can say that certain physical occurrences and events help to formulate the social climate of the times; attitudes both interpretative and evaluative form about the physical events and are reflected in public opinion, and certain cultural and social judgments and presuppositions always actively exert their influence by guiding perception and reflection.

All these elements combine to provide the social setting, or the climate of opinion, which acts as background for a specific communicative act. The climate of opinion heightens some attitudes, obliterates others, makes some considerations seem more important than others, calls forth certain values, and negates others. In public communication, specifically, the climate of opinion causes some messages to be prominent and others unimportant, and otherwise affects the way in which messages are received and interpreted.

Cultural Context

We must finally broaden our focus to include those habitual mannerisms, customs, attitudes, and institutions that form the cultural patterns whose influence is a significant factor in human affairs. Each community possesses its peculiar cultural characteristics which the larger cultural patterns of a whole people in turn subsume. These cultural patterns facilitate and strengthen both the communion and the communication of a people and at the same time control human behavior so subtly that they are often unnoticed. Anyone who has studied anthropology is aware of the influence of such cultural institutions as religion, family, home, and education. With these institutions we must include such cultural factors as patterns of behavior and manners, customs and traditions, and rituals and myths, which shape perceptions, attitudes, and judgments. All these and other factors form a *cultural screen* through which man receives his experience; thus man's perceptions of reality and consequently his behavior are already largely determined for him.

It is impossible to categorize and illustrate all the ways in which cultural differences can affect communication. Language differences reflect cultural differences, and, since language controls thought processes to some extent, there are obviously differences in patterns of thinking from one culture to another. Different cultures attach varying meanings to the same word and so interpret a communicative message in different ways. They have differing images of what constitutes communicator respectability and credibility; some cultures favor a thoroughly reasonable approach (by Western standards) when a cause or policy is being advocated, while others are susceptible to a more intuitive, emotional stance; some cultures place great value on the pragmatic workability of suggested proposals and appeals, while others appreciate more idealistic conceptions. And always the common attitudes, beliefs, values, and knowledge which accumulate through cultural influence largely account for the success or failure of communication and the variations in audience response. We do not mean to indicate here that man has no freedom whatsoever. We do, however, want to emphasize that man's behavior is controlled far more by his cultural heritage than he is ever aware.

The Interaction of Variables

Now that we have examined the basic variables that constitute and surround the process of public communication, we must picture them interacting with each other in order to arrive at a more holistic and realistic description of the total process. Each of the variables is present and influential whenever public communication occurs. But they do not all exert equal force on the receiver; some predominate over others, and the precise qualitative nature of each variable changes from situation to situation or even from moment to moment. How influential each variable is depends upon the particular perceptions of the individual receiver—his perceptions about himself, about his relationships to others, about his immediate needs in relation to the content of the message and the communicator, etc.

All these differences make it very difficult to understand exactly why a receiver hears, remembers, or behaves the way he does as a result of a specific message. We must draw generalizations concerning the influence of public messages with care and usually must state them in terms of probability or possibility rather than certainty.

1. Aristotle, *Rhetoric*, trans. Lane Cooper (New York: Appleton-Century-Crofts, 1932), pp. 8–9 (1356^a).

2. Kenneth Andersen and Theodore Clevenger, Jr., "A Summary of Experimental Research in Ethos," *Speech Monographs*, XXX (June 1963), 77.

A Good Talk: C.O.D.
(Content, Organization, Delivery)

Robert Haakenson

One afternoon a Roman Emperor was entertaining himself at the Colosseum by feeding Christians to the lions. Several Christians were sacrificed and the crowd screamed for more.

The next martyr said something to the lion, and the beast slunk away. Then a second lion; same result. And a third. The amazed throng began to shift its sympathies to the Christian. The Emperor announced that the Christian's life would be spared. He insisted, however, that the martyr appear before him.

Organizing messages around a body of information of interest to listeners will enhance your effectiveness as a speaker.

"I am sparing your life," said the Emperor, "but before I release you, I demand to know what it was that you said to those beasts."

"I merely said to each lion: 'After dinner, of course, you'll be expected to say a few words.'"

As community-minded adults, each of us faces a pretty good likelihood he will be "asked to say a few words" at least once during the coming year. The audience may be eight or eight hundred—or more likely—forty, a typical community group audience. How do you feel about it? When someone says to you, "Of course, we'll expect you to say a few words after dinner," do you—like the lions—run in dismay? You shouldn't. You should welcome the opportunity. Here are some helps.

FIMP—For Instances Meat and Potatoes: Content

Speech content, what the speaker says, really consists of two things: the topic and the supporting particulars. The most effective particulars are "for instances"; they become the meat and potatoes that put flesh on the speech outline skeleton.

Topics

The topic may be assigned or it may be left to the speaker's choice. It may be narrowly defined, even specifically phrased, or it may be suggested in the most general sort of way. The speaker may believe the more strictly he limits the topic the more he simplifies his assignment. This is not necessarily true. The decision must be made on the basis of analysis of the audience and commitment to meeting its believed needs.

If the speaker believes a general introduction to the subject is the most useful for the audience, then he will conceive of his topic as a broad survey. He may, on the other hand, determine he will be more helpful if he limits the topic to a narrow aspect and then will develop it in depth.

In the early stages of preparation he should approach the topic comprehensively, but keeping in mind the audience's believed interest. Later on, especially when phrasing his central idea (to be described later), he will sharpen his concept of the topic, covering only what he wishes to cover and taking into account the response he hopes to win from his hearers.

Supporting Particulars

Now, regarding supporting particulars amplifying details, specifics, or FIMP, let us ask: What forms do they take? How do we go about finding them? How do we select them for inclusion?

Types   Following is a list of types of particulars. It is not exhaustive, but illustrates the possibilities:

>   Instances
>   Case histories
>   Events
>   Examples, illustrations: real or
>   hypothetical
>   Narratives: true or fictitious;
>   serious or humorous
>   Definition
>   Description
>   Contrast/comparison

>   Enumeration/listing
>   Figures/statistics
>   Humor: quip, pun, repartee
>   Quotation: witness testimony,
>   authority opinion
>   Figure of speech: allegory, per-
>   sonification
>   Audio-visual aid

Sources   The speaker should be active in four ways in conducting his research: *reflection* (taking stock of what he already knows); *reading* (reviewing all types of printed material); *conversation* (formal and informal talks with experts and lay people, informal polls or questionnaires); *observation* (some topics lend themselves to direct investigation, e.g., community improvements, institutions, organizations, landmarks, nature).

Some tips: begin with *reflection*. Almost always we will surprise ourselves on what we already know on any given topic. Jot down notes during this inventory-taking. Second, do at least some or all of the first three, and —if at all possible—the fourth. Varied research activities provide both perspective and riches of specifics. Third, gather materials voraciously. Our speaker should wind up with at least four times as much material as time will allow him to include in the talk.

Criteria   As our speaker sits down with his voluminous notes, he needs guidelines on what to include and what to reject. Here are four standards:

1. Relevance. No matter how dramatic and appealing the narrative may be, how compelling the instance, it is not worthy of inclusion if it does not amplify the point under consideration. This, therefore, must always be the first test: Is it pertinent? Does it apply?

2. Accuracy. When we are satisfied that the specific applies, then we must satisfy ourselves that it serves truth. Is it representative, typical? In argumentation (speaking to convince), we must concern ourselves with documentation, revelation of sources. Information has a way of being as good as its source. Conversely, highly respected sources have a way of giving credence to data, e.g., "If it came from *Encyclopedia Britannica* it must be true." To that end, we will be careful to note details on printed and spoken sources: person, place, data, time, other circumstances; publication, date, page, etc.

3. Human interest. On a logical basis, relevance and accuracy certainly are the overriding criteria for good speech materials. On a psychological basis, human interest factors rise to the top. "No matter how good your data are," a pragmatist might say, "if they don't capture listeners' attention, they are wasted.

Here are some of the time-honored factors of attention and interest: narrative ("once upon a time . . . "), action, conflict, variety, novelty, the familiar in an unusual context (unexpectedly encountering a neighbor 1000 miles from home), humor, the bizarre or abnormal.

Dr. Russell Conwell, who founded Temple University, was famous for his "Acres of Diamonds" lecture. By giving this talk 7000 times, he earned seven million dollars, many of which were devoted to the education of deserving young men at Temple University. "Acres of Diamonds" is made up of *one story after another*, developing his theme that opportunity lies everywhere about us if we will scratch the surface. Like a skilled composer, Dr. Conwell lost no opportunity to develop his theme.

4. Adequacy. This is a tough criterion. When do we have enough specifics — enough for our listeners' understanding, conviction, motivation? This can only be answered in the crucible of actual speaking.

We can offer a suggestion on the length of a talk, however. A veteran pastor was asked by his new assistant, "How long should I preach when I give my first sermon next Sunday?" "That's up to you," came the reply, "but we feel we don't save any souls after twenty minutes."

Also, we can suggest a formula: "Balance the specific with the general." Use the case history or specific instance, thus providing narrative quality and something with which the listener can identify. Then, lest the listener charge that the specific is atypical or unrepresentative, the speaker advances the appropriate statistic or authority opinion to demonstrate that what is true in the instance cited is generally true. Balance the specific with the general.

Show and Tell: Audio-Visual Aids
A special type of FIMP is audio-visual aids: maps, graphs, charts, tape recordings, phonograph records, flannelboards etc. They are special because they simply present other types of specifics in audible or visual form, e.g., statistics on a graph, description on a photo, authority opinion on a tape recording, etc.

Use of a molecular model in a talk about prescription drugs illustrates many of the principles of effective visual aids. The speaker begins with the octagonal "benzine ring," representing the volatile, poisonous industrial solvent benzine. Then the speaker adds a cluster of red and yellow atoms at the top of the octagon and he has another compound: this time a food preservative for catsup and jellies — benzoic acid. Then the speaker adds another group of atoms and the compound is not volatile or poisonous, not harmful in ordinary doses, but remarkable in pain-killing properties: *aspirin*.

The molecular model illustrates some "RSVP" principles of effective audio-visual aids usage:

Relevant: The aid visually depicts the exact point under discussion: the significance of tiny molecular changes in pharmaceutical research.

Subordinate: The aid is an aid. Too often audio-visual aids dominate, making the speech an audio-aid to a demonstration. A good test is: the point can be made successfully without the aid, but is better because of it.

Visible (audible): Too often, aids are too small, too faint or too complex to be fully clear to all members of the audience. Simplicity and boldness should prevail. Also, the aid should be in sight only while in use. The red, black and yellow balls of the molecular model made it adequately visible for an audience of 800. Further, it offered the great advantage of the speaker keeping it between the audience and himself, keeping unity in focus of attention.

Portable: Most talks are presented in public meeting places.

The speaker must get his aids there and back. Huge billboards, bulky models, weighty devices become big problems. Imaginative use of paper, cloth and slide or filmstrip projections can provide size with minimal inconvenience.

The molecular model also illustrates some of the following desirable practices:

Action: Adding to, or taking away from the aid heightens interest; marking up a map or graph achieves the same.

Use a modest number: A good rule of thumb is one aid per main point. No talk should have more than five main points.

Use a variety of aids: A chart listing main points, a map, a model, a statistical graph, a tape recording.

"Roll your own": Personally-created aids can achieve the simplicity and boldness desired. What they lack in polished artistry may be more than made up for by relevance and impact.

Stow the visual out of sight when not in use. Otherwise it is a distraction, competing for attention. For the same reason, *only in exceptional cases* should aids be distributed to members of audiences. (Handouts may be distributed *after* the talk). (An exception on aids being stowed out of sight is the so-called "organizational visual." This is a card, blackboard, flannelboard or other device listing the main headings of the talk. This visual is introduced when the speaker previews his main headings, kept in sight and referred to as each main point is introduced, and used for the final summary, then put down out of sight before the "haymaker.")

"BUY A CIGAR AND A PAIR OF SPECTACLES."*

°Winston Churchill on how to become an effective speaker

Courtesy of Houghton Mifflin Company.

Tell, Tell and Tell: Organization

Some authorities regard *organization* as the basis of truly versatile eloquence. Let us consider *schema, central ideas, main headings,* and *transitions.*

Schema

We may properly think of almost any communication in this simple schematic:

```
_____
  _____
  _____
  _____
```

The long first line represents the *central idea.* If the communication has unity, it should have a single major theme, thesis, controlling purpose or thrust. Then this central idea should be based systematically on appropriate *main headings,* here represented by the three shorter lines. There should be not fewer than two main headings nor more than five, and the most typical number is three.

Central Idea

How does the speaker come up with the central idea? It may be automatic. He is asked to speak on his opposition to a sales tax for his state. His thesis declares itself: "We must defeat the proposed state sales tax."

Equally often, however, his central idea will be elusive. He is asked to speak on state finances. What does he wish to say? Does he wish to praise or find fault? Does he wish to inform, convince, motivate, inspire, entertain? Does he wish to discuss the broad topic or some limited part? Does he wish his listeners to do something about his recommended program?

When the central idea is elusive, the speaker should give long and hard thought. He may ask himself, "After the sound and the fury, the tumult and the shouting have died, and the details have faded, what is the ultimate 'residue' I would like my listeners to retain?" When he can answer that in a simple declarative sentence, he probably will have his central idea.

Incidentally, when the central idea is simple exposition ("The Community College movement is expanding rapidly"), we call it a *theme.* When it takes sides on a controversial issue ("U.S. should pull its military forces out of Southeast Asia"), we call it a *thesis.* Theses may be stated in different ways calling for different patterns of main headings (see below).

Even if the central idea pretty well decides itself, give it long thought, especially in terms of the response wanted from the audience.

Main Headings

When the central idea has been declared, it is usually relatively easy to come up with the main headings (main points). We wish to wind up with not fewer than two nor more than five: fewer than two, we are not subdividing; more than five, we are not grouping properly. A major purpose of grouping is to serve memory—the audience's *and the speaker's.* Also, almost any central idea will subdivide itself very nicely into two, three, four, or five main headings that cover the subject and are parallel. The most frequent number, as you will see, is three. Some persons trace this to the religious Trinity; others to the fact that any continuum has two extremes and a middle ground.

Items, events and phenomena in our universe tend to organize themselves into four major patterns. Following are those four with illustrative "stock designs" for each:

1. Chronological or time sequence: past, present, future

   Lincoln's Gettysburg Address, which had its 100th anniversary on November 19, 1964, is a classic example: "Fourscore and seven years ago . . . Now we are engaged in a great civil war . . . It is for us, the living, rather to be dedicated here . . ."

2. Spatial (topographical or geographic)

   federal, state, local
   metropolitan, suburban, rural
   inside, outside
   near, mid-distant, far
   left, center, right
   forward, midships, aft
   top, middle, bottom
   East Coast, Midwest, Rockies, Southwest, Far West
   Cook County, Downstate Illinois
   upper peninsula, lower peninsula
   land surfaces, water surfaces

3. Topical (distributive or classification)

   who, what, where, when, how, why (sometimes)
   theory, practice
   quality, price, service, beauty
   background, problem, methodology, findings, implications
   flora, fauna
   animal, vegetable, mineral

A very useful device both for preliminary analysis of a complex subject and later selection of main headings is the so-called decachotomy: political, social, economic, religious/moral/ethical, philosophical, educational, scientific, cultural/esthetic, military, psychological. If we were to investigate a subject such as electoral college reform, we might use this list to decide that the most important implications are political, social, and philosophical. Later, in making the talk, we might elect the same three as the best main headings.

4. Logical

> problem, damage (consequences), solution
> need, desirability, practicality
> cause, effect

There is good reason to believe that the most used stock design is the chronological (past, present, future). This is not surprising. When we consider almost any topic, it is natural to reflect: "What is the background; how did we get into this? Where do we find ourselves now? What is the next step?"

The most-used stock design probably should be problem, damage, solution. This is because we speak purposefully, to meet needs, to resolve problems, to achieve progress. Damage is included because it is the springboard of audience involvement. If, for example, we develop the problem of the electorate's persistent defeats of proposals to fluoridate the public water supply, and the recommended solution is to enlighten the electorate by a program of education, the listener might nod his head in agreement. "Yes; quite right; good sense"; but all at arm's length. If, on the other hand, the speaker drives home incontrovertibly that while this problem continues, *it is these very listeners* and *their children who pay the*

consequences (dental decay, pain, cosmetic unattractiveness, inconvenience, financial cost), the listener not only agrees but is ready to act—no longer arm's length, now shoulder-to-shoulder.

The problem-solution design, of course, is a foreshortening of educational philosopher John Dewey's reflective process: define the problem—nature, extent, cause(s); list all plausible alternative solutions; weigh and evaluate each alternative solution; select the best alternative solution (or best compromise or combination); recommend action to implement the solution selected. Then, at that point, reflection ceases and action begins.

Occasionally we hear of a fifth pattern of analysis, called the "psychological." Here the intent is to match the listener's reaction, meeting his interest (or disinterest) as we predictably will find it, and moving ahead as it (human nature) would. Richard Borden's "Ho Hum" formula is a good example:

> Ho hum
> Why bring that up?
> For instance
> So what?

The "AIDA" formula for successful advertising is another: attention, interest, desire, and action. Purdue University's Alan Monroe advanced a "motivated sequence," blending the logical problem-solution with psychological factors: attention step, need step, satisfaction step, visualization step, and action step.

Earlier we referred to central ideas that develop partisan stands on controversial issues being called theses. And we said that when these are stated in certain ways, they call for the development of main headings (contentions or arguments) in corresponding patterns. A thesis

may be stated as a question of fact, quality, degree or policy. When we argue whether a thing exists or is real, we declare our thesis as a question of fact. We will find that developing our main headings to establish theory and practice will be wise. ("Cigaret smoking causes lung cancer"; "Extrasensory perception is a fact.")

When we argue whether a thing is good, beautiful, dependable, we state the thesis as a question of quality, e.g., "Television is good entertainment"; "Modern art is ugly"; "The sales tax is unfairly discriminatory." We will find that using criteria as main headings will serve well, e.g., "U.S. compact autos provide fine transportation" (thesis) and quality, price, service, safety, beauty (main headings).

When we argue whether a thing is better or worse than, larger or smaller than, prettier or uglier than something else, we are stating the thesis as a question of degree, e.g., "U.S. compact autos are superior to foreign-made." Again we will be well-advised to develop main headings as criteria, e.g., "Radio news coverage is superior to television's" (thesis) and speed, accuracy, comprehensiveness, clarity (main headings).

When we argue whether something ought or ought not to be done, we state the thesis as a question of policy, e.g. "We should fluoridate the public water supply"; "We must stop the military conflict in Southeast Asia"; "The United Nations should not admit Red China to membership." Main headings here should establish problem, damage, and solution, e.g., thesis: "We should support programs of planned parenthood in all developing nations"; main headings: "1. The problem of world overpopulation

A STUDENT CAN BE CONFIDENT

ABOUT ASSIGNMENTS IN

if he knows about

is acute. 2. Dire consequences are starvation, grinding poverty and political exploitation. 3. Expansion of birth control programs is a practical and desirable solution."

Transitions

Structure of the speech should emerge boldly. If the listener can visualize the framework he can help the speaker fit the component parts together in their intended relationships. Nonetheless there should be smooth transitions that tie part-to-part and part-to-whole. The best transition is a partial summary, e.g., "Thus we see there is a critical problem of overcrowded classrooms. Secondly, let us consider the consequences while this problem continues . . . " Other transitional devices include enumeration (e.g., "Secondly, consequences"), questions (e.g., "Next we may ask: who is affected by this situation?"), directional phrases (e.g., "Let us move then"), audio-visual aids (e.g., "Consider now, please, this portion of the display").

Model Outline

The following is a model outline, employing the recommendations above, but not including the actual supporting particulars (specifics) that flesh out the skeleton.

  I. Introduction
    A. Icebreaker
      1. Reference to audience's (Olympia Civic Association's) contributions to mental health programs
      2. Reference to the speaker's own service with the Mayor's Committee
      3. Reference to the day's news item on the Committee's proposal

4. Case history of John D., whose rehabilitation was botched by archaic mental health services

B. Preview
1. We must all help in establishing the Olympia Community Mental Health Center
   a. Problem of out-dated mode of treatment
   b. Damages to patients, families and community
   c. Workability, desirability and bonuses of Committee's Plan

II. Body
A. We all must help in establishing the Olympia Community Mental Health Center
1. Problem of antiquated approach to treating mental and emotional illness
   a. Olympia facilities are antiquated ("specifics")
   b. Olympia modes of treatment are consequently archaic ("specifics")
2. Damage
   a. Patients suffer longer and more intensely than necessary ("specifics")
   b. Family is distraught and inconvenienced unnecessarily ("specifics")
   c. Olympia taxpayers and citizens generally bear the brunt ("specifics")
3. Solution
   a. Mayor's Committee's proposed plan to im-

and understands the purpose and application of

as well as the elements of effective

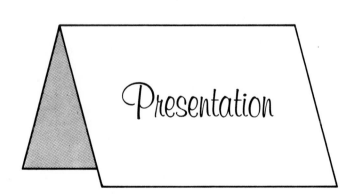

plement Community Mental Health Center is practical, dealing with problem at its roots ("specifics")
    b. Plan is desirable, consistent with highest precepts of community action for local problems ("specifics")
    c. Plan offers several "extras," bonus advantages ("specifics")

III. Conclusion
  A. Summary
    1. We must all move directly and speedily to establish the Olympia Community Mental Health Center
      a. The problem of outmoded treatment is a civic disgrace
      b. The consequences touch every Olympian, certainly the community leaders here assembled
      c. Support of Olympia Civic Association members will help implement Committee's eminently practical and highly desirable plan.
  B. Haymaker
    1. Recall case of "John D."? Never again need this tragedy occur if we will act now.

From the foregoing it can be seen that the heart of this outline is the schema: central idea and main headings. The speaker will "tell 'em what he's gonna tell 'em, tell 'em, and tell 'em what he told 'em"—preview, body and summary. Then to this basic pattern he adds an icebreaker to begin, and a haymaker to conclude.

The purposes of the icebreaker are two: (1) to call attention to, and arouse interest in the speaker and his topic; and (2) to create common bonds and warm rapport between speaker and audience.

Chief icebreaker items are narratives (preferably of the case history type); references to the audience, topic and/or occasion (latter includes "outside world," e.g., news of the day); humorous anecdotes; participation, such as show of hands, rhetorical questions; sensational "shocker" statements; definitions; quotations of Scripture, maxims, poetry; audio-visual aids, and the like.

If time is plentiful the speaker may wish to use several of these items to arouse interest and build rapport. Perhaps the best icebreaker is the case history type of narrative. It attracts attention (we never outgrow the magic of "let me tell you a story") and arouses interest. Properly selected it creates mutual ties among speaker, topic, audience and occasion—definitely identifying the speaker with topic—and clarifies the talk's theme.

The purposes of the haymaker are to bring the talk to a climactic finale, and for the speaker to land his final blow for his central idea. (Ancient orators made much of the *peroration* in which the speaker made his final eloquent plea for his central idea.)

The speaker may use for his haymaker many of the selfsame items he uses for the icebreaker: quotation, rhetorical question, humor, participation. It is particularly esthetically satisfying if the haymaker can revert back to the icebreaker, bringing the talk full-circle. Possibly the best combination, therefore, is, for an icebreaker, a case history type narrative that illustrates the talk's central idea, and, for a haymaker, another reference to that narrative,

"Well, I see my time is up . . ."

Reprinted from *The Saturday Evening Post,* July 25, 1959. Used by permission of Joe Zeis.

possibly completing the story or bringing it up to date.

Animated Conversationality

Can you recall a recent experience when you went all out in friendly persuasion? You wished to persuade some friend of yours to a point of view or action not for your good, but for his good as you saw it. These things were happening—all intuitively: You brought into play every reason, contention, emotional appeal, instance, description, story, comparison, quotation, figure and statistic that would build your case. You thus employed all the substance or *content* at your disposal.

Secondly you structured your persuasion. You may have said, for example, "All right, we are agreed up to here, are we not?" Then you would venture off into no-man's land, penetrating as deeply as you thought you could before experiencing rebuff. Then you would fall back and regroup, consolidating your gains, then venture off on another tack into no-man's land. Thus you were structuring, adding *organization* to your persuasive armamentarium. Thirdly, your personality ran its gamut and all the techniques of effective presentation came into play as you pled your case.

You were alternately friendly and stern, forceful and humble. Your voice ranged from shouting to whispering and the inflections varied persuasively. Your enunciation was crisp, biting out the syllables of key words with telling precision. You moved about freely, sometimes towering above your friend, sometimes almost on bended knee before him. You gestured freely. Your face was expressive, characterized chiefly by alertness and a friendly smile.

Your eyes rarely left those of your friend as you studied and adapted to his responses. Your language was eloquent; you expressed yourself dynamically in compelling words, phrases and sentences.

If you deliver a speech with animation and enthusiasm, your audience will receive it better.

In short, you were intuitively bringing into play every facet of personality and every aspect of *delivery* (psychological set, voice, articulation, bodily expression and language) that would enhance your persuasiveness. And equally important, you were totally unselfconscious as you immersed yourself in the project of *eliciting the desired response*, winning your friend over to believe and act as you know best for him. These are the selfsame things that should characterize our platform presentations: a lively, communicative personality; a rich, varied vocal expressiveness, with accurate pronunciation and distinct enunciation; bodily expression that is plentiful, meaningful and spontaneous: movement about the platform, stance, gesture, facial expression and eye contact; and language that is accurate, vivid, appropriate for the conceptual and vocabulary level of the listeners, action-oriented and rich in imagery.

When our speaker takes the platform we wish him to achieve the following:

1. A lengthy focal or initial pause, with a friendly facial expression (preferably a smile) as he looks out over the audience. This pause enables listeners and speaker to settle down in preparation for their respective "duties," and also builds suspense.

2. A rather full, and certainly genial and spontaneous salutation: "Thank you, Program Chairman Ellery Webb, for a sparkling sendoff; Mr. President Montgomery, Reverend Young, Judge Cloud, officers, guests, and members of the Olympia Civic Association." The most important parts of the salutation are the acknowledgment of the introduction and addressing the members by their organization's name. The speaker's salutation can virtually simulate his response if he were being introduced to these folks around a living room in a social setting.

3. "Parry and thrust" ad lib remarks to achieve a smooth transition into the text of the talk itself. At best these remarks will call attention to the speaker and his topic, arouse interest in them, and create common ground and rapport among speaker, audience, and topic. References to the audience, the occasion (including news of the day), the speaker himself, and the topic all can be effective.

4. Impressive presentation of the talk itself: "situation well in hand" authority; "think the thought" involvement; "elicit desired response" communicativeness; "persuasive vitality" in vocal expressiveness (with crisp enunciation); "plentiful, meaningful, spontaneous" physical expressiveness; and felicitous language, alive with action and rich in imagery.

5. Triumphant finale: knowing his closing sentences "cold," our speaker brings the talk to a resounding climax. He concludes with a terminal pause, holding eye contact, and avoids (as he would the plague) limping off on the weak crutch of "Thank you."

The Rights of Listeners

William Norwood Brigance

From a speaker, listeners have the right to expect interesting and useful ideas

The average educated person hears approximately one hundred speeches a year. Why listen to so many? Why listen to *any*? Not because we are forced outwardly, for outwardly we are free to listen or not. We are rather driven by forces within us. We are human beings, living in an entangled world. In that world we face problems which must be understood by responsible people; we are beset by choices and temptations; we are haunted by the shadows of fear. We listen to speakers because we hope they will illuminate life and make irrelevant facts seem significant. We listen because we hope they will give us new information, new ideas, or will simply water and cultivate old ideas. We listen because we want to be given encouragement, to renew our faith, to strengthen our determination. We listen because we want to be shown the beauty, the goodness, and the glories of life. We listen perhaps because we want to escape from reality for a time, to laugh and forget our troubles.

These are the services expected of speakers, and listeners have the inalienable right to demand that every speaker who consumes public time shall deliver the services expected. The following are three types of parasites who do not so deliver, and who ought to be put out of business:

1. *The Bafflegab*—who uses words that cover everything but fit nothing, like this:

The extent to which we control the future depends upon our adherence to the ideals that have made us great.

If you ask what these noble words mean you won't find out, not from the Bafflegab. He deals in generalities. The Bafflegab also winces at straightaway English. His sentences are shapeless bundles of words. Here is a specimen bundle:

In most cases where retirement dissatisfaction existed, advance activity programming by individuals had been insignificant. [In straightaway English this means "Most people who did not want to retire had not planned how to use their leisure time."]

Not only does the Bafflegab use imprecise words and rumple them into shapeless bundles. He ties his bundles together with what Sir Winston Churchill called "woolly phrases" that could "be left out altogether, or replaced with a single word":

It is also of importance to bear in mind the following consideration. . . . [Meaning "also."]

How do speakers get that way? Face it frankly. Clear thinking is hard work. Clear thinking takes time. The Bafflegab's foggy language comes from foggy thinking. He does not take the time to think himself clear. He does not take the time to find the right words, or to line them up in the right order. He does not make the effort to illuminate thought by an illustration, or to relieve a tired audience with humor. Of him it could never be said what Charles I said of Edward Coke, that listeners were "never weary with hearing him, he mingled mirth with business to so good purpose." The Bafflegab, in other words, does not meet the test. He fails to water and cultivate ideas with clear ideas, plain facts, and precise words.

2. *The Witless Wit*—who believes in the salvation of man by funny stories. He is determined to set the audience in a roar, and comes armed with twenty anecdotes—but no thought. He recites with gusto his hodgepodge of jests, which illustrate no theme, and measures his success by the amount of laughter. To listeners who have previously heard part or all of the jokes, they are no longer funny.

3. *The Phonograph*—who reproduces a magazine article and thinks it makes a good speech. The Phonograph is a common species among students. He puts off preparing a speech until the night before, then evades the issue by seizing a magazine article, swallowing it and attempting to reproduce it undigested, as a speech. He does not plagiarize outright; that is, he does not recite verbatim the words of the article. But he does reproduce the outline and the contents, and he adds nothing of his own. He is a Phonograph, and his speech is a failure, because even a good article when recited is not a speech. "The voice is Jacob's voice, but the hands are the hands of Esau." The magazine article was written six months or a year ago. It was intended for a reading audience of perhaps a million people, a people of varied educational levels, scattered over the entire United States and in foreign lands. In contrast, the speech is to be given *today* to *one* particular group of thirty people who have already heard two speeches on the same topic during the past month, and it is given by a student whose voice and manner proclaim loudly that he knows nothing about the subject except what he is reciting from the magazine. In other words, the student has failed to focus the speech on the particular audience meeting at a particular place on a particular day. Being a Phonograph, he simply reproduces another person's thoughts.

Listeners also have the right to see and hear a human being who talks with the audience, and not a dull or nervous creature who talks to himself

Some people, of course, believe that "delivery" is not important. A speaker, they think, needs only to "say what he thinks" and these thoughts will find their way into

"That's not fair! I listened to the others."

How Not to Speak at a Meeting

Few meetings produce, nor do they require, much golden-throated oratory. But the ability to stand up and talk—lucidly, convincingly and sometimes persuasively—is a must at any meeting. The rambler, the mumbler, the man who doesn't really know what he's talking about or *how* to talk, how to communicate, is worse than a nuisance; he's a dead loss.

These visuals depict a few of the all too common mistakes unpracticed speakers are likely to make.

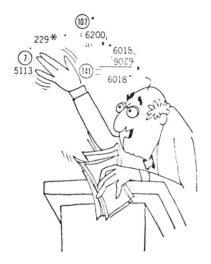

The Great Scientist: He may be a brilliant speaker. Unquestionably, he's a brilliant man. Unfortunately, he's as abstruse as he is brilliant: there may be only nine other men in the world who fully understand him— and none of these are in his audience. Translating *technicalese* into laymen's language is one of the toughest problems many speakers face today.

The Deadly Sleeper: This man is simply dull. He sometimes looks as if he might drop off to sleep . . . and his audience does.

(continued on page 193)

Abridged from "How Not to Speak at a Meeting" in *Association & Society Managers,* August/September 1969. © 1969 Society of Association Managers. Used by permission.

the minds of the listeners. A fair summary of this belief is, "It does not matter how you deliver a speech; the only important thing is what you say." Now this is a comfortable belief. It relieves a speaker from any responsibility beyond writing a paper. But the belief does not square with the facts of life. It assumes that you literally do "deliver" a speech in the same way you deliver a loaf of bread. It assumes that when delivered, the speech, like the loaf of bread, arrives intact and cellophane-wrapped no matter how long the delivery man took, whether he arrived drunk or sober, or how many detours or breakdowns he had along the way. These are grand assumptions indeed, but only assumptions. Actually there is no such thing as delivering a speech. The very word "delivery" is a turn of expression and not a statement of fact.

Why Speakers Fail in "Delivery"

The following are common types of speakers who create barriers that prevent their creating full thoughts in listeners' minds:

1. *The Fidgeter*—whose actions distract the listeners' attention. The eye is quicker than the ear. What the listener sees takes priority over what he hears. Hence the Fidgeter's actions interfere with his words. Behold his behavior: If his hands are in his pockets, he takes them out; if they are out, he puts them in. If his coat is unbuttoned, he buttons it; if it is buttoned, he unbuttons it. If he is at one side of the platform, he paces to the other side; when he gets there, he paces back again. He rocks from heel to toe. He stands on one foot, and hoists the other

as though to cool off the sole of the shoe. His hands and feet are always in the way, and he has the air of having too many of them.

2. *The "And-Er" Vocalist*—those pauses mutilate instead of punctuate. Instead of a clean pause at the end of a thought unit, he creates static like this:

I—*Er*—want to compare the—*Er*—stage plays of—*Er*—today—*Er*—with those of a—*Er*—century ago.

To *Er* is human. But the most unforgivable human *Er's* are those inflicted on suffering audiences by speakers who neglect their home work. They deserve cruel punishment. They should be forced to listen to a recording of their own voices.

3. *The Mumbler*—who can hear himself and does not care about anyone else. He looks at the ceiling, at the floor, or out the window, but not at the audience. He keeps his mouth closed "like the front room in an old-fashioned farmhouse," and opens it only to eat and yawn. His lips and tongue are on vacation. His jaw is fixed, like the Rock of Gibraltar. His voice is flat, and his tones are weak. He believes that talk is cheap, and his talk *is* cheap.

4. *The Sleeping-Pill Voice*—whose listless tones lull listeners into intellectual slumber. He talks loud enough to be heard, of course, but his words have no color, warmth, life, friendliness, or informing inflection. "Though the earth be moved and the mountains be carried into the midst of the sea," he gives nothing any meaning. He is a *tranquilizer* who leaves the listeners unmoved, untouched, and undisturbed. Over two centuries ago a famous author and clergyman, Jonathan Swift, warned a young man entering the ministry

(continued from page 192)

The Moving Target: This fellow walks off his nervousness. Listening to him is like watching a tennis match. He detracts from his own talk and, more important, may well "walk himself" away from some of the principal points he planned to make.

The Comedian: A joke is fine . . . but don't begin to mistake yourself for a scintillating night club comedian.

The Musician: This fellow accompanies his talk with a rendition on the change, keys and so on in his trouser pockets . . . and in short order his audience is busy trying to recognize the tune he's playing instead of listening to him. Many practiced speakers take their change and keys out of their pockets before they approach the podium.

The Nearsighted Note Nibbler: Most speakers use notes . . . but the best ones don't act like it. Usually, over-reliance on notes simply means the speaker is ill-prepared. But if he doesn't find his material important and interesting why should his audience?

(continued on page 194)

(continued from page 193)

The Fumbler: The Fumbler, at the podium, is about as popular as the fumbler on the football field. A good many speakers now use visual aids regularly. Their first rule is: Know thy equipment.

The Preening Peacock: He never gets his tie quite straight or his coat adjusted or his hair smoothed to his satisfaction. Chances are he's nervous. Chances are he doesn't know he's repeating these nervous gestures. But his audience knows it—and his audience is distracted.

against such speaking; and his words are as apt today as then: "If your arguments be strong, in God's name offer them in as moving a manner as the nature of the subject will probably admit." Or as Emerson put it: "Eloquence wants anthracite coal. Coldness is the most fatal quality."

Of course, it is self-satisfying for a listless speaker to imagine that it does not matter *how* he talks, that *what* he says is the only thing that counts. But whosoever says that varnishes nonsense with the charms of sound. Down the centuries wise men have known better, and experimental evidence has given statistical validity to their wisdom. This evidence suggests that listeners will remember only about 40 per cent as much of what speakers say in a listless voice as compared with what they say in a lively voice having emphasis, inflection, and tone color. Imagine two speakers. Both talk loud enough for every word to be heard, but one speaks with color, warmth, and informing inflection; the other speaks in a dead-flat tone. The audience will remember only about 40 per cent as much of what the listless speaker says as compared with what the lively speaker says.

To summarize: *In speaking, the know-how as well as the know-what is important; and listeners have the right to demand that speakers have both.*

Characteristics and Organization of the Oral Technical Report

Roger P. Wilcox

Main Purpose of Oral Technical Report: to Inform

A speaker may attempt to secure any one of three basic responses from his audience. He may want them to be entertained or interested (as in the case of the after-dinner speaker); to believe or act differently (as in the case of a safety talk); or to understand (as in the case of directions on how to operate a machine). Basically, the oral technical report is expository or informational. The speaker should strive for all three basic responses, but his main purpose is to advance the audience's understanding of the topic under discussion.

If the main purpose of the oral technical report is to inform, the speaker must be objective and impartial towards his material. Even though he may present strong advantages in favor of some recommendation, he scrupulously presents its disadvantages as well. The speaker stops short of playing the role of the advocate arguing for the adoption of a special point of view. He is more like a scientist reporting his latest findings to a group of fellow scientists.

In keeping with the objective point of view, the development of the oral technical report is primarily factual. Although an occasional anecdote may be valuable for illustration or enlivenment, the body of the report should consist of such objective data as explanations, descriptions, definitions, statistics, and expert opinion. Any conclusions offered should be based strictly on the facts available.

Yet, the speaker must take care that emphasis on the data does not obscure understanding of what the data support. An example of this is the speaker who is so preoccupied with explaining certain equations employed in his study that he never makes clear what his equations were intended to prove, nor what results they produced.

Although an oral technical report does not necessarily need the use of visual aids, they are usually recommended. Graphs, diagrams, models, and samples are employed freely for such purposes as explaining mechanisms and processes, presenting statistics, and stating objectives or listing main points. Because it is so easy to use visual aids ineptly, a few suggestions are:

- Charts and diagrams should normally be prepared before instead of during the presentation, when valuable time may be needlessly consumed.
- Aids should be kept simple, focusing only on what is most pertinent.

A public speaker is someone who seeks to inform or influence an audience.

Abridged from "Characteristics and Organization of the Oral Technical Report" by Roger P. Wilcox in *General Motors Engineering Journal*, Oct./Nov./Dec. 1959. © 1959 General Motors Corporation. Used by permission.

Evaluation of the Oral Report

YES NO

Introduction

_____ _____ Did the speaker effectively capture the interest and attention of his review group right from the start?

_____ _____ Did the speaker give the necessary explanation of the background from which the problem derived?

_____ _____ Did the speaker clearly state and explain his problem?

_____ _____ Did the speaker indicate the method(s) used to solve the problem?

_____ _____ Did the speaker suggest the order in which he would report?

Organization

Was the plan of organization recognizable through the use of:

_____ _____ (a) Sufficient introductory information

_____ _____ (b) Successful use of transitions from one main part to the next and between points of the speech

_____ _____ (c) Appropriate use of summary statements and re-statements?

_____ _____ Were the main ideas of the report clearly distinguishable from one another?

_____ _____ Was there a recognizable progression of ideas that naturally led to the conclusion?

Content

_____ _____ Did the speaker have adequate supporting data to substantiate what he said?

_____ _____ Was all the content meaningful in terms of the problem and its solution? (Avoidance of extraneous material.)

_____ _____ Did the speaker present his supporting data understandably in terms of the ideas or concepts he wasy trying to communicate?

_____ _____ Were the methods of the investigation clearly presented?

(continued on page 197)

Source: "Characteristics and Organization of the Oral Technical Report" by Roger P. Wilcox in _General Motors Engineering Journal_, Oct./Nov./Dec. 1959. © 1959 General Motors Corporation. Used by permission.

- Each drawing or chart should be adequately titled and labeled.
- Diagrams and labels should be large enough to be fully legible to those seated farthest away.
- Charts should have a professional look. Drawings and lettering not neat in appearance detract from the report.
- Normally, materials should not be distributed during the presentation since they divert attention from the speaker.
- Aids should not be revealed until they become pertinent in the presentation.

Proper Organization Important for Effective Report

As in any form of communication, the pattern of development is very important. The organization of the oral technical report can be most conveniently discussed in terms of the three major divisions of the report: body, introduction, and conclusion.

The _body_ is normally organized in terms of the steps involved in the problem-solution sequence. They include (a) an analysis of the problem to show what is wrong (the evidences of effects of the problem), the conditions which brought about the problem (the causes), and a statement of what is desired (the criteria or expectations); and (b) an explanation and analysis of one or more solutions in terms of their advantages and disadvantages in solving the problem and meeting the criteria.

The report need not always follow the entire sequence. Sometimes it may only analyze the causes of a problem or explain and evaluate a solution to a problem.

The discussion of each phase of the analysis should close with a statement showing the sub-conclusions arrived at during that phase.

The *introduction* prepares the audience for the body of the report. This is done by motivating the listener to want to hear what the speaker has to say and orienting the listener as to what the report contains.

You can develop an effective informative speech by following the pattern of an oral technical report.

Motivating the audience depends on two steps. First, the speaker should dwell briefly on the importance of the problem so the listener will have the feeling, "Here's something I want to find out about." Second, the speaker should establish the distinct impression that he has something worthwhile to offer on this subject. This can be done indirectly by referring to the speaker's interest and background concerning the problem and particularly to the amount of time spent and methods used in his investigation. Another way is to create an impression of competence, both in the introduction and throughout the report.

Orienting the listener is accomplished by (a) identifying and defining the problem by showing its relationship to the area from which it was taken, making clear what phases of the problem will be included in the report, and being explicit as to the exact purpose of the report; (b) providing whatever background is necessary concerning how the problem arose; and (c) giving a preview of what the main divisions of the report will contain.

(continued from page 196)

Visual Aid Supports

———— Did the speaker effectively use charts, graphs, or diagrams to present his statistical data?

———— Did the speaker use clear drawings, charts, diagrams or blackboard aids to make his facts or explanations vivid to the review group?

———— Did the visual aids fit naturally into the presentation?

———— Did the speaker give evidence of complete familiarity with each visual aid used?

———— Did the speaker clutter his report with too many visual aids?

Conclusion

Did the speaker conclude his report with finality in terms of one or more of the following:

———— (a) The conclusions reached

———— (b) The problem solved

———— (c) The results obtained

———— (d) The value of such findings to the corporation or industry at large

———— (e) Recommendations offered?

The Question Period

———— Did the speaker give evidence of intelligent listening in interpreting the questions?

———— Were the speaker's answers organized in terms of a summary statement, explanation, and supporting example?

———— Did the speaker show freedom in adapting or improvising visual aids in answering questions?

Delivery

———— Did the speaker use a natural, communicative delivery?

———— Did the speaker use adequate eye contact in maintaining a natural, communicative delivery?

———— Did the speaker use sufficient movement and gestures?

———— Did the speaker use good clear diction to express himself?

———— Could the speaker be heard easily by everyone?

———— Was the speaker confident and convincing?

———— Did the speaker display enthusiasm when communicating his ideas?

When the introduction is completed, the listener should be motivated to want to listen to the report and should know what it will cover and in what order.

The *conclusion* normally fulfills three main functions. First, the various subconclusions presented during the report at the close of each unit are summarized. Second, general conclusions, in the form of generalizations drawn from the subconclusions, are presented. And finally, any recommendations, arising from the general conclusions are offered.

A Politician's Guide to Success on the Stump: Hire a Heckler

John P. Keating

When President Nixon took to the campaign trail in last year's elections, a small but vocal group of hecklers seemed to show up at every rally. These hecklers probably were unaware that their mere presence may have given the President his biggest dividends of the campaign. A series of studies in the last decade shows that the distraction that hecklers create could be the catalyst to swing the votes of the uncommitted or wavering.

Vaccine

In the early 1960s William McGuire attempted to explain how people resist persuasive arguments against their dearly held beliefs. Seeing an analogy with the way the body resists an attacking virus, he put forth the inoculation theory ["A Vaccine for Brainwash," *P.T.*, February 1970]. Just as inoculation wards off an attacking virus, McGuire maintained, people persist in their positions by developing antidotes that counterattack arguments against them. If people practice and develop counterarguments, they remain secure with their old convictions, and attempts to change their opinions are futile.

To demonstrate his theory, McGuire worked with such cultural truisms as "Everyone should get a yearly chest X-ray." Because these truisms rarely are challenged, people have little chance to develop counterarguments, and resistance to an attack is poor. When white prospectors carried the tubercle bacillus to Alaska, Eskimos had no resistance to it because the bacteria had not previously existed among them, and tuberculosis became a plague. Similarly, as McGuire suspected, when without warning subjects heard an attack on the cultural truism about chest X-rays they could not counterattack; they wavered in their belief, thinking that radiologists had hoodwinked society into the dangerous practice of once-a-year chest X-rays. But given a little

---

practice at resisting arguments against truisms before attack, subjects developed their own resistance and continued to beatify time-honored cultural practices.

It seems that the tool employed to conserve opinions in the heat of attack is the counterargument. In political campaigns counterarguments are readily available. The favored campaigner will provide inoculation against opposing views. He may not cover the whole gamut of possible arguments, but he primes his constituents to manufacture their own antibodies and remain inoculated against the possibility of defection. The more concentration they exert at the time of the attack, the more efficiently they will produce counterarguments and the more firmly they will remain ensconced in their old positions.

Din

The inoculation theory piqued the curiosity of other psychologists. What would happen if people were distracted during an argument and could not devote all their attention to the attack and to the production of counterarguments? Would they still hold to their comfortable positions? Or would resistance lessen, enabling the persuasion to raise doubts or change their convictions?

You can develop an effective persuasive speech by following the pattern of political speaking.

Leon Festinger and Nathan Maccoby sought an answer. Fearlessly walking into a bastion of loyalty to tradition, they exposed

a group of fraternity brothers to an attack on fraternities. At the same time, they showed an amusing film to some of the men. As expected, all the men rejected the message. But the ones who had their attention divided by the film accepted more of the points made by the attack than did the ones who merely listened to the attack.

Distractions from hecklers can increase the acceptance of a politican's arguments.

These investigators concluded that people counterargue, actively but subvocally, when they encounter disagreeable messages. When distraction interferes with this process of counterargument, it weakens resistance to the persuasive communication.

But commentators disagreed with the interpretation. Some suggested that the amusing nature of the film made the attack more palatable, provoking less animosity and more acceptance. Some thought that the novelty of the situation may have resulted in more learning and thus more attitude change. Others argued that in order to justify the greater energy expended in listening to the message through the distraction, the men gave the communication more merit than they normally would have.

Machine

Though the explanation was hazy, the result—greater acceptance of the negative communication—was certain. To clear away the haze, Robert Osterhouse and Timothy Brock went a step further. They reasoned that if they

could (1) remove the amusement factor from the distraction, and (2) equalize the novelty and the energy that subjects expended in listening to a negative communication while they were distracted or not distracted, then explanations contradictory to Festinger and Maccoby's would be discounted.

Osterhouse and Brock constructed a distraction machine—a black wooden panel, similar to those used in airplanes, with four numbered lights that could be flashed at varying intervals. They told their subjects, students at Ohio State University, that they would hear a faculty member present a report that advocated doubling tuition. Some were distracted while they listened to the report—they were instructed to monitor the panel by calling out the number of each light as it flashed. With this simple distraction device, students who monitored more lights tended to agree much more with the tuition increase proposal than did those who had less or no distraction. Osterhouse and Brock concluded that calling out the numbers on the panel hindered the ability of the students to counterargue with the professor and led to greater agreement. Even though the students had bags full of arguments against increased tuition, they needed time to subvocalize these arguments and counterattack. Interference with their concentration debilitated their resistance.

Mix

It seemed clear from this study that if the counterargument mechanism could be shut down or interfered with, a person would be much less immune to disagreeable communications. But one last question remained. Osterhouse and Brock had designed their distraction study to interfere with the subvocalization of counterarguments. Would resistance to persuasion be equally broken down by distractions that did not call for vocalizations?

At Tim Brock's suggestion I attempted to answer this question in an experiment using the same kind of tuition-increase message that Osterhouse and Brock had used. While exposing some students to no distraction whatsoever, I had other students monitor either 10 or 25 light flashes each minute by one of three methods: I asked some to respond to the panel vocally, others to monitor the board by pushing the flashing light with their fingers to extinguish it, and still others to do both at the same time. I found no appreciable difference in acceptance of the communication between those who called out the numbers and those who monitored the panel manually. Those who performed both operations simultaneously were the most accepting. And, as expected, those who were the most distracted—with 25 lights each minute in each of the operations—agreed more with the communication than did either of the other two groups.

I undertook this experiment somewhat timorously, since the tuition issue was a hot one at the time; frequent advertisements in the campus newspaper condemned any proposed increase. But even though the students were aware of the issue and were forewarned of the nature of the communication, they still needed uninterrupted concentration and time to produce adequate counterarguments to buttress their resistance. It was also apparent that they did not have to contribute to their own distraction by actively vocalizing. And surprisingly, those who were most dis-tracted retained as much information from the communication as did those who were less distracted.

Stump

But how do distraction machines in a university laboratory relate to the campaign trail? We know that people resist change in thought by counterattacking any disagreeable message. The campaigner trying to swing votes to his side by persuasive arguments would be well advised to prevent his audience from launching reasoned counterattacks. The distractions and confusion inherent in campaign rallies can provide such interference. Instead of engaging in repartee with hecklers, a wise politician would continue with his stock speech, hoping for the distraction to grow louder—though not so loud that his voice could not be heard above the clamor. The dissident demonstration would distract potential voters at the rally or in front of television sets. And as we have seen in the series of studies starting with McGuire's, distraction would make these potential voters less defensive against the candidate and more accepting of his arguments, whatever they might be. These studies, of course, used communications whose ideas were diametrically opposed to the audience's views. In political campaigns, where the issues are more complex and ambiguous, politicians could anticipate even more success than the laboratory psychologist would predict for them.

I had a dream the other night about what I fancy would be the acid test of this theory. Jerry Rubin was addressing American Legionnaires while the Iron Butterfly performed its loudest music and a claque of paid hecklers shrilled in the audience. And Rubin won the Legion's endorsement.

How to Listen to Campaign Oratory If You Have To

Robert Bendiner

To help voters make their choices this year, enough words will be spoken to fill three thousand books, each the size of *Gone with the Wind* and each rating that title. Fortunately, most of this outpouring will not get into print. But you will probably catch two or three volumes' worth, and maybe you will want a guide through the verbiage.

The first rule for penetrating the underbrush of words is to keep always in mind that a candidate is not out to explain anything to you. It is not your mind he is after: it is your glands. He is out to show you, above all, that he is *your* kind of man—only more so. For this reason, a good campaign talk always starts out with the speaker finding a link to his listeners—no matter how hard he has to stretch for it. Here is the same candidate addressing three different audiences:

Reprinted from "How to Listen to Campaign Oratory If You Have to" by Robert Bendiner in *Look* October 11, 1960. © 1960 Robert Bendiner. Used by permission of the author.

To a veterans' convention—"I am proud to be here, among my former comrades in arms. I was not 'big brass,' but I think I know the thoughts and feelings of a humble soldier . . ." (He was, in fact, at Camp Yaphank in World War I, when the Armistice happily cut off his military career.)

At a county fair and ploughing contest—"My Grandfather Richards, on my mother's side, had a small farm, like most of you folks here, and many's the day I spent getting to know the backbreaking work that makes the farmer this country's forgotten man . . ." (He spent three summer vacations there as a growing, eating boy.)

In a trade-union hall—"I am delighted to be here, because this is where I belong. I am proud to have in my pocket right now a membership card in one of the great trade unions of this country . . ." (An honorary card bestowed on him by a bricklayers' union when, as an alderman, he laid the cornerstone for a new local.)

Where the audience is a mixed group, the speaker finds a quick kinship in geography. He will always have a soft spot for Devil's Gulch, Ariz., because his mother was born 18 miles from there. Or for East Overshoe, Ill., because his Uncle Henry ran a poolroom there in 1912. At worst, he can always call a town his "second home" on the ground that he once stayed overnight at the local hotel and had his laundry done.

Once past the amenities, our man is ready to plunge into serious matters, equipped as he is with a life belt of ready-made phrases to keep him afloat. The kind he chooses depends on whether his party is in or out of office. If he belongs to the "out" party, government expenditures

They Say	They Mean
My opponent is making a political football out of this grave and complicated issue.	He has a good thing going for him there. If my party was on the paying end of that issue, I'd sure know what to do with it.
Let us return to spiritual values.	Let's put my party in again and see what happens.
Clean up the mess in Washington (or Boston or Albany).	Clean up their mess in Washington (or Boston or Albany). It will take a few years before we have a mess of our own.
We will conduct a vigorous, fighting campaign.	We will smear them.
They are trying to smear us.	They are conducting a vigorous fighting campaign.
It is time to close ranks.	It is time to close ranks behind us. (If the opposition wins, it is time for honest criticism.)
I am not here to make a speech.	I mean to talk for another 40 minutes. Don't anyone leave.
I am not suggesting that my opponent is personally dishonest.	He is a willing dupe.

This is the speech *they* wrote for me, but I'm going to throw it away and speak from the heart.

I cannot go into the details now, but I think I may say without fear of contradiction that our policies have proved to be sound.

We will take the American people into our confidence.

They are playing into the hands of our country's enemies.

You may hear talk that they have reformed, my friends, but the leopard doesn't change its spots.

We have had enough of their defeatist talk.

They have made a tragic blunder, for which we must all pay the price.

They slipped me tomorrow's speech, which would lay an egg with this audience.

All sound.

We will let them in on all the opposition's scandals we can uncover.

They are criticizing us again.

We haven't been able to get anything new on them lately.

Let's forget the facts for awhile. Things are tough all over.

They have had a nasty break, and it looks as though we can cash in on it.

are *criminal waste and extravagance*. And all members of the executive branch of government automatically become *bureaucrats*.

If our man belongs to the "in" party, government expenditures are *the best return on his dollar the American taxpayer has ever had*. As for executive personnel, they are *dedicated public servants*, who daily sacrifice themselves for you and me when they could be making millions in some other job.

There are, of course, turns of phrase that are common to both the "ins" and the "outs." In this category are the diminutives—*little man, common man, small businessman, small farmer* and the like. In an election year, we seem to have an enormous population of midgets. The candidate's immediate audience, however, is never made up of these wee folk; it is made up of *the great people of this great state*. That's you. The little people are your relatives and neighbors. They don't happen to be there, but on their behalf, you will no doubt appreciate this unselfish champion of the underdog.

Having mastered these semantic twists, the student of campaign oratory is ready to move on to those tags that politicians hang on each other in the hope that voters will treat the wearer like a medieval leper. In this category are the various Red labels, ranging from *pro-Communist* to *fellow traveler* to the newest variants, *soft on communism* or *soft on Russia*. Every candidate has to run against two opponents— the other party's candidate and Nikita Khrushchev. It might be assumed at this stage in history that every American politician is against communism, just as he is against barracuda in the bath. But unless his views are the exact opposite of the Russian leader's on everything from astrophysics to the can-can, he may be put down as *playing into Khrushchev's hands*. In common with certain head-hunting natives of Borneo both John F. Kennedy and Richard M. Nixon relish a good meal, but it would probably be wrong to assume on that evidence that either of them is soft on cannibalism. Unless this particular trick is held in check, anyone who lights a match may be put down as soft on arson.

In a milder category are the hundreds of clichés, rubber stamps and warmed-over metaphors, mixed and unmixed, that make the padding of campaign oratory. Most of them are so washed out by waves of repetition that they call up no pictures at all and are intended only to get the speaker from one sentence to the next with the least resistance. He thinks it sounds good to work in references to *our Founding Fathers, Old Glory, hearths and homes, our children and our children's children*. These are not really words at all. They are red-white-and-blue cement.

Now that you have been warned, how are you to get through the next few weeks? Here are a few rules that may help:

1. Spend a preliminary month in a Trappist monastery, so that the sound of even a politician's voice, no matter what he says, will have a certain welcome freshness.

2. Decide in advance on three or four questions that a candidate ought to deal with in this year of 1960. If he dodges or skirts all four of them the first time you hear him, ignore him the next time and go back to Bat Masterson.

3. If he answers even one of these questions to your satisfaction, give him a second try. If he answers two or three, vote for him. And if he successfully answers all four, go out and work for him.

4. Try listening to a candidate in the company of someone who generally opposes your views. If the two of you can't get up a good row about the talk afterwards, the chances are that the speaker didn't say anything.

5. No matter how frighteningly the campaigners warn you that the salvation of the world depends on their winning, remember that on November 9, half of them will be wiring congratulations to the other half on their great victory and promising to co-operate fully in the predicted disaster.

June Is Speakers' Month

Howard Mumford Jones
Harvard's Abbott Lawrence Lowell Professor of Humanities, Emeritus

In the month of June the voice of the commencement orator is loud in the land. The commencement speaker is, I think, a purely American invention, like chewing gum and baseball.

He inhabits no other country, and he comes in four sizes.

(1) He may be a Very Important Personage, who might conceivably announce a Very Important Policy Change in foreign affairs, or business, or religion, or the income tax, theoretically to the graduating class but actually to the newspapers, all to the glory of dear old Siwash.

(2) He may be the recipient of an honorary degree. The recipient of an honorary degree is of course a Very Important Person but he is not necessarily a Very Important Personage, and commonly all he is expected to do is to point with pride on the one hand and to view with dismay on the other.

(3) The father (or uncle) of somebody in the graduating class may serve. He is usually unequal to the task, and embarrasses his young relative.

(4) Anybody. I think I have heard better commencement speeches from Anybody than I have from any member of categories (1), (2), and (3).

Commencement oratory suffers from some built-in difficulties. The first is that as nobody suggests a topic, a theme, or a proposition, the orator is like a blindfolded man sailing a boat on a sea without shores to a port he never arrives at.

The second is the miscellaneous and conflicting interests of his audience—or audiences. To the graduating class he is simply delivering another required lecture. The college president hopes for the best. The main hope of the trustees is that the guy won't talk too long and that he won't say anything "radical." They don't want to embarrass the current fund drive.

As the parents think that everything is just too wonderful, they would be quite as pleased if the orator recited "Alice in Wonderland" until it came time for John to cross the stage. The newspaper boys already have copies of the speech and couldn't care less.

As for the general public, what with graduating classes getting larger, alumni associations growing bigger, and the faculty becoming more numerous, not to speak of the inability of the college gymnasium to expand in our space-time world, it mostly isn't there.

Over the decades commencement orators have developed a number of gambits that sometimes lend certainty to their undertaking but do not improve it as oratory. One is to congratulate the graduates and then tell them that their education is just beginning—a reflection that would annoy the faculty, except that they have heard it so often, it no longer stings.

A second is to admit the complete failure of the older generation, represented by the orator, and to turn the world over immediately to the graduating class. Despite the universal rebellion of individuality in the graduating class, symbolized by their universal long hair and their universal short skirts, the graduates commonly do not want the world—they want to know about the draft and a job and matrimony.

A fourth ploy is Leadership. The seniors are informed they are the Leaders of Tomorrow's World. As we graduate some thousands of students from all sorts of institutions annually and semi-annually and quarterly, it seems clear that the Future is going to be filled up with Leaders who will have nobody to lead.

The commencement orator is part of a ritual, a rite of passage, and perhaps it doesn't make any difference what he says, just as it would be simpler to mail the diplomas to the graduates. But they come to the platform and get them. It is all part of a show. The show at least allows parents to glory in what they think they have paid for, and substituting tape recordings won't do.

Still, commencement is a climactic point in education. It is the last, and sometimes the first, occasion when the graduates as an organized group confront the world they are about to be catapulted into. I think somebody ought to build a better bridge between the campus and the world outside than that offered by the usual American commencement speech, even if it is only a Bailey's bridge.

Somebody might indicate clearly and passionately what you can

Courtesy of the Boston Globe: June Is Speakers' Month by Howard Mumford Jones, June 1966

and what you cannot do with a liberal education, now that you have got one. Somebody might reasonably assess the place of the college in a world in tension. Somebody might indicate that, higher education being an exposure to a world of ordered intelligence, other persons have found ordered intelligence of this kind to be in some limited degree useful, or enriching, or annoying, or stabilizing in business or matrimony or the entertainment world or Madison Avenue. In such a case the commencement speaker would have to address the graduates and not the universe at large. This is probably asking too much. It is far easier to address the universe.

Prods

1. Think of two large organizations (e.g., university, state government, business, city police, hospital) with which you are familiar. To what sector of the public are they responsible? Is it likely that speeches by representatives of these organizations would be different? Why?

2. How does a political scandal affect the credibility of the President of the United States? In what ways would it affect what he says in a public speech?

3. If you were speaking to a group of publishers about laws governing pornography, what would your central idea be? Using the chronological pattern of organization, state three main headings for your talk. State three others for the topical pattern.

4. Watch and listen to a public speaker deliver a speech before a live audience. Describe his or her delivery. Was it animated? Did the speaker have any problems in delivery? Did you think he or she was more or less effective because of delivery?

5. You are to speak to an audience of oil company executives about industry research for alleviating the energy crisis. State two main ideas you might include in this report. What kinds of visual aids could you use?

6. Listen to a political campaign speech. How did the speaker try to win over his or her audience? Were there any hecklers? What would you have done differently from what the speaker did?

". . . Furthermore . . ."

From *The Saturday Evening Post* courtesy of Reg Hider.

To the Cause of Better Communication

I solemnly pledge that I shall conscientiously and seriously strive to improve my relationships with others—regardless of what they do to me—through a judicious application to my own behavior of what I have learned by reading this book.

I had a friend one time.
He died.

—a prison inmate

Many relationships wither under the strain of misunderstandings, thoughtlessness, and even cruelty as well as differences in status, location, and experience; and yet people persist in seeking to share understanding. We cannot deny that some people seek advantage over others or deliberately try to hurt them. If such designs were the rule rather than the exception, surely we would see the end of human cooperative behavior. As you seek to improve your relationships with people, we can promise only a fierce struggle and the possibility of occasional peace and happiness.

You will be wise to ponder your new knowledge. With caution and humility, approach each communicative event as a new experience, honestly trying to do your best. Only in that way will you find it possible to narrow the communication gap.

Throughout this book we have sought to present some basic ideas about human communication—its personal, message, and environmental components and the four fundamental relationships in which people interact. Taken together, these components and relationships comprise a fairly complete picture of human communicative behavior, which may help you analyze and comprehend human interaction and to develop specific skills to improve your communication with others. We hope that from our presentation you have gotten a sense of what it means to communicate with others as well as a good feeling about the subject of human communication. Aware of our strengths and weaknesses as human beings, we can at least resolve to do better next time. Nevertheless, the only reality we can offer is the challenge of improved communication in a world in which perfection is a lie.

The Ending

I Never Promised You a Rose Garden

Hannah Green

Most of the time Helene was out of contact and not to be reached; sometimes a bitter sentence or two broke like glass, sudden and brittle, and sometimes an attack as hard as it was surprising, but Deborah knew in the quiet, unspectacular way of her clear moments that Helene, as desperately ill as she was, had the unknown quantity of strength or will or *something* that it took to get well. Helene, she knew, could make it. Because of this, her feelings toward Helene were a texture of envy, respect, and fear.

Once, she had been cruel to Helene; she had told her that she thought she could get well and had seen the terror build in the muscular body. Deborah had not realized fully her own tormenting then. Helene had told her in a fine and reasonable voice that if she, Deborah, didn't move away and fast, she, Helene, would break every bone in that dung-stinking head. Deborah had complied.

The light went on and both of them groaned softly at the revelation of the lurid spectacle of themselves and each other after the beauty of the star-darkness. Ellis came in alone, and walked swiftly to Helen's bed to take her pulse.

Normally the nurses and attendants spoke as they entered, in order to introduce slowly the presence of the world, of which they were representatives, to those who might be midhung and con-fused, and usually they waited for their presence to be acknowledged even by an eyeblink. The suddenness of Ellis' coming was too much in so vulnerable a place; when he went for Helene's head to capture her temple-pulse and force from it a number for his report, she pulled hard away from his hand. Movement of the head was a person's whole repertoire in pack; Ellis grabbed Helene's face and held it with one hand while he tried to catch the bird-pulse with the other. Again she fought away. Then he straightened a little, not angry, only deliberate, and began to hit her in the face. The blows landed sure and hard. She spat up at him, a diffused and angry spray, and Deborah, watching, saw what would be to her forever after the symbol of the impotence of all mental patients: the blow again, calm and accurate and merciless, and the spitting back again and again. Helene did not even reach him, but after every attempt he met her at the end of his arm with full force. There was no sound except the pursing sputter of the now dry lips, her labored breathing, and the blows falling. They were both so intent that they seemed to have forgotten everything else. When he had slapped her into submission, he took her pulse and Deborah's and left. When he went out, Helene was coughing a little on her blood.

The next day Deborah became her own Yri enemy—a voluntary sharer, an eyeless-and-utterly-naked, which Yri called *nelaq tankutuku*. She went to the nurse and asked to see the ward doctor when he came to sign the orders for the week.

"Why do you want to see him?" the nurse asked.

"I have something to tell him."

"What is it?"

"That a pacifist is one who uses his open hand."

Nurse gave way to ward nurse. The theme again. Ward nurse to head day nurse; the theme again. The cloud was beginning to darken under the ceiling, lowering toward Punishment, but Deborah had to tell the doctor somehow and get it off her own conscience that she had been a witness and thus, in some obscure way, a sharer in the experience of both victor and victim. The nurse was skeptical and Deborah had to plead, with the cloud pressing closer and the wind coming up. At last she got permission to see the ward doctor. She told, sparely and dryly, what she had seen, trying for the world's semblance of sanity so that he would believe her. She did not use the expense of the telling to show him how important it was, nor did she speak of Ellis' propensities, which she knew were secret simply because he had the keys and the patients didn't. When she got finished, the doctor sat looking at her, watching her hair grow. She knew from long experience that he did not see the cloud, feel the dark wind, or sense the Punishment. He sat in another season—springtime, maybe—beneath a separate sun whose rays ended at the periphery of her eyesight, her reality, and her kingdom.

At last he said, "Why doesn't Helene tell me this?"

"Helene left right after it hap-

pened." She was about to add that it was like Helene to blank out and leave her holding the bag, her way of getting even for the time when she had told Helene that she saw the possibility of wellness in her. She saw that this was unwise, but the realization stopped her mind on it, like cloth caught on a nail, and she could say no more.

"We are interested in stopping any brutality going on around here, but we can't take something without proof. You were in pack

---

Although gaps between people occur again and again, it is possible to understand and narrow the communication gap between yourself and others.

---

because you were upset, you know. Something perhaps you believe you saw . . ."

"Ask Ellis at least. With his Soul . . . he's going to have trouble with it anyway if he has to lie."

"I'll make a note of it," the doctor said, making no move toward his ubiquitous notebook. He was clearly giving her what Lee Miller called Treatment Number Three: a variety of the old "fine-fine," which went, "Yes, yes, of course," and was meant to placate without changing, silence without comprehending, and end friction by doing nothing. As she looked at him, Deborah thought about her sedative order. She had wanted an increase in her sedation and she knew that if she asked now he would give it to her. But she

There Will Never Be a Gap Gap

We suffer from, among other things, gaposis, or a plethora of gaps. Among them are the Credibility Gap, the Communication Gap, the Culture Gap and the Missile Gap, the Sputnik, Power, Credit, Technological and Ecumenical gaps. And what household is not familiar with the ever-present Financial Gap?

Long before there were any of these gaps, of course, there was a Delaware Water Gap. God gave us that gap, but it is relatively small, dividing only the states of New Jersey and Pennsylvania. The great gaps are man-made, and we lead the world in producing them. We are also rich in headline writers grateful for a three-letter word to cover them all. Last week the New York *Times* garden section even produced a Skilled Plantsman Gap, which it called nationwide. Washington alone has created more gaps than all the other world capitals put together (although this statistic must be hedged because Moscow does not make figures of this kind available). Washington also produces a ceaseless flow of Stopgaps.

The greatest of all gaps, because it is one of the oldest and grows exponentially, is the celebrated Generation Gap. It has been the subject of much confused interpretation. To set this straight, it is necessary to understand what a gap is and what a generation is.

A gap, of course, is an interstice, an absence. It separates this from that, I from Thou. The last man to experience existence without an interpersonal gap was Adam. As soon as Eve made her appearance, the Communication Gap was born. Neither knew how ignorant they both were. From the first bite of apple they started to find out. In the attempt of each to convey a vision of reality to the other, the gap widened, and it has been widening ever since. Ours is the most abyssal Communication Gap ever achieved, because in an age of specialization we have uncovered such a vast number of things to be ignorant about. The only way to halt that widening would be to stop learning. The Generation Gap came with Cain. A generation is the space between father and son, the smallest and the greatest distance the universe knows. Of one blood and bone, they are achingly alike; of different times, they can be galaxies apart.

Generation is one of our most abused terms. A generation's span cannot be stated in years. Fathers—and mothers—have been as few as five and as many as 90-plus years older than their offspring. A school generation may be six, eight or nine years, depending on the school system. A college generation (undergraduate) is usually four years. Generations of computers (we're into the third now), of space capsules, missiles and antimissile defense systems get shorter all the time.

President Kingman Brewster of Yale was referring specifically to students in the colleges as of 1968 when he labeled their generation the Cool Generation—using the adjective in its inverted, McLuhanesque sense of committed, motivated. Who, though, qualifies to be included among their predecessors, the so-called Silent Generation, those unquestioning, uncaring Bachelors of Arts who are alleged to have strolled out of Academe during the Eisenhower years? Where did they leave off and the Cool Generation begin? With the class of '61 (three and a half years under Ike, one semester under Kennedy)? The Class of '65 (no Ike, about 800 of Kennedy's thousand days and a year and a half of

(continued on page 211)

didn't want to buy sleep with Helene's swallowed blood, and she let him go, murmuring, "Chloral hydrate generosity, and charity in cc's." She watched the worms that were dropping out of the cloud. The doctor left. Never mind; she would tell Dr. Fried, The Fire-Touch, about it.

Furii, or Fire-Touch, was the new Yri name for Dr. Fried; it recalled the fearsome power that had scarred Deborah's arm with an invisible burning.

"Did you tell the ward doctor this?" Furii asked.

"Yes, and he gave me the Number Three With Smile: 'yes-yes.'" She felt ridiculous in her honorable abstinence from the heavier sedation that she had wanted. She wished that she had at least got something from what was bound to be so costly.

"You know," Furii said, "I am not connected with the running of your ward. I cannot break into ward policy."

"I'm not saying that policy should be changed," Deborah said, "unless the policy is beating up patients in pack."

"I have no say in discipline of ward personnel either," Furii said.

"Is Pilate everybody's last name around here?"

At last Furii agreed to mention it in the staff meeting, but Deborah was not convinced. "Maybe you doubt that I saw it at all."

"That is the one thing that I do not doubt," the doctor said. "But you see, I have no part in what is to be done on the wards; I am not an administrative doctor."

Deborah saw the match lighting dry fuel. "What good is your reality, when justice fails and dishonesty is glossed over and the ones who keep faith suffer. Helene kept her bargain about Ellis and so did I. What good is your reality then?"

"Look here," Furii said. "I never promised you a rose garden. I never promised you perfect justice . . . " (She remembered Tilda suddenly, breaking out of the hospital in Nuremburg, disappearing into the swastika-city, and coming back laughing that hard, rasping parody of laughter. "Sholom Aleichem, Doctor, they are crazier than I am!") . . . and I never promised you peace or happiness. My help is so that you can be free to fight for all of these things. The only reality I offer is challenge, and being well is being free to accept it or not at whatever level you are capable. I never promise lies, and the rose-garden world of perfection is a lie . . . and a bore, too!"

"Will you bring it up at the meeting — about Helene?"

"I said I would and I will, but I promise nothing."

(continued from page 210)

L.B.J.)? After what cutoff birthdate is a parent of today declared ineligible for membership in the Depression Generation? The Postwar Generation?

Since human beings are born every second, it is glib and often dangerous to label generations. Each man knows he is his father's son, and that is his generation. Oh, he may have a way of identifying with coevals: seeking out others who fell in love to the melody of *Star Dust*, or *I Left My Heart at the Stage Door Canteen*, or *Rock around the Clock*. But contemporaneity is not generation: there is no genesis in it. Generations flow from specific fathers to specific sons. Each newborn infant is a tiny piece of the future and however much he and his father are alike, they are as different as two tenses. To decry it is to protest against time itself.

To call it a Generation Gap gives it an impolite burden of meaning. To the young it's what separates them from those committed to hypocrisy and false values. To their elders it's the separation from those who don't appreciate the nuances of life, the complexity of motives and the arts and necessities of compromise. Trouble is, once people blame their differences on age, they feel it useless to argue them out. And so what they call a Generation Gap becomes the worst Communication Gap of all.

We've Only Just Begun

LYRIC BY PAUL WILLIAMS   MUSIC BY ROGER NICHOLS

far left: Bert Fox
near left and below: T. Zannes

Brent D. Peterson

Gerry Goldhaber

R Wayne Pace

Major articles in this book are in 9-point Primer; illustrative articles are in 9-point Helvetica Light. Display lines for both are Bodoni Bold.

The book was set by the American Can Company, Clarinda, Iowa, and printed by Kingsport Press, Kingsport, Tennessee.

Project Editor   **Gretchen Hargis**
Designer   **Joe di Chiarro**
Sponsoring Editor   **Frank Geddes**
Cover Photo   **Charles Harbutt/Magnum**

5236

DATE DUE

7 05 '84	
7 31 '85	
2.14 '85	
3. 21 '85	
5. 25 '88	
6. 08 88	
JUL 14 '93	
Ret. 7/26	
JAN 16 1996	
JUN 3 0 1998	

BRODART, INC.   Cat. No. 23-221